For Anne
with every good will
Affection atly

GW00775921

HELPING WITH INQUIRIES

Some other books by the same author

Jewish Prayer
We Have Reason to Believe
Jewish Values
Principles of the Jewish Faith
Seeker of Unity
Faith
A Jewish Theology
Teyku

HELPING
WITH
INQUIRIES

An Autobiography

LOUIS JACOBS

VALLENTINE, MITCHELL

First published 1989 in Great Britain by
VALLENTINE, MITCHELL & CO. LTD.
Gainsborough House, Gainsborough Road,
London, E11 1RS, England

Copyright © 1989 Louis Jacobs

British Library Cataloguing in Publication Data
Jacobs, Louis
    Helping with inquiries.
    1. Great Britain. Judaism, history
    I. Title
    296'.0941
    ISBN 0–85303–231–9

Library of Congress Cataloging-in-Publication Data
Jacobs, Louis.
    Helping with inquiries: an autobiography/Louis Jacobs.
        p. cm.
    Includes index.
    ISBN 0–85303–231–9
    1. Jacobs, Louis. 2. Rabbis—England—London—Biography.
3.Orthodox Judaism—England—London. 4. London (England)–
–Biography. I. Title.
BM755.J23A3 1989
296'.092'4—dc19   88–36674
[B]   CIP

Printed and bound in Great Britain by
BPCC Wheatons Ltd, Exeter

TO MY CONGREGATION

THE NEW LONDON SYNAGOGUE

IN APPRECIATION OF THEIR
COURAGE, SUPPORT AND LOYALTY
THROUGHOUT THE YEARS

CONTENTS

ILLUSTRATIONS

ILLUSTRATIONS

PREFACE

I doubt very much whether the story of my rather uneventful life would have been worth recording had it not been for the so-called Jacobs Affair in which I had a central role. I cannot claim that in the following pages an objective account of the Affair is presented. After all, as one of the protagonists, I look back to see it in terms of my own personal experience and my bias hardly needs to be mentioned. Nevertheless, while this book cannot be considered objective history, I have tried to present the arguments and activities of my opponents without distortion of their views and with as much fairness as I could muster.

My wife, Shula, has kept, with admirable thoroughness, scrapbooks containing practically all the newspaper cuttings and other material on the Affair. I am indebted to her for everything I have written but this book in particular could never have seen the light of day without her painstaking work of recording the material on which it chiefly relies. On the twentieth anniversary of the formation of the New London Synagogue, Anne Cowan, using the material Shula had collected, edited a good deal of it under the title *New London Synagogue: The First Twenty Years*. This has helped considerably for the chapters on the Affair. For the earlier chapters of the book I have relied chiefly on my memory. These chapters are not directly relevant to the Affair but indirectly do have a bearing on it.

It would have been quite impossible to avoid details of my personal life in telling my story. For the same reason I have been obliged to mention the members of my family – Shula, Ivor, Naomi and David, and their families – but I know that they prefer me to do as I have done, that is, to concentrate more on ideas than on personalities. I still hope that enough has been said about the various persons I have known (and, in some cases, fought against) to save the book from dullness.

PREFACE

The title of the book is self-explanatory. All the fuss was really about whether traditional Judaism could be seen as a quest rather than as a corpus of dogmas fixed for all time by divine *fiat*.

Finally, I want to express my gratitude to the Honorary Officers, Council and Members of the New London Synagogue and to all my other friends who have been unstinting in the encouragement they have given me to 'help with inquiries'.

1

CHILDHOOD

The city of Manchester, where I was born on 17 July 1920 – famous for its alleged anticipatory thinking, for the Hallé Orchestra, the Free Trade Hall and the splendid Town Hall (a cathedral to business, as it has been dubbed), from the tower of which one could, on a clear day, see the Blackpool tower over forty miles away, – had, and still has, the largest Jewish population in the United Kingdom outside the metropolis. In those days the majority of Manchester Jewry lived in the Cheetham and Hightown districts of north Manchester and its neighbouring Salford, together with a sprinkling in the posh district, also in the north of the city, of Heaton Park. The Jews of north Manchester were prominent in the raincoat and waterproof industries, both as manufacturers and as the work force. Most of them hailed originally from Russia, Lithuania and Poland. Contrary to the conventional picture of English Jews in the twentieth century as solidly middle class, there was a sizeable Jewish working class in Manchester, as well as in Leeds on the other side of the Pennines.

The Jews of south Manchester, on the other hand, were either of German extraction or were Sephardim, Oriental Jews from Syria and other Near Eastern countries, engaged for the most part in shipping. My mother used to refer to these as 'Turks' and I had a vision, derived from the pictures of Turks in the comic books, of them wearing a fez and curled, pointed shoes.

The epithet 'Mancunian', after the old Roman city on the site, was sometimes used of Manchester citizens. When I visited a congregant in London soon after I had taken up a rabbinic position there, she said: 'You are a Manchurian, aren't you?', to which, with my dark features and rather sinister goatee beard, I could but reply: 'I only look like one.'

1

My parents were married for over ten years before their only child was born, with the consequence that I suffered from the disadvantages of that state and wallowed in its advantages. I had no living grandparents so the essential 'spoiling' for which they would have been responsible was carried out quite adequately by my parents and by a host of aunts, uncles and older cousins, both my parents belonging to large families.

My paternal grandparents, Yehudah Laib (after whom I am named) and Sarah, both came from the town of Telz in Lithuania, the home of the famous *Yeshivah*. My grandfather's great hero was Rabbi Yitzhak Elhanan Spektor, the illustrious rabbi of nearby Kovno, whose *Responsa* on Jewish law are authoritative to this day. My grandmother (my *Zaide's* second wife) was either the daughter or grand-daughter (I have never been able to discover which) of Rabbi Laib Hasid, a well-known figure in nineteenth-century Lithuanian Jewry, who, despite his appellation, was no '*Hasid*' but a saintly Litvak.

Grandfather was strictly observant. My father once told me that he had received a smack across the face, when he was a grown man, from his father for failing in some religious duty. For all that, the old man's authority could not have sat too heavily on his children, who always spoke of him fondly. My father and his two brothers always managed somehow to evade parental watchfulness when they went along to watch Broughton Rangers, the Rugby team, playing on the Sabbath. Through my father's influence I, too, became a Broughton Rangers fan.

My father also liked to tell how, after long years hoping for a child, his father, no longer alive, came to him in a dream and said to him: 'Harry, begin to put on *tefillin*. You will have a son.'

Grandfather, I am also told, had remarkable skills in bone-setting, and for a time he was a milkman. By these and various other occupations he managed to eke out a living in a strange land. Yet he seems to have been easily adaptable to the new environment. At first he lived in Canterbury of all places, where there was a small Jewish community with its own synagogue, but later he moved to London where my father was born, in Brick Lane, I believe. When my father was four years of age the

2

family moved to Manchester, my Zaide becoming a prominent member of the little synagogue in Julia Street, Strangeways, just across the road from the forbidding prison. The Telzer and Kovner Hevra, as its name implies, was founded by my Zaide's *landsleit* who had preceded him there. Yiddish was the language in the home but Zaide learned to speak broken English with a Manchester accent. A photograph I have of him and my *Bubbe* shows him resplendent in a smoking jacket with velvet lapels and an embroidered smoking cap set rakishly on his head. With his snow-white, patriarchal beard he looks like a cross between an Edwardian dandy and an old-time rabbi.

My mother Lena's parents, Carl (Kasriel) and Agnes Myerstone, came to England from Mittau, near Riga, in Latvia. Like most Latvian Jews, they were more Westernised, certainly far more than my father's parents. They, too, spoke Yiddish but in a more Germanic mode. My mother was the youngest of eight children. Her older brothers established themselves in Manchester, Hyman as a retail clothier, Wolf as a jeweller, both helping to support the large family. These two uncles quickly adapted themselves to life in this country. Hyman eventually became President and Wolf the Treasurer of the Great Synagogue in Manchester, the English *Shul*, as it was called to distinguish it from the more 'foreign' and less decorous synagogues in the city. There my parents were married. The rabbi of the Great Synagogue was Dr Saloman, a graduate of the Orthodox Hildesheimer Seminary in Berlin. Chazan Newman, the synagogue cantor, was a highly gifted musician with a fondness for good food. It was rumoured that when the cost was being negotiated for a wedding banquet, the caterer would ask: 'With or without Chazan Newman?' I can still recall standing in line with other little Jewish boys and girls as Dr Saloman's *cortège*, taking him to his last resting place, proceeded solemnly through the streets.

Both my parents attended the Jews' School. My father did well at the school, winning a place at the prestigious Manchester Grammar School. He was unable to accept, his father requiring an extra breadwinner to augment the family's meagre income. All his life, his not inconsiderable intellectual talents were consequently wasted as a worker in Jewish-owned rain-coat factories. He himself never saw it that way. He was always proud to be a working man, sticking his neck out on more than one occasion on behalf of his fellow-workers against the 'bosses', though he was never a member of the Labour party. The majority of Jews at that time voted Liberal. Whenever a famous Liberal speaker came to Manchester, my father and his friends would make a point of being there and perhaps being introduced to the speaker. My father really did know Lloyd George!

My mother also took well to her schooling. She loved English literature in particular and could recite huge chunks of narrative poetry, such as *The Pied Piper of Hamelin*, by heart. To supplement my own schooling, she would spend hours with me reading Arthur Mee's *Children's Encyclopedia*. In a different age and in different circumstances she might have carved out a career for herself, but there were no opportunities in that direction for poor Jewish girls in Manchester. She was a particular fan of Gilbert and Sullivan. I was brought up on songs from Gilbert and Sullivan; *The Mikado* was a special favourite.

My father volunteered to serve in the Army before the compulsory conscription in the First World War but he was rejected on grounds of ill-health. Instead he became a special constable. (His highly polished, embossed 'truncheon' now assists the decor in my son David's flat.) He would often regale me and my cousins with tales of his prowess in defeating crime, though he never fought against desperate criminals with the odds heavily against him, as I would romantically have liked to hear him tell. In the Second World War he again served as a Special Constable, this time as a traffic controller. His friends and members of the family would make a point of crossing the road where, resplendent in his neat uniform and policeman's cap, he would stop the traffic for them.

My father, like my mother, had an excellent memory. Unlike her he did not read much apart from the daily paper, but he remembered everything he had ever read and could come up with an apt quotation whenever he was called upon to speak, acquiring something of a reputation as a public speaker. At family celebrations he was always invited to give the toast of

Grandfather – Yehudah Laib Jacobs, b. Telz,
Lithuania

Grandmother – Sarah Jacobs, b. Telz, Lithuania

Father at Jews' School, Manchester – class photograph

Author at Jews' School, Manchester – class photograph

the evening. I never saw him prepare beforehand a speech he was to deliver but he generally got by very adequately without preparation.

Both my parents loved the old-fashioned music hall. Regularly, every Saturday night (baby-sitters had not been heard of) my parents *shlepped* me (not unwillingly) to partake of the comedian's 'I say, I say, I say', the acrobats and jugglers, the sentimental songs like 'Daisy, Daisy', and the *risqué* turns, some of which I precociously understood, or thought I did, but was shrewd enough to pretend I did not. So far as my parents were concerned I was a complete innocent. Sex was not so much a taboo subject in our home, it was never mentioned at all. Together with other boys of my age my sex education was gained in the school playground. In later years, when I came across an explicit reference to sexual topics in the Talmud, I used to say to myself: 'I remember Basil Cohen telling us that', Basil Cohen being the school's Havelock Ellis (or, more appropriately, Kraft-Ebbing).

I was born in Penrose Street in the Hightown district of Manchester. The names of the surrounding streets were derived from the place-names and flora of the Lake District, the source of Manchester's water supply. There was a Thirlmere Street, an Elm Street, and a Sycamore Street—the 'Magnolia Street' of Louis Golding's novel, where Jews lived on one side of the street, Gentiles on the other. Penrose Street was rather more ghettoised, only two non-Jewish families living there, the Robinsons and the Ridleys. I was a close friend of Norman, the younger of the two Ridley boys, but stood in awe of his father, a policeman. The Jewish mothers in the street, including mine, would threaten their unruly children with: 'If you don't behave yourself I'll tell Constable Ridley.' Mrs Ridley in particular did not take kindly to the position given to her husband of honorary watchdog for Jewish juvenile delinquents.

There were two Jewish grocery shops: Dardik's at one end of Penrose Street, Sheinberg's at the other. Meat and chicken were bought at the kosher butcher-shop, just around the corner, in Heywood Street, owned by a Mr Kahn, whose son was studying at the Telz Yeshivah. I had heard much about Telz from my father, who had heard it from his father, but it was Mr Kahn's talk about his son's prowess at the Yeshivah that captivated me, although, at that time, I had no more than the vaguest notion of what a Yeshivah was. Other shops in the district were Radivan's the greengrocer's, selling huge, luscious pickled cucumbers; and an all-purpose store, owned by non-Jewish people, whose name I have forgotten, patronised by Jewish children for its mouth-watering array of sweets and chocolates. Long strips of liquorice and large sweet concoctions known as 'gob-stoppers' were the main draw on our meagre pocket-money. At this shop we bought our comics – the *Beano*, the *Magnet* and so forth. We were aware that there really existed public schools with characters like Billy Bunter and Harry Wharton, where Latin was taught and where brothers were addressed as Smith major and Smith minor, but it was all as remote from our own world as the adventures of Weary Willie and Tired Tim.

Relations between Jews and Gentiles were fairly good in Manchester generally. In Hightown, they were cordial. Jewish boys had non-Jewish friends but we were warned not to eat *terefa* food when we visited our Gentile 'pals'. On the whole they managed to avoid any sly digs at Jews, as we were careful never to ridicule Christian practices. Occasionally, however, chiefly in fun, organised battles took place between Christians and Jews. During one of these fights in the school playground, I was captured by the Christians who tied my boot-laces together in order to incapacitate me from continuing the struggle. With my non-pugilistic, not to say cowardly, record, I doubt that I would have been much good even with my laces untied. A useful function of the non-Jewish boys of the neighbourhood was to light the fire in Jewish homes on the Sabbath in winter, a task they gladly undertook since the few pennies they received in payment were very welcome.

Although most of the Jewish working men in Manchester did not work on the Sabbath, most of them did not go to synagogue either. But they sent their children to the Friday night and Sabbath morning services. I used to go to a little synagogue in Elm Street, where I had my Bar Mitzvah. I recall being amazed, when I was little, at the ease with which the worshippers could rattle off the lengthy Hebrew prayers, convinced that I would never be able to gain fluency in the strange language. On special occasions, my father would take me to the splendid Great Synagogue with its stained-glass windows, its top-hatted wardens and prayer-books with English translations on pages facing the Hebrew. When I saw the heading 'Hymn of Glory', not having come across these words before, I concluded that it must somehow be a reference to my Uncle Hyman, President of the synagogue.

At the age of five I was enrolled at the St John's School, also in Elm Street, a crumbling, neo-Gothic monstrosity of a building with cracked walls and outside toilets, scheduled for demolition within the year. Whatever the demerits of the building, the atmosphere in the school was relaxed and pleasant. My earliest recollection, still very vivid, is looking through the railings of this school at the age of about three to gaze at my cousin Marje, playing with her friends in the playground, my mother saying: 'That's where you are going to go when you are a little older.' I have questioned many people over the years about their very early recollections. Their memory of very early events in their lives has generally been the same as mine; that perception in infancy does not differ in kind from that in adolescence and adulthood. Of course, a little child has far fewer objects of perception and far less ability to reflect on his experiences, but that which he does experience seems to be perceived with the same clarity as that of grown-ups.

When the school closed, I was enrolled at the school which my parents had attended, the Jews' School in Derby Street at the bottom of Cheetham Hill Road. I still have a school photograph of Class Four in the school and another of my father in the same class some fifty years earlier. The resemblance between the two of us is uncanny; both of us with the same very dark features and both wearing the school cap askew in exactly the same way. My dark complexion was an acute source of embarrassment to my mother and her sisters. My maiden Aunt Ettie would often take me on an outing to the pictures or to a restaurant for tea, but, before we set out, she would give my face a liberal sprinkling of face powder. Once she overdid it and a women friend stopped us in the street to say: 'The little boy is so pale. Is he well?' My mother did not look at all Jewish. On one occasion she took me along with her to buy something in a Jewish-owned shop, where she overheard the shopkeeper say to his wife in Yiddish: 'Take a look. A *shiksa* with a Yiddisher *yingel*.'

The Jews' School in Manchester, like its counterpart, the Jews' Free School in London, was established in the last century with the aim of helping the children of Jewish immigrants to become fully integrated into English society. All the teachers were staunch English patriots. The day began with prayers and hymns in English; a popular one was sung to the rousing tune of 'Deutschland, Deutschland, Über Alles' – naturally, it was given words more appropriate for Jewish boys and girls in England. On Armistice Day at 11 o'clock in the morning, we all had to observe the two minutes' silence, after which we were treated to a patriotic speech extolling the virtues of the great country that had been so hospitable to the Jews, many of whom had given their lives for her in the Great War. For all that, our thoughts were directed frequently towards Palestine, Manchester Jewry being strongly Zionist in outlook. On *Tu Bishvat*, we would be given the blue and white boxes of almonds from the Holy Land, by courtesy of the Jewish National Fund. In my teens I joined the Young Zionist Society and would go around with my friends soliciting contributions to the Fund.

At the age of eight, I suffered a severe attack of appendicitis and was rushed off to hospital to have my appendix removed. The operation was successful but I still have a huge scar on my abdomen to show for it. Anaesthetisation was a tricky affair in those days. It was done with a chloroform pad placed over the nose and mouth. I remember the anaesthetist asking me up to what number I could count. 'To a million', I replied. 'Go ahead and count', said he, which I did, succumbing when I reached nine. My mother was a religious woman in her own way and was not averse to seasoning her religion with a dose of superstition. She would never sew a button on my clothes while I was wearing them unless I chewed on something while she was doing the sewing, otherwise, she had been told, I would acquire 'a cat's head' (*a katz in kop*). I remembered this years later when I read in the Talmud that since cats eat mice and since whoever eats food from which mice have eaten forgets his learning, it follows *a fortiori* that the cat, unlike the dog, is a forgetful creature. Naturally, then, when I was taken to hospital my mother heeded the advice of a local rabbi that my name be changed. A prayer is recited in the synagogue for a severely sick person in which it is stated that X's name has been changed to XY so that any evil decree on X no longer applies, since he is now not X but XY. Joshua Trachtenberg refers to the process in his *Jewish Magic and Superstition*. So Hayyim ('Life') was added to my name and, for years afterwards, I was called to the Torah as Hayyim Yehudah Laib, but eventually dropped this, not out of a brave defiance of superstition; it just happened.

Like most Jewish mothers in Manchester, my mother was afraid of the evil eye. A poor woman with a powerful squint was particularly suspected of possessing this baneful power. This woman, meeting me with my mother, did not exactly say: 'What a lovely little boy!' – that would have been too blatantly untrue – but she did look at me, making some complimentary remark. No sooner had the woman left us, than my mother spat three times, placing a little of the spittle on my face, evidently in the belief that this was effective in preventing the consequences of the evil eye.

My mother's faith in miracle workers was given expression when a niece of hers was lying dangerously ill in hospital. Mother consulted a rabbi who gave her some kind of amulet to place under her niece's pillow at the hospital but warned her it would only work if she kept silent, not speaking to a soul, on her way to perform her mission. Off she went but as luck would have it she met one or two friends on the way, whose greetings she met with stony silence. 'What's the matter with Lena Myerstone?' her friends declared. 'She's become very stuck up lately.' Undeterred, mother carried out her task. Her niece made a miraculous recovery, thanks to the skill of the doctors, said those not in the know. Mother knew better. It was due to the rabbi's amulet and her ability to carry out his instructions to the letter.

After my operation, my parents treated me as if I was wrapped in cotton wool, which, due to the large bandage I was now obliged to wear round my middle, in a sense I was. I recall being terribly embarrassed when seeing tears in their eyes while we watched the film in which Al Jolson sang the horribly sentimental 'Sonny Boy'. The outcome of all this coddling was my transfer to a third school, the Jews' School being thought by my parents to involve too long a journey for their delicate offspring. The new school in which I was enrolled, Temple School, a few blocks away from home, had excellent teachers and was housed in an attractive modern building. The boys and girls (like the other schools, it was co-educational) were encouraged to read widely and to express their own thoughts in writing. The English teacher had stamps with the picture of an elephant which he would stick on to the first page of a particularly commendable essay produced by a pupil. I won my 'elephant' for an essay on the trite subject, 'A Visit to the Zoo', in which I wrote that the monkeys I had seen there were so like humans that they supported Darwin's theory. I began another essay on the economics of coal with: 'Coal, that great saviour that has enriched mankind', or some such pretentious one-upmanship. The teacher read this out to the class with an ironic smile but he still gave me my 'elephant'.

That such topics were discussed at all by eleven-year-olds and younger speaks eloquently for the advanced methods of Temple School. But all good things come to an end. Elementary schooling was only up to the age of eleven. On reaching that age I was obliged to go elsewhere. I had the ambition to win a place at the Manchester Grammar School, like my father, but no arrangements were made for this at Temple School. Of course, I cannot say whether I would have won the place in any event, but I was not given the opportunity to find out. Instead off I went to be enrolled at the Manchester Central High School for Boys, second in prestige only to the Manchester Grammar School. The entrance examination for the school consisted of an interview in which three teachers (a *Beth Din*) fired questions at the candidate to test his IQ (the term itself had not yet been invented). Among other questions I was asked: 'Who is the King of Spain?' (he had been deposed, so it was a trick question) and 'Describe an umbrella.' To ask the latter of a Jewish boy without expecting him to use his hands was to try his patience considerably.

The teacher of Ancient History at the school humbly consulted the Jewish boys in his class whenever there was a need to discuss the Biblical period. On Friday afternoons, the English

Literature teacher would read aloud from *The Wind in the Willows* in a melodious voice and gently led us into an appreciation of captivating English writers.

Most of the Jewish boys at the school came from more or less observant homes. We were exempt from attendance at Christian prayers; the Jewish sixth-formers tried to share with us, in a room set aside for the purpose, their somewhat perfunctory knowledge of Judaism. Their favourite method was to read passages from *Ethics of the Fathers* without explaining them very much. They repeated Hillel's famous saying so frequently that 'If I am not for myself who is for me?' became a catchword for the younger boys, who jokingly used it whenever trying to defend their rights. We did not eat the school meals but brought sandwiches which we ate at a separate table in the dining hall. The Jewish boys met with little anti-Semitism, except from a group of boys who lived in at the Chetham's Hospital, established in the seventeenth century as a home for orphans. These boys were obliged to wear an outfit, dating from the eighteenth century, with long skirts and silver buckles on their highly polished shoes. Looking ridiculous and resenting it, they vented their spleen on the Jewish boys, most of whom lived in terror of these cherubic toughies. When they taunted us with the cry 'Yid' or 'Sheeny', none of us dared retaliate with 'Girlie' or 'Cissie' and we had to grin and bear it. On only one occasion I plucked up enough courage to engage in fisticuffs with a Chetham's Hospital boy. I lost, of course, and earned a black eye, to the consternation of my mother and the pride of my father, who was fond of saying: 'Always stand up for yourself. No one else will' – little knowing that he had been anticipated by Hillel.

Unfortunately, my father's income was such that my attendance at the Central High School became too heavy a drain on the family resources so I moved to my fifth school, the Cheetham Senior School, also close to home. Mr Chapman, the headmaster of the school, ruled with an iron hand, doling out floggings (on the hand, with a cane) with alarming regularity. But the pupils in the top form, to which I was admitted, were allowed by him to go their own way to a large extent. The prefects, as we were grandiloquently called, were permitted a certain latitude in attending classes. Instead, when we were not lording it over the youngsters and telling each other off-colour jokes, we organised such things as school plays and classes in public speaking. We also spent a good deal of time oiling the cricket bats for the use of the school team, in which I was wicket-keeper. 'Howzat' became my favourite shout in dreams and while awake. When I put on my tefillin after Bar Mitzvah, if there was a match that day, I used fervently to pray that I might succeed in stumping out a record number of the opposing side. My fondness for the game had been nurtured by my father who, in summer, when there were no Broughton Rangers fixtures, would take me (on the Sabbath, I have to say) to watch the cricket at Old Trafford. My moment of glory came while sitting, with other boys, just near the boundary at a Test match. Don Bradman, the famous Australian cricketer, was fielding and made a magnificent catch just within the boundary, to fall at my feet with the ball held firmly in his hand.

With a good deal of effort and the help of a Jewish printer I knew, we also managed to produce a school magazine, in which my first little piece in print appeared – a hideous poem praising the school. Years later, when I was a rabbi in my home town, I paid a courtesy call on the headmaster, who had retained the only copy of the magazine to have been published, which he gave to me, perhaps only too glad to be rid of the memory of what, by any standards, was an unruly lot of boys. His first words were: 'So you are one of those people who think they can put the world to right. Humph!' – after which he relaxed sufficiently to discuss his problems with me over coffee. He and the other teachers were blunt, forthright Lancashire men and women whose caustic manner concealed their real sense of vocation. Against the odds, they persevered in trying to impress a degree of learning and culture on very unpromising material. It will have been noticed, however, that my general schooling has been desultory and I have suffered from it.

My Jewish education was equally varied and uncertain at first. Boys, but not girls, were expected to spend an hour or two each day at one of the Hebrew schools, of which there were many, privately run by *melamdim*, Hebrew teachers possessing varying degrees of competence. There was an excellent Talmud Torah in Manchester using modern pedagogical methods but run on completely traditional lines. The Principal of the Talmud Torah in my day was Dr I. Slotki, who was succeeded by his son, Dr Judah Slotki, both renowned educationists. My father had received his Hebrew education at the Talmud Torah. He was fond of reciting the Hebrew poem he and the other boys had to learn in order to welcome Sir Samuel Montagu (later the first Lord Swaythling) when that worthy paid a visit to Manchester. For some reason I was not enrolled in the Talmud Torah but attended a succession of Chedarim. The first of these was conducted by a Mr Hirsh, an elderly gentleman whose English was inadequate so he tried to teach us in Yiddish, a language of which we knew nothing. It soon became evident that it was a complete waste of time, so my parents sent me to learn Hebrew and the other requirements at the house of a young man in Penrose Street itself. This young man had studied at Manchester Yeshivah and was a capable teacher. I still recall him reading with us the narrative in Genesis of the war of the four kings against the five and making it all come alive. Unfortunately, he contracted tuberculosis (this was before the discovery of penicillin) and had to be admitted to a sanatorium, where he lingered until his death some years later. My next Cheder was run by an optician with a good knowledge of Hebrew and Jewish literature, Mr Nachman Engelsberg. Mr Engelsberg, a staunch Zionist, introduced his charges to the niceties of modern Hebrew literature and Jewish history, enlivening the lessons with Jewish jokes of all kinds, most of them stale but for us very fresh. Nachman soon emigrated to *Eretz Yisrael* and lived to witnesss the establishment of the State of Israel. I was again on the move, this time to a Cheder that changed my life.

Reb Yonah Balkind opened his Cheder at the age of nineteen. At the time of writing, almost sixty years later, Balkind's Cheder is still headed by this extraordinary pedagogue (may he live to be a hundred and twenty!). In my time the Cheder was situated in a barn-like structure in Elizabeth Street, Hightown. Reb Yonah took the lessons in a large room on the ground floor. Helping him to keep order was the non-Jewish caretaker and general factotum, a Mr Peart, of whom the boys stood in almost as much awe as of Reb Yonah. The upper floor had been converted into a recreation area, serving as a boy's club for the youngsters of the Cheder and the neighbourhood, all Jewish of course. Here were installed a fine billiard table and tennis table. Reb Yonah and Mr Peart taught us how to play both games. One or two of the Cheder boys acquired such prowess at ping-pong that they became world champions.

Rebbe Balkind, as most people referred to him, was beyond doubt the most naturally gifted pedagogue I have ever met, in spite of the fact, or possibly because of it, that he was self-taught in the art of teaching. (He gained his vast knowledge of Judaism in his native Gateshead and at the Manchester Yeshivah.) He had constant recourse to practical illustration. For instance, when we studied the portion dealing with the construction of the Tabernacle in the wilderness he would take us to the floor upstairs where we would proceed, equipped with the necessary tools, to try our hand at constructing a scale model. Inevitably we met with difficulties, pointed out by the critics, but it was part of the fun to see whether we could make the model stand without collapsing, which it never did. (According to some of the critics, the Tabernacle was an ideal structure, based on Solomon's Temple, but the boys at Balkind's, and I imagine Reb Yonah himself, had never heard of Biblical Criticism.) Or when we arrived at the portion (we studied the biblical portion of the week with complete regularity) in Exodus dealing with the ox that falls into a pit we would be led outside into the earthen yard where some of us would actually dig the pit while others would act out the part of the ox.

Rebbe Balkind conducted the Cheder purely out of his love for Judaism. He had to live, of course, but, compared with the other Chedarim, his tuition fees were laughably low. The poorer boys (of which, when my father was out of work, I was one) were given free tuition. He was single at the time. When he married and had to support a wife and family, he had to be a little more realistic, but he remained indifferent to a fault to financial gain. Whenever I wish to understand something of what the Talmudic Rabbis meant by *Torah lishmah* ('Torah study for its own sake'), I cast my mind back to Rebbe Balkind and his dedication.

In the higher classes of the Cheder, we studied the weekly portion together with Rashi's commentary for which we were

Author, aged 10, with parents Harry and Lena

Mr Balkind and the Old Boys of his Cheder at the wedding of one of them
Mr Balkind – second from left; author – second from right

Shula in 1942 at Kibbutz Shivat Zion in Bromsgrove,
Worcestershire

Manchester wedding, 1947

first obliged to master the 'Rashi script'. A particular innovation in Rebbe Balkind's Cheder was the 'speed test'. Each boy would be required to read, as quickly as he could, a given number of lines from the Hebrew while the Rebbe took a mark off for every mistake and Mr Peart stood by with a stop-watch. The mark taken off for a mistake was made to count as an extra second, the idea being to see which boy could get through the lines with the greatest speed. On a chart the name of the boy who did it in the fastest time each week was displayed, efforts being made to break the record – held for weeks, I recall, by Sidney Olsberg, a real champion who managed to read the lines in just over two minutes. Nowadays educationists may throw up their hands in horror at such a method of teaching. All I know is that it succeeded in producing hundreds of youngsters who were never embarrassed in later life by their lack of fluency in Hebrew.

I have always seen Reb Yonah as my teacher *par excellence*. Even when a rabbi in Manchester, I stood in awe of him. He frequently came to the synagogue to hear me speak or preach but he made me feel inadequate, without intending to do so, because my boyhood teacher stood before me in my mind's eye. It was characteristic of the man that even when I had blotted my copy book in his eyes, he refused to denounce me but tried to understand why I held such strange views. I am afraid that I did not even try to convince him, realising that such an attempt would be quite fruitless. He was set in his ways as I had become set in mine. Unwilling to embarrass this kindly teacher, I have never tried since to communicate with him. On more than one occasion I was tempted to send him something I had written but, rightly or wrongly, resisted the temptation. In the words of the Talmud, 'A mountain has raised itself between us.' If he reads these remarks or has them conveyed to him, I hope he will understand them for what they are: a sincere tribute to a great teacher to whom, more than any other, I owe whatever appreciation of traditional Judaism I may have.

A particular favourite of Reb Yonah was the Commentary to the Bible by R. Moses Alsheikh, the preacher in sixteenth-century Safed. The *Alsheikh* ('the Sheikh') is, of course, homiletical. One would not normally go to it for serious Biblical exegesis. Yet, in Reb Yonah's skilful exposition, we youngsters could not help admiring the brilliance of the sage of Safed, gifted, so Reb Yonah would tell us, with *ruah ha-kodesh* ('the holy spirit'). In other than its strict theological sense, the *Alsheikh*, and Reb Yonah himself, were truly inspired.

Reb Yonah was a fundamentalist but so was every other Orthodox teacher I had in those days and later. Perhaps it is too imprecise to state it so baldly. It was not that he and my other teachers positively rejected historical methods. They were simply unaware of their existence. Traditional views on all matters were the only views they entertained or wished to entertain. There was a narrowness in their approach but this was offset by their appreciation and great love of the *Torah*, and the *mitzvot*. Reb Yonah was born in England and spoke (and largely thought) in English. But his spiritual home was the Lithuania of the famed Yeshivot, the learned rabbis, the pious householders, with never an unworthy thought allowed to intrude. He would no doubt consider me to be one of his failures, but his successes were many – pupils won to traditional Judaism by this dedicated man. Having said this, I cannot pretend that I have regrets for having moved eventually out of that world with its weaknesses as well as its strengths.

Although neither my parents nor my aunts and uncles were strictly observant Jews, there was a traditional Jewish atmosphere in our home. No one in our family, for instance, would ever have dreamed of belonging to a Reform synagogue. The degree of observance may have been less than perfect, otherwise, but father did not go to work on the Sabbath, neither did my uncles, and they recited *kiddush* and grace after meals on the day. Dressed in my Sabbath best, I would visit my Uncle Hyman and Aunt Bertha and Uncle Joe and Aunt Mary. They lived respectively in Maud Street, on one side of Penrose Street, and Crummock Street on the other. Uncle Hyman had acquired a collection of adventure stories in his boyhood. On my weekly visits I would read chapter after chapter of these as well as the *Arabian Nights*, from which latter I learned captivatingly of Sultan Al-Rashid, Sheherezade, djinns, the ghouls and the magicians.

16

On Passover, we would enjoy Aunt Bertha's hospitality for the first *Seder,* Aunt Mary's for the second. During a lull in the proceedings at both homes my cousins would regale us with songs from the musical comedies, not quite relevant to reflection on the Exodus but very enjoyable nonetheless.

On Passover afternoons I would be taken to visit my mother's relations who lived along Cheetham Hill and then to my father's who lived in Strangeways, where we sampled the ginger and *eingemachts,* a mixture of beetroot and syrup prepared by my aunts and female cousins. Later we would discuss which of the relatives excelled in the art, Aunt Bertha usually winning hands down.

Passover, in Manchester, was the season when games with nuts came into their own. Boys and girls who had acquired skill in these games would come home with pockets bulging with nuts to be scolded by their parents for ruining their best suits and frocks. It being *Yom Tov,* no one played for money. Only the most lax youngsters handled money at all on the festival. Consequently, without our consciously being aware of it, a semi-religious atmosphere was imparted to the games.

Uncle Hyman was a gramophone buff. He also would try to get the right station on his 'cat's whisker' radio, a fascinating object for me. On one occasion, Uncle Hyman had a Caruso record on the gramophone, and just as the singer had completed his aria in popped the *shamash* of my uncle's synagogue to collect the dues. I was a little boy and a gullible little boy at that, so when Uncle Hyman jokingly remarked that the *shamash* was Caruso who had popped out of the gramophone, I believed him. The *shamash* had a long beard and my mother had a habit of referring to anyone with a long beard as a *rov.* For years afterwards, the result of it all was that my mind was totally confused as to the real identity of *shamashim,* rabbis and Caruso. Tiny though I was, I am still ashamed to confess that I thought the few old, bearded men in the little synagogue around the corner somehow went home after the service to live in the gramophone. I must also confess that I still share with some of my colleagues some uncertainty about the role of a rabbi in the Jewish world of today.

On the eve of Yom Kippur my father would carry out the *kapparah* ceremony as he had seen it done by his father. The ceremony, originally done with a cockerel, for which my father, like his father, substituted a sum of money, was denounced by the author of the *Shulhan Arukh* (code of Jewish law) as superstition, but Isserles gives it as the Ashkenazi custom. Father would wrap the money in a handkerchief and swing it first around his own head (one has to find atonement for oneself before one can help others to find it), then around mother's head, then around mine, saying (in Hebrew): 'This is the atonement. This money will be given to charity while I (you) will proceed to enjoy good and long life.' The Biblical length of days is the traditional Jewish blessing. But the greeting to those who have lost a near relative, 'I wish you long life', is peculiar to this country and is unknown in other countries where Jews live. It would be of interest to learn how the practice originated and why only in Anglo-Jewry.

Before going to synagogue for the *Kol Nidre* service, father would go the house of a friend and neighbour just down the street, also named Jacobs, though no relation, to say (in Yiddish): 'May we succeed in our supplications (*ausbetten*) for a good year.' We would then go to the service in the hall of my first school, St Johns, which was still standing even though the school itself had been demolished. (There cannot be anything to it, but it is a coincidence that my synagogue is in St John's Wood and was once known as the St John's Wood Synagogue.) The hall was lit by naked gas flares. Whenever I hear the *Yigdal* hymn being sung to the traditional melody, I am taken back to that hall with the worshippers chanting this hymn with the same melody while the gas lights flickered to provide a strongly numinous atmosphere.

Of all my aunts, Aunt Sarah was the most observant. She was the daughter of a Hasid from Austria and followed, as best she could, the pattern of Jewish life she had witnessed in her home. Her preparations for Passover were most stringent. Everything had to be thoroughly scoured before Passover, including the tables so that there was not the slightest possibility of even the minutest bit of leaven being left in the house. Once I confessed to her that I was afraid of the dark. Read the *Shema*, she said, before you go to bed and nothing will harm you or make you afraid. It did not quite work but it helped. Aunt Sarah was the second wife of my father's older brother, Alec. Before he could marry Sarah, he had to obtain a *get* from his first wife. Little as I was, when I heard Alec discussing the *get* with my father, and being very uncertain what a *get* was, I naturally thought it was something to do with marriage that Uncle Alec had to 'get' and for which he had to pay some of his hard-earned cash – which, in fact, it was.

As a boy I belonged to the 'Penrose Street Gang'. We were far less sinister than the name suggests, our main activities being to play cricket in summer and football in winter with rival 'gangs' and fight these on occasion, and to collect wood for the bonfire on Guy Fawkes' night. We were all great jazz fans, with Cab Calloway our special hero. Many years later, Stefan Grapelli performed at one of the concerts instituted by the New London Synagogue. Afterwards he remarked to the Chairman of the synagogue that he was gratified to see the rabbi tapping his feet to the melody of 'Tea for Two'.

On Saturday nights we would all go in a group to the pictures with Mars Bars for refreshments. Whenever we could we liked to watch gangster films starring Humphrey Bogart, James Cagney, Edward G. Robinson and Paul Muni. The last two, we felt, were the greatest since they were Jewish. When a horror film or other films declared unsuitable for children were being shown we would plaster our hair with brilliantine and tell them at the ticket office that we were sixteen, the age when admittance to such films was allowed. We usually got away with it.

Fed, like the majority of Jewish boys in my neighbourhood, on a diet of piety of a very undemanding kind, the joys of the cinema, the excitement of sport, the appeal of jazz and the affection of the family, my boyhood was far from unhappy. Manchester may have been a rainy city; it was never a gloomy one, at least, not for a boy growing up in the Jewish district. I cannot say that my schooldays were the happiest days of my life but they were not the worst by any means.

2

MANCHESTER YESHIVAH

One day, immediately after my Bar Mitzvah, Reb Yonah
Balkind said to me: 'Jacobs, have you thought of going to the
Yeshivah?' Although I had heard from Mr Kahn the butcher all
about the Telz Yeshivah in Lithuania, where his son had been
sent to study, I was extremely vague about what a Yeshivah was
really like. As for the Manchester Yeshivah, all I recalled of it was
walking past the Yeshivah building years before with my father
(I must have been no more than seven years old at the time). It
was fairly late at night and my father, pointing to the shadows
moving across the curtained windows, said: 'These are young
men studying to be rabbis.' Red Yonah explained that there
was an after-school class at the Yeshivah into which I would
fit. My parents declaring, 'Why not?' I was duly enrolled in this
class, where I found myself in the company of boys from strictly
observant homes, attending various schools in Manchester and
Salford.

The curriculum at the Yeshivah proper (the full-time course)
was confined entirely to the Talmud, but the afternoon class
I attended was somewhat broader in scope. We studied Rashi,
the Humash, the other Biblical books (the prophetic books),
Jewish history, Hebrew grammar, and, of course, elementary
Talmud. The teachers were Mr Chaim Meyers and Rabbi
Golditch (later Dayan Golditch of the Manchester Beth Din).
The Yeshivah received a grant from the Jewish Memorial Coun-
cil, in return for which the examiner of the Council, Mr Herbert
Adler, paid an annual visit to see if the requirements of the grant,
including a good knowledge on the part of the students of Jewish
history and Hebrew grammar, were being met.

The whole thing was treated as a huge joke. Did not the
Tosafists, in mediaeval France, say that the Babylonian Talmud

20

contained all that was necessary for Jewish studies? Once the Yeshivah knew the date when 'Uncle Herbert' was due to arrive, all the students, full- and part-time, began madly to rehearse the facts they had totally ignored during their uninterrupted studies (at least by the full-time students) of the Talmud. The Yeshivah rang with students singing, in the traditional *Gemara* tune, 'cardinal numbers and ordinal numbers' and the names of the kings of Judah and Israel. When the examiner finally showed up, we looked in wonder at this strange, very Anglicised figure, as if he had come from another world, which in fact he had. He quoted the saying, 'From Moses to Moses none arose like Moses', asking us who was the second Moses referred to in the saying. Thinking to ourselves, 'That's an easy one,' we shouted out, 'Moses Maimonides.' 'No,' was the answer, 'think again.' 'Moses Isserles,' we suggested; a personality not quite up to the standard of Maimonides, but who could know what was going on in the mind of this stranger from the wilds of the Jewish Memorial Council? 'No,' again. 'We give up,' we said in unison. 'Very simple,' Uncle Herbert replied, as if astonished that we could be so ignorant. 'The reference is, of course, to Moses Mendelssohn.' Collapse of all present in comic protest. Only a complete stranger to the Yeshivah world would dare to mention Mendelssohn at all in a Yeshivah, still less compare the 'heretic' with *Moshe Rabbenu* and imply that he was greater than the *Rambam* and the *Rama*. The bemused Adler, to whom we must have seemed as odd as he was to us, nevertheless gave us a favourable report. After all, we had been able successfully to rattle off the names of the kings of Judah and Israel and to conjugate the verb *katal* ('to kill'); trust the strange Londoner, we thought, to choose this example, little knowing that this was the usual choice in scholarly circles. No sooner had he departed than the full-time students reverted to the study of the Talmud with an unspoken apology to the melody for having used it for purposes for which it had never been intended. We part-time students, however, continued to study the other semi-'profane' subjects.

Rabbi Golditch was a superb teacher, erudite, witty and imaginative. It was he who awakened my interest in Bible studies. His father, Reb Susya, was a Hasidic Rebbe – the only one in Manchester – and Rabbi Golditch would share with us his first-hand acquaintance with the world of Hasidism; unexplored territory, except for the one or two boys who were themselves from Hasidic homes. One afternoon (this was when I had become a full-time student at the Yeshivah) Reb Susya came to the Yeshivah on his father's *Yahrzeit* to take the *Minhah* service. Although the Litvaks were aghast at this invasion, they had too much respect for the venerable Rebbe to say him nay. Two huge brass candlesticks were set up on the reading desk, into which long white candles were inserted and lit. As part of the ritual, the Rebbe then smoked an aromatic Turkish cigarette, representing, his sons patiently explained, the incense offered in the Temple. The Rebbe then led us in prayer, his face, adorned with a snowy white beard, illumined by the light of the candles, reminding us, Litvaks though we were in outlook, of the shine on Moses' face. This, the aroma of the cigarette and the Rebbe's melodious voice ringing out in fervour, was the nearest any of us had ever come to a mystical experience. The lone voice of the Yeshivah sceptic was heard remarking afterwards: 'Very pleasant. But can he learn?' This was my first introduction to the Hasidic/Mitnaggedic debate, helping me a little to understand both sides of the fray, when, years later, I wrote on Hasidism.

At Reb Susya's home, I saw displayed a photograph of a painting supposed to be of the founder of the Hasidic move-ment, the Ba'al Shem Tov, looking very much like Reb Susya himself with his marvellous face. Alas, Reb Susya, and the many Rebbes who display this photograph, imagining it to be a true likeness of the Ba'al Shem Tov, have been misled. The painting is by the famous Anglo-American artist, John Copley, and is of another Ba'al Shem, the adventurer Samuel Jacob Hayyim Falk, the 'Ba'al Shem of London'.

A boy at the Yeshivah with whom I became friendly, Shalom Dressner, was the son of a devout Belzer Hasid who lived the life of a Hasid in all its detail as if his home were in Galicia. Reb Wolf Dressner had a reputation for integrity in business as well as for Hasidic piety. One Sabbath afternoon, Shalom and I were taking a stroll and we met his mother walking along towards us. I raised my cap to her, after all I had been brought up to be polite, but realised my mistake when I saw the look of consternation on her face. I learned afterwards from Shalom of her surprise that a boy studying at a Yeshivah could have been guilty of aping the gentile practice of raising his hat to a woman. In Belz circles a Yeshivah student would not have been aware that a female was there at all. She had no doubt begun to wonder whether a boy who raised his hat to a lady could possibly be anything but a bad influence on her son.

Shalom's uncle, Mr Carwen, also a Belzer Hasid, loved to describe how the previous Belzer Rebbe, R. Issachar Dov Rokeah, had taken the service on Yom Kippur in Belz, where thousands of Hasidim had assembled to hear the prayers of the saint. 'Incomparable delight,' this true Hasid used to say. 'Why, even if the High Priest himself had suddenly appeared to lead us in prayer, instead of our beloved Rebbe, we would have sent him packing!'

Shalom Dressner's older brother, Baruch Hirsh, made a pilgrimage to Belz. On his return, full of the wondrous things he had witnessed, he solemnly informed his fellow students at the Yeshivah that he was engaged to be married, the Rebbe having chosen a bride for him; she was daughter of a Belzer Hasid in Germany who had to be rescued from the looming Nazi threat. 'Is she pretty?' we asked, only to be told that Baruch Hirsh did not know himself since he had never seen his bride-to-be and would only meet her face to face on his wedding day, as was the custom of the Belzer Hasidim. 'But', we protested in pseudo-innocence, 'the Talmud states explicitly that it is forbidden to marry a woman whom one has not previously seen.' The young Hasid witheringly replied: 'And everything else in the Talmud you follow?'

The Yeshivah was in no way to blame, but like so many impressionable youngsters exposed to religion in an intense form, I became an insufferable little prig and religious fanatic, driving my poor parents frantic with my absurd demands. My bewildered father would protest in vain that his father, himself a very *frum* man, had never done this or that, whatever my stupid act of super-piety happened to be. I am too ashamed, even now, to refer to many examples, such as the particularly odious act of burning a book on science, given to me as a Bar Mitzvah present, because it accepted the theory of evolution, contrary, as I thought, to the Bible. Preparations for Passover became a nightmare for my mother, to whom I would tactlessly quote the example of my extremely devout Aunt Sarah. 'But she is a foreigner', my mother would protest, 'while you are an English boy.' I did not see myself as 'English' and looked down on the English ministers sporting their inverted collars, little dreaming that one day I would belong in their ranks. Had I been old enough to grow a beard I would undoubtedly have grown one, but by the time hair did begin to sprout on my face I had acquired a modicum of common sense and like the other boys at the Yeshivah, removed my facial hair, not with a razor (that was forbidden by the law) but with a noisome depilatory purchased from a local pharmacist. This brought further trials to my parents. The horrible substance smelled like rotten eggs and my mother was obliged to fumigate the house after each usage. By now my parents, though ashamed of it, had become a little accustomed to the odd behaviour of their spoilt only child. I, too, had grown up a little and began to appreciate the wisdom of R. Israel Salanter's famous maxim: 'One must never be *frum* on the shoulders of others.' For all the negative effects (and they were many) of my trip into religious extremism, it had the salutary result of breeding in me a hatred of extremism itself bordering on the fanatical. (Krochmal long ago observed that it is possible to be a fanatical liberal.) When parents have consulted me regarding the problems they have with their *ba'aley teshuvah* offspring, I have said to myself: 'I know what you mean. I have been there.'

It was taken for granted that I would leave school at the age of fourteen to obtain some form of gainful employment. My father had negotiated with a Jewish printer for me to be apprenticed to him, receiving a small wage while I learned the trade. The teachers at the Yeshivah, however, managed to overcome my parents' resistance to my becoming a full-time student. After all, they argued, it does not mean that he has to become a rabbi. After a year or two at the Yeshivah he will be equipped to become a religious journalist. Notwithstanding this, having a religious journalist for a son was not, in my father's eyes, much better than having a rabbi. However, enter the Yeshivah as a full-time student I did. I was now a fully fledged Yeshivah *bochur*, remaining at the Yeshivah for seven years, studying the Talmud and attaining a degree of competence. In seven years it would have been hard to achieve anything less.

Only a handful of the full-time students were from Manchester itself. Most of them were from out of town. These stayed either in private houses or (the older students) in the Yeshivah dormitory. The older students took their meals in the Yeshivah dining hall. The younger ones ate *teg* ('days'); that is, each day they were provided with meals in a Manchester home, where it was considered an honour to help on the study on the Torah in this way. One of the students had a 'day' at our home, where he enjoyed my mother's cooking as much as I did. Mother was hardly a *cordon bleu* cook, but she was a dab hand at fish and chips. This, in true Lancashire fashion, was washed down with strong tea, liberally sweetened. She also prepared a good soup dish which she had been taught by her mother. This was known, in my grandmother's Latvian Yiddish, as *puster fisch* ('fishless'), because, while containing all the ingredients of a good fish dish, it contained no fish!

The Yeshivah students received a small amount of pocket-money from the coffers of the Yeshivah. Many of them earned a little extra by private tutoring and reading the Torah in one of the Manchester synagogues. I earned a few shillings a week reading the Torah in the little *Shomrey Shabbat* synagogue in Elizabeth Street, just across the road from Balkind's Cheder. The members of this conventicle were Lithuanian Jews who followed all the Lithuanian Jewish customs as formulated in the School of the Vilna Gaon, including the reading of the *Haftarot* from hand-written scrolls. My function was to read not only the Torah from the *Sefer Torah* but also the Haftarot from these scrolls as well as the five *Megillot*, each from its own scroll. There were five different melodies for the cantillation: for the Torah itself, for the Haftarot, for the book of Lamentations, for the book of Esther, and, finally, one for the three books of Canticles, Ruth and Ecclesiastes. In this comparatively easy way I managed to acquire familiarity with a good deal of the Hebrew Bible which I can still recite more or less by heart.

This was important since only Talmud was studied at the Yeshivah.

In a house near the Yeshivah in Heywood Street there lived two very learned but very eccentric Talmudists, father and son. It was rumoured that years earlier the father had been a candidate for the post of *Rosh Yeshivah*, 'Head of the Yeshivah'. Since he had a very scruffy appearance, his sponsors had advised him to spruce himself up a little before his interviews with the appointment board. 'That's all very well,' he replied, 'but what if I do this and do not get the job?' The son, Reb Yossel, was slightly deranged, poor man. He used to go around like a tramp with a sack on his shoulders containing all sorts of strange objects. The more imaginative students thought Reb Yossel was a *Lamedvovnik*, one of the thirty-six disguised saints in whose merit the world endures. He was certainly no saint so far as his temper was concerned. When discussing Talmud with the Yeshivah students, he would sometimes feel that they were mocking him and would then fly into a terrible rage, making his exit with a fierce slam of the door while uttering imprecations under his breath. One evening after the teachers had gone home, some of the students were larking around instead of studying. R. Yossel, who was sitting by the fire, in a surprisingly good mood, deftly quoted: 'In those days there was no king in Israel; every man did that which was right in his own eyes' (Judges 21:25).

As in the majority of Yeshivot then and now, the students spent most of their time studying unsupervised usually with another student, attending lectures for only an hour or so each day. Studying was done in the large hall of the Yeshivah, which reverberated to the sounds of fierce debates and the chanting of passages from the Talmud by students studying in this way. I quickly adapted myself to the noisy background, so much so that for years afterwards I was unable to concentrate properly on my studies unless there was some noise, if only that of a radio turned on in an adjacent room. My children were allowed to make as much noise as they wished while I was studying without it disturbing me at all. On the contrary, strange though it may seem, I welcomed it as an aid to concentration.

The teaching, involving detailed exposition of the Talmudic tractate we happened to be studying page by page, was given by the only two full-time teachers: the Rosh Yeshivah, Rabbi Moshe Yitzhak Segal, and Rabbi Yitzhak Dubov, a prominent Lubavitcher Hasid. The Rosh only took the top class; Rabbi Dubov had the remaining two classes. In my day it was a very small Yeshivah with no more than around thirty students. The major fault of the system was the total absence of anything like an organised scheme of studies. Every student was expected to thoroughly study the tractate (sometimes more than one) chosen for the school term but beyond this he was free to study wherever his fancy took him, on the basis of the Talmudic observation: 'A man can only study a topic successfully if his heart is in it.' This was a godsend for lazy students. Partners supposed to be studying could engage in idle gossip, there being no end-of-term examinations and no mapped-out course of study. They usually got away with it, except when caught out by the Rosh on one of his regular perambulations to check whether the students were wasting their time. The greatest sin a Yeshivah student could commit was *bittul zeman*, 'wasting time'.

The advantage of this comparative do-as-you-please attitude on the part of the faculty was that the industrious were able freely to peruse the many books in the Yeshivah library. I used to devour book after book, especially the *Responsa*, which were only names to me and were never actually studied in the Yeshivah. There was neither catalogue nor an adequate arrangement of the books in the library but, quite by accident, I came across a beautifully-produced edition of the *Responsa* of Rabbi David Ibn Abi Zimra (the *Radbaz*), the renowned Halakhic master of sixteenth-century Egypt. This authority's felicity of style and clarity in expressing the most abstruse legal topics taught me that the great Halakhists of the past never engaged in mystification and would always prefer simplicity to woolliness, even when discussing difficult theological matters. When I came to write my *Theology in the Responsa* I realised that my interest in the subject had been aroused by the *Responsa* of the *Radbaz* long before.

The Rosh was a somewhat forbidding figure, stern and unbending, before whom all the students stood in awe. His spotless grey-white beard was always neatly combed, his long black frock-coat always immaculately tidy. Like all the rabbis of the

27

old school in Manchester, he wore a hard black Trilby hat on weekdays and a tall, highly polished silk hat on the Sabbath. I never got over my feelings of uneasiness in his presence but realised, when I came to know him better, that beneath his stern demeanour there beat the heart of a deeply humane teacher, totally concerned for the well-being of his students. His off-putting manner was a cloak he donned in order to preserve discipline in the Yeshivah. We never saw him in his shirt-sleeves in the Yeshivah. The only time I ever saw him without his frock-coat was when he dusted his books before Passover. As a reward for helping him in this task, he gave me a copy of Rabbi Elhanan Wasserman's notes to the Talmud, through which I became familiar for the first time with the analytical methods practised in the Lithuanian Yeshivot. When Dr Altmann, Communal Rabbi of Manchester, delivered the eulogy at the Rosh's funeral, he spoke of him as 'the *Tzaddik* of Manchester', a fitting title for a man whose every breath breathed piety and who was never heard speaking of anything but Torah. To hear him recite the *Shema*, slowly and precisely, with obvious total concentration of the meaning of every word, was to have an object lesson in *yirat shamayim*, 'the fear of the Lord'.

Rabbi Segal, the Rosh, had come to England as a young man after years of study at the Navarodock Yeshivah in Russia. Here Rabbi Yoisel Horowitz, 'the Old Man of Navarodock', taught his own version of the teachings of the Musar movement, founded by Rabbi Israel Salanter. The students at Navarodock would be encouraged at times to adopt bizarre practices for the realisation of their spiritual goals. To cultivate, for instance, the attitude of indifference to fame and worldly opinion, they would go out of their way to court humiliation by such actions as calling out in the synagogue, on an ordinary day, that the New Moon prayers should be recited or by entering a pharmacist to ask for a packet of nails. Reb Yoisel himself lived as a hermit for several years, the better to equip himself for his life's work, the spread of knowledge of the Torah, to which all personal ambition required to be sacrificed. His pupils followed in their master's footsteps. It was not an unusual sight to witness a group of young Navarodockers setting up a revivalist campaign in the market-place of a town. There they would preach repentance and the essential importance of Torah study, and would refuse to be on their way until the townsfolk had agreed to found a Yeshivah.

Although the Rosh appreciated that what was sound doctrine in Navarodock was not necessarily the final word in the vastly different spiritual climate of Manchester, his presentation of Judaism was in the best (or worst, depending on how one sees it) Navarodock traditions. His Judaism was rigorous, severely demanding and, I have in honesty to say, almost completely joyless. The note of admonition was rarely absent from his discourses. Moreover, he brooked no opposition and his every word was law. It was not until a number of students who had escaped from the Nazi terror in Czechoslovakia were enrolled in the Yeshivah that his authority was challenged. He refused to meet certain demands the students had made with regard to conditions of study at the Yeshivah, whereupon they went on strike, to the utter amazement of the docile English students who had come to look upon any criticism of the Rosh as a criticism of the Torah itself.

Before he came to Manchester, the Rosh had been a *shohet* in London. His wife was born in London and they were married in that city. They had five sons, one of whom, Reb Yudel, studied at the Mir Yeshivah in Poland and eventually became his father's successor in Manchester. The Rosh knew English but rarely spoke it. I once overheard him giving instructions to a man who had been engaged to mend a door. The carpenter spoke with a broad Northern accent, the Rosh with an equally broad Cockney accent, but, somehow, they managed to understand one another sufficiently for the door to be repaired. Although my parents spoke Yiddish they only used it at home when they did not wish me to understand what they were saying. But it was no hard task to master enough Yiddish to follow the tuition in that language in the Yeshivah.

In the collected letters of Rabbi A.I. Kook, the famous philosopher and mystic who became the first Chief Rabbi of Palestine, there is a letter to the Rosh, who had inquired of the Rabbi to provide him with guidance on how to foster *yirat shamayim*, 'the fear of the Lord', among the students in the

Yeshivah. The letter (No.998) should be quoted in part, at least, since the Rosh evidently based his approach on Rav Kook's advice:

> Greetings to my dear friend, Great Luminary, Treasure Store of Torah and the pure fear of Heaven, spreading Torah to his flock, our Teacher, Rabbi Moshe Yitzhak Segal, long may he live, Rosh Yeshivah of Manchester. May God protect him. From his brother who greets him with great affection.
>
> Your Honour has made my heart glad that he has begun to teach his students a little Musar and the wisdom that is the fear of the Lord, from the holy books . . . How else can we stir the heart of those young in years, to open their eyes to the splendour, beauty and illumination of the Torah, if not through the study of the true wisdom of the fear of Heaven through the words of the great men in Israel who have delved deeply into the wisdom of this pure fear . . .?
>
> Now I am unable at the moment to provide your Honour with a detailed programme suitable for your dear students. It is especially difficult to adapt ideas of the sacred to the capacity of students, of whose way of thinking, abilities and psychology I am ignorant. Nevertheless it would seem that priority should be given to expounding to all the students the great principle upon which all success in Torah study depends, namely, on the degree of *yirat shamayim* and the holy depths of pure faith rooted in the soul of the mind and its intense application depends on the deep psychological intent regarding the appreciation of the value of the subject one studies. Since it is the Torah, the words of the living God, in which the student is engaged, the quality of loving application depends on the point of the holy fear of the Lord which resides in the heart of one who studies the Torah.

Rabbi Kook continues in this vein, hardly concealing his reluctance to offer concrete advice in a situation of which he is ignorant, contenting himself with rather vague reminders that the really important thing, or at least the priority, is *yirat shamayim*. Progress in Torah study depends on a deep appreciation that the Torah is the word of God. This was the watchword of the Rosh throughout his career, but in practice his students sensed little of the mystical fervour of which Rav Kook wrote in his letter. At the third meal of the Sabbath, for instance, of which the students partook at the Yeshivah, the Rosh's discourses were usually all to the same effect – that the students should not waste their time but apply themselves unceasingly to their studies, with little emphasis on why the study of the Torah was so important and certainly without any philosophical discussion of the significance of Judaism in the contemporary world. Even the *zemirot* were sung to a mournful tune and there was such an air of general gloom that most of us experienced a fast-day rather than a Sabbath mood. Navarodock transplanted in Manchester soil simply did not take root.

It used to be said that anyone who has studied in a Yeshivah may go to Heaven but he will never be able really to enjoy this world. In that sense the Rosh's approach was successful. In later life few of us interpreted Judaism in worldly or utilitarian terms. In my work of Jewish theology I have been saved from any reductionist thrust by my years at Manchester Yeshivah as a student of the Rosh.

Rabbi Dubov was a totally different teacher, jovial and always in a good mood, as a true Hasid should be. The students had the utmost respect for Rabbi Dubov but they never stood in awe of him as they did of the Rosh. I can still see the picture of Rabbi Dubov, with his straggly beard, pipe in his mouth, interrupting his lecture to tell us Hasidic tales or discuss with us the merits of rival tobacco mixtures. He was, of course, a strictly observant Jew but was sufficiently human to warn us against religious excess. On one occasion we were reading the passage in the *Shulhan Arukh* about the need to eat and drink and satisfy the other bodily needs solely 'for the sake of Heaven'. Rabbi Dubov wryly remarked that nowadays it took all our efforts to pray 'for the sake of Heaven', let alone eat and drink. On another occasion, when we were discussing our future careers, he observed that in his opinion every student at a Yeshivah, whatever his ambitious motivation, studies the Torah 'for its own sake'. For, he said, if he has the brains to study the Torah, even if he does so in order to win fame or a career (as a rabbi), he could have equally achieved his ambition by studying to be a doctor or a lawyer. Even if his basic motivation is a self-seeking one it is still untainted since, after all, he caters to it by studying God's Torah.

The *Habad/Lubavitch* tendency in Hasidism, of which Rabbi Dubov was a prominent representative, was founded by R. Shneur Zalman of Liady (1747–1813) and represented the intellectual, contemplative movement in Hasidism. Rabbi Dubov used to pray in the Habad mode, his heavy, woollen *tallit* over his head, singing or humming a yearning melody as his thoughts soared aloft to the 'upper worlds' of which the Kabbalah speaks.

Rabbi Dubov came to England in his middle age. After experiencing at first hand the rigours first of Czarist then of Communist Russia, he loved the free atmosphere of England in whose praise he was unceasing. On a royal occasion – I think it was the jubilee of King George V and Queen Mary – he was seen climbing on to the roof of the Yeshivah building to hoist there a Union Jack. But he never adopted English ways. When he was chided by a charlady in the Yeshivah who saw him spit into the sink – she called him a 'dirty foreigner' – he quizzically exclaimed to us: 'Isn't it better to get rid of the spittle in the sink than unhygienically carry around a soiled handkerchief in the pocket?' He had nothing but scorn for English ministers and their head, the Chief Rabbi. He was furious with the Honorary Officers of the Yeshivah for inviting Dr Hertz to preside at a Yeshivah prize-giving, seeing in it the hand of God when the Chief Rabbi was prevented from accepting. He loved to scoff at the Chief Rabbi's grandiose title. 'If a Reverend is a *goy*,' he would say, 'it must follow that a Very Reverend is a great *goy* (*a grosser goy*).' He had a melodious voice and served as Chazan in the Lubavitcher synagogue, the *Adath Israel*, enrolling some of us in the choir for Rosh Ha-Shanah and Yom Kippur as well as for Selichot. Before the midnight Selichot service, he would take us to his home, where his wife would prepare a concoction of milk, sugar and raw eggs for each of us which he called a 'goggle-moggle' after the sound made by the nauseous mixture as it went down. This was intended to make us sing more sweetly but, judging by our actual performance, it was not terribly effective (perhaps this should have been rephrased as 'it was effectively terrible'!)

I was first introduced to Habad thought at Rabbi Dubov's home and in the *Adath Israel* synagogue. Rabbi Dubov would read with one or two of his favourites (not for him were modern notions of pedagogical impartiality) passages from the *Zohar* and Habad literature on Sabbath afternoons. It was all very mysterious and beyond our heads but there was life in it and the joy that was almost totally absent in the dry atmosphere of the Yeshivah itself. The Hasidic master, R. Pinhas of Koretz, used to thank God daily for the *Zohar*, which, he said, had saved him from being lost to Judaism (*hat mich derhalten bei Yiddishkeit*). Certainly it was the Hasidic, mystical approach of Rabbi Dubov that saved the students for the religious life of Judaism. (Incidentally, Rabbi Dubov was an excellent teacher of Talmud, explaining the most difficult passages with keen insight and referring us constantly to the opinions of the commentaries and super-commentaries printed around the text and at the back of the volume.)

The rabbi of *Adath Israel* was the very learned Rabbi Rivkin (from whom I later obtained *Semichah*), the *Av Beth Din* of Manchester. Rabbi Rivkin, a gentle soul with a thin, extremely soft voice, used to deliver recondite discourses on Habad thought on Sabbath afternoons. The first time I attended one of these (at Rabbi Dubov's invitation) I noticed that the men sitting around the table were glassy-eyed and uncomprehending, with the exception of one old gentleman who, at appropriate stages of the discourse, interjected an 'Ah', apparently of pleasure, at understanding what was being said. 'This man must be a genius,' I said to the others, who sat in respectful but stony silence. 'Nothing of the kind,' they replied, waving away my admiration. 'The man is as ignorant of what the rabbi is saying as the rest of us. It is simply that he has been attending these discourses for so many years that his reflexes tell him when to say: "Ah"'!

Rabbi Rivkin, with his long, snow-white beard and the silk hat he wore on weekdays as well as on the Sabbath, presented, for all his gentleness, a patriarchal picture to the Manchester community, in which he was held in the highest regard. He wore a little earring made of silver dangling from one ear. The story he once told me in explanation of this adornment was that his brothers had died in infancy and in order to prevent him from meeting the same fate, his mother had been advised by a Hasidic Rebbe to fashion the earring out of silver taken from a Sefer Torah ornament. 'Your little boy must always wear the earring,' said the Rebbe, 'and he will live long.' Whatever one thinks of such miracle-working, it was effective for Rabbi Rivkin, who lived to a ripe old age, suddenly collapsing, without previous illness, as he ascended the steps of the synagogue on the eve of Yom Kippur.

Hasidic Jews wear two pairs of *tefillin*, those of Rashi and of Rabbenu Tam, the normal practice being to wear Rashi *tefillin* only. The extremely pious, in the privacy of their homes, also don the *tefillin* of *Shimusha Rabba*. During one of my visits to Rabbi Rivkin's home for my *Semichah* examination, I discovered him taking off his *Shimusha Rabba tefillin*. I noticed how embarrassed he was to have been caught in the act.

Sermon-tasting was a favourite pastime for the Yeshivah students. Occasionally, we would go to listen to the preachers in English at the various synagogues. Generally we were unimpressed by these *derashot* (sermons) in English. We considered them to be too thin for our taste, preferring the full-blooded, Yiddish sermons of the Maggidim, the itinerant preachers who frequently descended on Manchester to deliver *derashot* in the synagogues on Sabbath afternoons.

The usual practice of the Maggid was to wrap himself around with a huge *tallit*, kiss the curtain of the ark (in apology for having his back to it while addressing the congregation) and then proceed to deliver his *derashah*, speaking softly at first and then working himself up to a frenzy of eloquence. At suitable stages of the *derashah*, the Maggid would burst into chant for added emphasis. I recall one Maggid hotting up and walking in agitation along the platform before the ark, suddenly ripping off his tight collar to balance it precariously on the rail surrounding the platform. Distracted by this, the congregation became less interested in what the Maggid was saying than in speculating when the collar would fall from its perch.

The majority of the Maggidim came to Manchester to solicit funds for the Eastern European Yeshivot. Naturally, their favourite theme was the high rewards promised to patrons of Jewish learning in the Yeshivot. Another favourite was Jewish martyrdom, a theme calculated best to achieve the Maggid's evidence of success – that he had moved the congregation to tears. One could almost hear the Maggid's sigh of relief when the women in the gallery began to sob, thereby demonstrating that his *derashah* was going well. No Maggid worth his salt would fail to tell, or rather chant, the story of R. Haninah ben Teradion. This martyr, according to the Talmud, was burnt at the stake by the Romans, with his body wrapped in a Sefer Torah. When he was asked what he saw, the saint replied: 'I see the parchment being destroyed by fire but the letters are flying aloft.' Here the Maggid would chant repeatedly the words: 'The parchment burns in fire but the letters fly aloft', reminding the congregation that the enemies of Judaism can only harm its exterior, never its soul, which is kept alive in the Yeshivot.

The Maggidim were both superb actors and masters of the art of illustration. One of these, seeking to convey how base is lack of fellow-feeling, asked why it is that the Torah allows fish to be eaten without first being killed by the less painful method of *shehitah* reserved for animals and birds. Unlike other creatures, fish eat other fish, preying on their own species, hence they deserve the worse fate. There was no discussion as to why God created fish to swallow other fish; however, the Maggid's message was not directed to the sceptic or to those who floundered in a sea of doubt. His aim was to strengthen the faith of those who already possessed it in good measure. The truth is that a major aim of the whole exercise was to conjure up the Eastern European way of Jewish living for which the older congregants nostalgically craved.

Another Maggid I heard waxed eloquent on the meaning of the eternal bliss promised to the righteous. He asked his audience to imagine a huge mountain composed of tiny seeds. Once, every million years, a bird takes away a single seed.

Think how long it would take for the bird to remove the whole mountain of seeds, and that vast amount of time is still not eternity. Think further of that huge mountain as constituting but a single seed in a far greater mountain. Think how long it would take for the bird to remove this larger mountain, and you would still not have eternity. And so the Maggid would go on producing ever greater mountains with the constant refrain, 'and that is still not eternity', until the mind reeled. Not for him was any consideration of eternity as beyond space and time altogether. Yet the impression on his audience was far greater when eternity was described so vividly as an endless duration in time rather than in terms of the mystic's eternal Now.

Yet another Maggid, wishing to impress upon his audience the value of carrying out their religious obligations, used a parable he attributed to the Hafetz Hayyim. A merchant travelled to a distant land where precious stones were found in such abundance that they had little worth in terms of cash. Fish, however, was hard to come by in that place and was a rare and costly delicacy. Influenced by the different scale of values in his new environment, the stupid merchant bought vast quantities of fish to take back with him, thinking he would make a fat profit. Of course, by the time he reached his destination the fish stank to high heaven and were worthless. The merchant's wife vented her spleen on her foolish husband for losing all his money on the crazy enterprise. (Here, to the delight of his audience, the Maggid proceeded to describe in detail how the shrew insulted the unfortunate adventurer, acting the parts of both husband and wife.) Exhausted by his ordeal the merchant fell asleep. To his amazement, when he awoke, he found the table laid with all kinds of good things, his wife, all smiles of welcome, greeting him with unaccustomed tenderness, as if nothing untoward had happened. She had looked through his pockets while he was asleep to find there one or two precious stones which she quickly sold and was glad to inform him that they had become rich. '*Oi vey!*', groaned the Maggid, acting the husband's part. 'Precious stones were in great abundance in the place I visited and yet I wasted my money on fish!'

When a Jew, concluded the Maggid, applying the illustration, has wasted his years on worldly vanities, he will have to suffer in

Hell when he has departed this life. But since there is no Jew who has never given to charity or has never answered 'Amen' in the synagogue, he will be admitted into Paradise as his reward. The exquisite bliss he will experience there will be a greater source of anguish to him than his sufferings in Hell, as he comes to realise how many such precious *mitzvot* were there for the asking while on earth, if only he had not been deluded by his folly.

During my years at the Yeshivah, I became aware of the Telzer 'way' (*derekh*) of learning, the analytical and logical methods of study cultivated at the famous Yeshivah of Telz in Lithuania, especially by Rabbi Simeon Skopf and Rabbi J.L. Bloch. This method stressed the importance of understanding the deeper meaning of a text and that this is far more worthwhile than to simply have a superficial knowledge of a large number of texts. At Telz they used to say of a student who could easily tell you where texts were to be found but without really understanding them: 'God knows the way thereof but he (only) knows the place' (an adaptation of the verse in praise of wisdom, Job 28:23).

I was attracted to Telz in any event because it was the hometown of both my grandfather and grandmother, and my father used to tell me stories of the place he had heard from them. One day a raffle was organised at the Yeshivah, the first prize being a slim volume of essays, published by the Telz Yeshivah, containing the ideas of the Telz teachers and students, past and present. To my amazement, I won the raffle and have cherished the volume ever since. It seemed almost as if it was destined for Telz to come into my life, which it did again when Rabbi Dubov asked me to teach his young son, about to become Bar Mitzvah, a piece of Talmudic exegesis to be recited on the happy occasion, prepared by another son of the rabbi who was studying at Telz. This piece, an analysis of the legal principle of agency, was a beautiful example of the Telzer *derekh* at its best. The young boy did not share my delight. When he came to our home for instruction, he preferred to talk cricket with my father.

The result of it all was that I made a firm resolve to get to Telz somehow and I hesitatingly broached the subject to my parents who viewed my stay at the Yeshivah as odd in itself and by now thought I was quite mad. It so happened (in my innocence I saw this as the hand of providence) that an emissary from Telz Yeshivah was visiting Manchester at the time. Aided and abetted by Rabbi Dubov, but discouraged by the Rosh, I spoke to this man who said, in so many words, 'No problems.' The tuition fees would be waived and all I had to do was to make my way to Lithuania. He even gave me precise directions on how to proceed from Kovno railway station. Off I went to the rather shabby Lithuanian Consulate in Manchester to make the necessary arrangements and was all set to realise my dream when the Second World War broke out. Although I had to give up, I still avidly read anything I can get hold of about Telz and about its famous Yeshivah, transplanted now to Cleveland in the USA and to Telstone, a hamlet near Jerusalem.

During the war years, I was exempt from military service as a theological student and could not serve as an army chaplain because I was too young, and had no training for such a position, even had I been old enough. No ignominy was attached to the exemption of *bona fide* theological students from military service. I had been at the Yeshivah for several years and had not joined, as one or two did, in order to escape conscription.

Nevertheless, I have since been haunted by severe feelings of guilt for not having engaged actively in the struggle against Nazism when so many of my former school friends gave their lives for the cause. When I was being interviewed as a candidate for the position of Minister to the New West End Synagogue, many years later, a member of the Council of the Synagogue (he later became a good friend) eyed me up and down and said: 'To be honest, we are impressed with your credentials but what of your military career (or rather lack of it) in the service of King and Country?' I could only stammer an explanation and although I did get the position I felt that I had been given a thick black mark, mentally at least.

My failure to travel to Telz only whetted my appetite for learning of the sort offered there. I had heard that it was to be found in the Rabbi of Sunderland, Rabbi Rabbinovitch, of whom it was reported that he knew the whole of the Talmud by heart. Feeling increasingly that I was getting nowhere in the Yeshivah I wrote in desperation to the Sunderland Rav asking if he could take me on as his private pupil; a ridiculous request, full of *chutzpah*, as I soon realised. In the letter I wrote to the Rav I enclosed a 'piece of Torah', a lengthy analysis, in the Telzer mode, of the Tosafists in tractate *Bava Kama* on the subject of the four bailees. Rabbi Rabbinovitch was evidently unimpressed by this youthful effusion. More probably, he had no wish to appear in any way critical of the Yeshivah administration. Whatever the reason, he did not reply to my letter, eagerly though I awaited the call of the postman bearing good tidings. When I was introduced to the Rav years later in Gateshead, he did remember that I had written to him but said: 'Now that you are studying in Gateshead you have nothing to worry about.'

Just when I was beginning to despair of ever having the opportunity of being subjected to real Lithuanian-type learning, the Gateshead *Kolel* was established and I applied for admission.

3

GATESHEAD

The Gateshead Kolel was founded by the *shohet* of Gateshead, David Dryan (he had founded the Gateshead Yeshivah several years previously) and Rabbi E.E. Dessler, an outstanding representative of the Musar movement. The word Kolel means 'comprehensive', referring to an institution developed in Lithuania in the last century, when the Yeshivah heads came to appreciate the need for an all-embracing programme of advanced studies for students who had already spent many years studying the Talmud but who now required the opportunity of engaging in further research, with the total dedication and application such a study required. This is an extension of the Yeshivah ideal – the study of the Torah *lishmah*, 'for its own sake'. The Kolel students were usually married men with families and they were supported, like the Yeshivot, out of communal funds.

From its beginnings, the Kolel institution was beset by tensions. On the one hand, it was unrealistic for advanced students to pursue their studies without any thought of a future career as rabbis or Yeshivah heads. Few were able or willing to be supported for too long by others, even if a sufficient number of patrons of learning could be found to provide the necessary funding. On the other hand, the ideal of Torah study for its own sake could not be abandoned and, rightly or wrongly, it was felt that for the students of the Kolel to think of any career, even a rabbinic career, was in some measure to compromise the ideal. For this reason, while the curriculum at the Kolel did sometimes cater to the needs of the practical rabbinate (by studying the Codes, for instance, as well as the Talmud), the main thrust was towards sections of the Talmud, such as those dealing with the sacrificial system, not normally studied in Yeshivot. To apply the mind, so it was argued, in the study of laws in abeyance since the destruction of the Temple, was supreme evidence that the

Torah was being studied 'for its own sake'. To opponents of the Kolel system it might seem odd to see studies that would equip a man to serve as a rabbi as somehow tainted by self-interest. But that is how many of the Kolel enthusiasts did see it.

To establish a Kolel in England during the war years seemed an impossible dream. England was no doubt, even in those years, far more affluent than nineteenth-century Lithuania, but were there enough people willing to give their money to the funding of an institution of purely academic learning in an Anglo-Jewry strong in philanthropy, but weak in an approach contrary to the pragmatism in which it took pride? More to the point, was there a sufficient number of seasoned Talmudists willing to risk their financial future in order to devote themselves to pure learning in a community where they would be looked upon, as Rabbi Dessler used to remark, 'like men from Mars'? Undeterred by these considerations, David Dryan and Rabbi Dessler went ahead with the project, confident that God would provide in England as He did in Lithuania. Tireless, amid conditions of extreme discomfort, travelling on midnight trains packed with members of the armed forces, Rabbi Dessler sold the Kolel idea to a number of wealthy men in London and in the provinces and managed to raise enough capital for the project to be set in motion. A large house was purchased in Gateshead, a town with a Yeshivah and a strictly observant community removed from the more vibrant centres, so that the Kolel students could study without distraction in a congenial atmosphere. A handful of scholars who had studied in Yeshivot made themselves available and the Kolel was established, with no fanfare or official opening but with an abundance of faith.

Nowadays, the Kolel institution has caught on in the Orthodox world; every Yeshivah of any size in Israel and the United States has a flourishing Kolel attached to it. The details are given in William B. Helmreich's *The World of the Yeshivah* (New York, 1982). But the Gateshead Kolel was a pioneer in the new world. Moreover, it was a quite separate institution from the Gateshead Yeshivah. Indeed, Rabbi Dessler, anxious to promote an elitist attitude, discouraged any close association between the Yeshivah and the Kolel. Evidently he believed that the tone of the Kolel, as befitting a place for mature scholars, could only be weakened if the immature youngsters at the Yeshivah were allowed even casual entrance into its august precincts. Graduates of the public shools may find their way eventually to Oxford or Cambridge University but no one has ever suggested that an 'Oxbridge' college be attached to Eton or Harrow or vice versa.

When I joined the Kolel, soon after its inception, the other members had all studied at one or other of the famous Lithuanian Yeshivot – Telz, Mir, Slabodka, Kamenitz, Baranowitz, Grodno and Radin – before coming to England, with the exception of a fiery young Hungarian, Zusya Waltner. The married students had their own homes in Gateshead. The three of us who were still single – Zusya Waltner, Moshe Schwalb and myself – had rooms in the Kolel buildings, where we ate our Sabbath meals. On weekdays we went across the road to eat at a small Jewish hotel.

On a bitterly cold winter's day, after I had received written confirmation of my acceptance as a Kolel student, I got off the train at Newcastle station, where David Dryan met me and took me to his home for a hot meal prepared by his wife. The couple had no children of their own but looked upon the students of the Yeshivah as their children, caring for them as they would have done for their own offspring if they had had any. The warm welcome I received from the Dryans made me feel less uncertain whether I was doing the right thing in venturing forth into such a strange environment. David Dryan took me to my room in the Kolel building. After a few minutes to allow me to survey my new quarters, I was taken downstairs to the hall of study, where I was at once plunged into the atmosphere of a Lithuanian house of learning of which I had long dreamed.

As the 'babe' of the Kolel (I was only twenty years of age, while some of my colleagues were several years older) and as one who had only studied in a Lithuanian Yeshivah in spirit (I was, so to speak, an honorary Telzer) I was welcomed very good-heartedly by the other members but with an amused tolerance. Immature as I was, I had the cheek on my first day at the Kolel to show off by debating Talmudic law with the learned scholars, but soon realised that I was no match for them. I had obtained my small amount of *lomdus* from books. They had sat at the feet of the great masters.

I have vivid recollections of several members of the Kolel, each of them an unforgettable character . . .

Rabbi Dessler himself was a member of the Kolel, which was run democratically. Each of us had a say in the administration, at least on paper, but we all knew that were it not for Rabbi Dessler there would have been no Kolel and that he was the real (albeit unofficial) Principal. We naturally deferred to him in all matters and none of us ever thought for a moment of casting a vote against his opinion. Yet he himself would always insist that we were equal partners in the enterprise and refused to accept that he was in any way more equal than the others. At times this extreme humility bordered on the disingenuous. At a wedding reception, he was introduced by the chairman in the most glowing terms, but when he rose to speak, protested 'I am only the *shamash* of the Kolel.' This moved the Rav of Gateshead, Rabbi Naftali Shakovitsky, himself a member of the Kolel and a Musar personality, to anger at what he considered to be a result of false modesty that could only bring the Torah into disrepute in the eyes of the lay public. The Rav contended that if you tell people often enough that you are a nobody, they will come to believe it.

Rabbi Shakovitsky, a powerful figure of a man with a huge, black beard and a deep, resonant voice, had been a rabbi in Lithuania before being appointed to his Gateshead position. He pursued unchanged his role as a rabbi of the old school, preaching only on rare occasions, the community accepting that the main function of a rabbi was to render practical decisions in Jewish law. In the strictly observant community of Gateshead there were sufficient questions for him to answer covering the whole gamut of life to keep him occupied, yet he managed to find the time to be present at the Kolel sessions. As the town Rav, he was our rabbi as well but he did not like us to refer to him as the Rav except in public. We used to address him as Reb Naftali. In fact, the title 'Reb' prefaced the name of each of our members. It was never 'Moshe' or 'Zusya', always 'Reb Moshe', 'Reb Zusya', a practice I found rather quaint.

The gentle, soft-spoken Reb Hayyim Shmuel Lopian was a son of Reb Eliyahu Lopian, another renowned Musar teacher and head of the Etz Hayyim Yeshivah in London. A number of Reb Hayyim Shmuel's brothers had been ordained as rabbis, including Reb Laib, an acknowledged genius in Talmudic learning even as a young man. Reb Laib also became a member of the Kolel not long afterwards. Both brothers were graduates of Telz (to my good fortune, thought I). Reb Hayyim Shmuel had already won fame as the author of the very erudite work *Ravha Di-Shemata* on the *Shev Shematata* by Aryeh Laib of Stry in Galicia. This and R. Aryeh Laib's *Ketzot Ha-Hoshen* were the staple diet for budding dialecticians in the Lithuanian Yeshivot. Like most of his contemporaries, Reb Hayyim Shmuel had no interest in historical questions. On one occasion I made some remark about the period in which a certain sage had lived, whereupon Reb Hayyim Shmuel shrugged it off with the Talmudic expression: 'What has been has been', as if to say, 'Who cares?' It was this complete indifference to historical studies on the part of the Yeshivah-trained scholars that eventually put me off Lithuanian *lomdus* to a certain extent, much as I admired its other aspects.

Reb Laib Grosnass (later Dayan Grosnass of the London Beth Din), a brother-in-law of Reb Hayyim Shmuel, had studied under R. Baruch Baer Leibovitch in the Yeshivah of Kamenitz. He was the Kolel's authority on R. Baruch Baer's analytical methodology. This was brilliant, logical and extremely subtle but was often no more than hair-splitting, unlike my beloved Telzer *derekh*. The recognition of acute distinctions between apparently similar concepts is useful in the study of the Talmud but it can be overdone, as I felt it had been in Kamenitz; later on, I must confess, I thought this true of the Telzer *derekh* as well, sad to say.

Reb Pinhas Gard was a native of Brisk, the town of which R. Hayyim Soloveitchick (Reb Hayyim Brisker) was rabbi. Reb Hayyim was succeeded by his son Reb Velvel, both of these giants of Talmudic dialectics helping to create yet another methodology, the Brisker *derekh*.

Reb Pinhas had a fund of stories about his native town of Brisk and its rabbis. Some of these stories were miracle tales. It is a mistake to imagine that only Hasidim tell of the supernatural powers of their saints; the Litvaks had their own wonders to relate of the rabbis who were their heroes. This is one of his stories: Reb Hayyim Brisker once informed his family that in every generation there is a single saint who is unique. He is the *had be-dora*, 'the only one in his generation'. The way to tell whether a rabbi could be said to qualify for this elevated status is to observe the manner in which his earlocks (*peot*) lie at the moment of death. Reb Hayyim is reported to have shared with his family this manner of recognising the outstanding figure of the generation, explaining that the earlocks have to lie in such a way that it is impossible for a dying man to arrange them himself, if his claim to extreme sanctity were inauthentic. Lo and behold, the story concluded, when Reb Hayyim died his sons observed that his earlocks were lying in the position that demonstrated that he was the true *had be-dora*.

Reb Shimon Danziger was the *menahel* (a kind of general overseer) whose job it was to see our letters were posted, our linen sent to the laundry, our meals prepared for the Sabbath and our books ready for us when we sat down to study.

Reb Shimon did not look upon the tasks he had to perform for us as demeaning. On the contrary he looked upon it as a rare privilege to 'serve *talmidey hakhamim*', as the Talmudic phrase has it. Reb Shimon was often to be seen lost in a reverie, which was not surprising since he had a wife and only daughter in Lithuania whose fates were unknown. Hoping against hope, he would share with us his dreams about life after the war when he would be reunited with his loved ones. All the anguish and yearning of a human being buffeted by fate yet holding on in his trust of God could be heard when Reb Shimon led us in prayer. Despite his lowly position in the Kolel administration, Reb Shimon was listened to with respect by his colleagues in the study sessions and general deliberations. He was a Talmudist of far from inconsiderable attainments who usually had something to contribute. More than anyone at the Kolel, Reb Shimon, for obvious reasons, lived in spirit in his native Lithuania. His alma mater, the Slabodka Yeshivah, was situated in the townlet of that name across the bridge from Kovno, just as Gateshead was situated across from Newcastle. When Reb Shimon went shopping in Newcastle, he would absent-mindedly ask, 'Can I get you anything when I go to Kovno?'

Reb Moshe Schwalb (later the spiritual mentor of Gateshead Yeshivah) was a German-born young man who had been sent by his thoroughly westernised but Jewishly observant parents to study in Lithuania in the Yeshivah at Baranowitz presided over by Rabbi Elhanan Wasserman. After spending several years at this Yeshivah, Reb Moshe returned to Germany more of a Litvak than the Litvaks themselves, speaking Yiddish with a Lithuanian accent and acting as if he had never had an extensive general education in his German school before he left for the Yeshivah. Soon after his return to Germany he was obliged to leave again, this time for England, in order to save himself from the Nazi terror.

Reb Moshe, too, was full of tales about the Lithuanian rabbis of note. He once told me that his teacher, Rabbi Wasserman, would tell the students of the Yeshivah on Purim how he had been present when the great Hafetz Hayyim had driven out a *dybbuk* from a young girl. Rabbi Wasserman and some other disciples of the Hafetz Hayyim, in the name of the saint, compelled the lost soul, pursued by demons, to leave the body of the girl which it did, but only after extracting a promise that *kaddish* would be recited by the disciples for its repose. There is a lengthy account of the exorcism in A. Sorski's *Or Elhanan,* the biography of Rabbi Wasserman.

Reb Moshe had thoroughly imbibed the Musar atmosphere of the Lithuania Yeshivot with all the tenacity of a 'Yekke'. As a staunch Musarist, he was constantly taking his own spiritual temperature, seeking to discover hidden faults of character (these were, in fact, few in number) with a view to self-improvement. This 'working on the self', *arbeiten auf sich* as the Musarists called it, could be very trying, especially when it spilled over to affect others. I once lost my temper with him for pointing out the faults in my character that I ought to remedy, but he calmly and rather patronisingly replied: 'I thought you had no feelings. Now I see you do have them.' He had a reputation at the Kolel of being a Zaddik, something of a saint. The two of us shared a room in the Kolel. At night he used to talk in his sleep. If I were awake, I was curious to listen to what he was saying. Invariably, he would quote to himself in his sleep verses from the Bible or passages from the Talmud and the moralistic literature. If this is any indication, he *was* a Zaddik.

My closest friend at the Kolel, formerly a fellow-student at Manchester Yeshivah, was Zusya Waltner (later head of a Yeshivah in Tangiers). This red-bearded, Hungarian cynic with a brilliant mind loved the Lithuanian methods of study (which was why he joined the Kolel) but enjoyed pouring scorn on the Litvaks, by whom he was so grossly outnumbered. Since I too was a 'foreigner' we recognised in each other a kindred spirit. We used to go for long walks in the evenings, discussing the books we borrowed from the Gateshead Public Library as a rest from our Talmudic studies. One of the books we found particularly fascinating was James Dunne's *An Experiment With Time*. Dunne's theories about the different dimensions of time tied in to some extent with Rabbi Dessler's discourses on time and eternity in Jewish thought. According to Dunne, in our dreams we can occupy a different dimension of time so that we can occasionally see into the future. He suggested to his readers that they keep a pencil and paper under the pillow to jot down their dreams on the moment of waking, while still fresh in the memory. Zusya and I tried the experiment and actually did discover one or two astonishing events anticipated in a dream. I recall jotting down on my pad a dream I had had of a cripple in a white suit walking towards us. On our stroll that evening we really did see a cripple in a white suit and I was able to show my pad to Zusya in support of Dunne's theory. Yet we were both too sceptical to see in this kind of thing anything other than sheer coincidence.

Reb Zusya came from a Hasidic background but that did not prevent him from scoffing at Hasidic claims that the Rebbes could work miracles. He loved to repeat the story of his business-man uncle who visited a little town where he posed as a Hasidic Rebbe, just for the fun of it. A childless householder in the town requested the 'Rebbe' to give him a blessing that his wife would give birth to a son. Keeping up the pretence, Zusya's uncle solemnly declared: 'In a year's time your wife will give birth to a son.' A few years later the uncle had occasion to visit the town again, taking care, as he thought, not to be recognised. But recognised he was by the man he had blessed, who, with great joy and admiration for the power of the saint's prayer, proudly introduced him to his wife holding a little boy by the hand!

The curriculum at the Kolel was better organised than at the Yeshiva but was still something of a hit-and-miss affair. In the major Lithuanian Yeshivot eight tractates of the Talmud were studied. These eight were *Bava Kama; Bava Metzia; Bava Batra; Yevamot; Ketubot; Nedarim; Gittin and Kiddushin,* the first three on general jurisprudence, the other five on marriage and divorce law. The complicated discussions in these tractates, it was felt, provided ample scope for the exercise of the mind in the keen analysis typical of the Lithuanian Yeshivot. There were two terms in the year, in each of which one of the eight tractates was studied, the cycle being repeated every four years. The aim was qualitative rather than quantitative. Far greater stress was placed on an in-depth analysis of the Talmudic texts and the commentaries than on a mere familiarity with the surface meaning. One who had mastered these tractates in the manner described qualified as a *lamdan,* 'a learned man', and the aim was *zu kennen lernen,* 'to be able to learn', that is, so to have assimilated the method that it became second nature and could easily be applied to all the other tractates of the Talmud. At the Kolel it was taken for granted that the members knew the eight tractates and were able to use the methodology. But, as the Gateshead Rav used to say, now that we can be assumed to be capable of learning, let us actually learn. Since we have acquired the method, let us apply it.

The Talmudic texts to which the methods were applied at the Kolel were all from the Order *Kodashim,* dealing with the sacrificial system in Temple times. Even when the tractates of this Order were compiled in Babylon, the topics were purely academic, since the Temple had been destroyed centuries earlier. To the outsider it would undoubtedly have seemed strange that a group of scholars should spend twelve hours a day discussing such things as the correct manner of sprinkling the blood of a sacrifice on the altar or the time allowed for the meat of various sacrifices to be eaten. But this was to miss the point. Every member of the Kolel believed in perfect faith that the Torah (written and oral) is the revealed word of God, therefore to study the Torah is to think God's thoughts after Him. It is to engage the mind in eternal wisdom and truth; to be wondrously united with the divine Author of the Torah. In a way the very fact that *Kodashim* is of hardly any practical significance (there are a few passages on the rituals followed today such as *tzitzit* and *tefillin*) was adequate reason for its choice since it demonstrated that the study of the Torah is the highest value in itself, quite apart from any practical consequences for the religious life. It *is* religious life at its highest. Moreover, this Order had rarely been studied in the Yeshivot so that there was now scope for the application of the methodology in a new area of study. The famous toast at Cambridge is not irrelevant: 'To pure mathematics. May it never be of any practical use whatsoever!' In one or two Yeshivot today the further motivation for studying *Kodashim* is to be in readiness for the coming of the Messiah, the rebuilding of the Temple and the restoration of the sacrificial system, as orthodoxy believes. The priests especially will then have to consult the rabbis on the details of how the sacrifices are to be offered. But this motivation was peripheral at the Gateshead Kolel.

When Professor Norman Bentwich visited the Kolel, he described its regimen as semi-monastic, which it was. The day began with prayers but these were soon over so that we could get on with our studies. After a quick breakfast, we studied all day and well into the night, interrupted only by afternoon and evening prayers and for the other meals of the day. In the pattern of the Lithuanian Yeshivot, each of us had a *havruta* ('company'), a study-partner with whom to read and analyse the texts. My study-partners were Moshe Schwalb in the morning and Laib Grosnass in the afternoon. There were no formal lectures but once a week each of us in turn would share his insights, real or imaginary, with his colleagues who were expected to challenge him and demolish his arguments if they could. Debate and discussion were of the essence.

Although Commentaries to *Kodashim* were few, we were able to use the collection of Commentaries produced in the seventeenth and eighteenth centuries known as *Asifat Zekenim* and works by the contemporary Talmudists, Rabbi Daniel Sachs's *Hemdat Daniel* and Rabbi Moshe Rozen's *Nezer Ha-Kodesh*. There were, in addition, the more general works in which many comments were to be found on the topics we were studying. Prominent among these were three works on Maimonides' *Code*, which has large sections on the sacrificial system: the *Novellae* of R. Hayyim of Brisk; the *Or Sameah* by R. Meir Simhah Kagan of Dvinsk; and the *Tzafenat Paneah* by R. Joseph Rozin also of Dvinsk. The views of these and other commentators were never accepted blindly but were resorted to chiefly for the location of problems to which we preferred to offer our own solutions, only falling back on what the great commentators had to say if we were stumped. The whole exercise was keenly critical as well as analytical. It must be said, however, that any criticism was aimed at the Commentaries, never at the Talmudic texts themselves, except of course where the text was uncertain. There was never any objection to considering different versions of a Talmudic text in order to establish the correct one. It was axiomatic that *Hazal* (the rabbis of the Talmud) were infallible supermen. The critical aim was never to show that the Talmud was wrong – that was as unthinkable as to imagine that the Torah could be wrong – but to show that it had often been misunderstood by its commentators. There was thus a blend of critical acumen applied to the post-Talmudic teachers, and of total acceptance as revealed truth of all the words of the Talmudic Rabbis.

A further point worthy of mention is that our questions of how, what and when were only addressed to the details of the sacrificial system. No one thought it proper to ask why there should have been a sacrificial system in the first place and why Orthodox Jews should be required to pray for its restoration in the future. Maimonides' *Code*, the *Mishneh Torah*, in which he states all the rules of the system, was studied in the greatest detail. But of Maimonides' *Guide for the Perplexed*, in which a section is devoted to the question of the purpose of the system, there was no mention at all.

To give one example among many of the kind of analysis in which we were engaged: the first Mishnah in tractate *Zevahim* states that if a sin-offering is offered up by the priest as any other offering it is invalid. Suppose, for instance, the priest declared that the sin-offering was being offered as a peace-offering, this would be an offering *shelo lishmah,* 'not for its own purpose', and the sacrifice would be invalid. However, the Talmud comments, if the priest offers the sacrifice without any intention at all, the sacrifice is valid. Since sacrifices are set aside to be offered as what they are – a sin-offering as a sin-offering and no other – it follows that *stama* ('anonymously', i.e. without *any* intention) is to be treated as if the sacrifice has been offered *lishmah,* for the purpose for which it has been intended.

At this stage our analysis began. The statement that the sacrifice offered without any intention at all is valid, because it is treated as if the sacrifice had been offered with the statement of purpose (*lishmah*), can be understood in two different ways. (1) Since the sacrifice has been set aside for that purpose, where it is offered without any intention it is considered as if it had been offered with the correct intention. (2) A sacrifice is not required to be offered with the express intention of a sin-offering as a sin-offering and so forth. The fact that it has been set aside for the purpose is sufficient. It is only when the sacrifice is offered *shelo lishmah,* that is, as a different sacrifice – a sin-offering as a peace-offering – that it is invalid. In other words, is it the positive intention of *shelo lishmah* that invalidates the sacrifice or is it the absence of *lishmah* that renders the sacrifice unfit? Put baldly like this, there appears to be no difference between the two ways of looking at it, but we were able to show that differences between the mediaeval commentators depended on which of the two ways they favoured.

It was all intellectually stimulating and I enjoyed it immensely, except for the half-hour Musar session at the end of the day just before the *Ma'ariv* service. The Musar movement was founded by Rabbi Israel Lipkin of Salant, Reb Israel Salanter, a very erudite Lithuanian Talmudist who considered Talmudic studies to be insufficient in themselves; they required to be supplemented by rigorous introspection with the aim of producing an ethically and religiously orientated 'whole' personality. The term 'Musar' means 'reproof'. It is used in this sense in the book of Proverbs. The basic idea behind the movement was to strengthen the faith of outwardly devout Jews by encouraging inwardness in religious life, thus counteracting the effects of the Haskalah ('Enlightenment') trend toward secular knowledge that was particularly powerful in nineteenth-century Lithuania. On the part of the traditionalist rabbis, there was at first considerable opposition to the new movement, much as they respected Rabbi Israel's great learning and piety. These rabbis believed that the study of the Torah was sufficient in itself to change the character for good. As the Talmudic Rabbis had said, God created the evil inclination, but provided the Torah as the antidote. Rabbi Hayyim Brisker once observed that Musar is like castor-oil, beneficial to the sick but useless or even harmful to the healthy. Rabbi Israel, on the other hand, when asked by a man what he should study if he only had one half-hour a day in which to do so, replied: 'Study Musar and you will find another half-hour!'

Dov Katz's six-volume work *Tenuat Ha-Musar* is still the most comprehensive account of the movement and the opposition to it on the part of the traditionalists. In his volume on the anti-Musar polemic, a typical opposition critique is quoted. According to this critique the Musarists were too morbidly introspective. A Musarist, it is reported, was sitting at a table laid with a number of delicacies and was invited by his host to partake of them. The Musarist declared to himself that he would dearly like to enjoy the good food but had to steel himself from tasting any of it as an exercise in self-denial. But he then thought that by denying himself he would be guilty of the sin of pride in that he would congratulate himself on his self-control. His thoughts thus vacillated between the desire to cultivate abstinence and the equally strong desire not to give way to pride. A reasonable person, the opponents of Musar argued, would simply get on with it without fuss, freeing his mind to be occupied with things that really mattered.

The study of the Musar literature, of which there is a considerable amount, dating from the Middle Ages and beyond, was engaged in by latter-day Musarists not so much as study proper but as an emotional exercise. The text from one of the holy books was repeated again and again in a mournful tune and with interjections in Yiddish in order to get the particular idea deeply imbedded in the psyche as a permanent possession. Reb

Israel Salanter, in some anticipation of Freud, believed that it was futile to try to engage in self-improvement on the surface level. Unless the unconscious mind were involved the character would remain unchanged. The only technique for influencing the unconscious was, he held, to rehearse Musar texts in the way described. The attempts to introduce Musar into the Lithuanian Yeshivot were at first strongly resisted, but eventually the leaders of the movement – Rabbi Israel's chief disciples – managed to win over the Yeshivot to their side. The major Lithuanian Yeshivot appointed *mashgihim,* Musar personalities, to give regular Musar discourses and generally to oversee the conduct of the students. The Telz Yeshivah had a Musar programme of its own, differing from the others in its intellectual rather than emotional thrust. As the printed discourses of Rabbi J.L. Bloch, the Rosh Yeshivah of Telz, show, the Telzer discourses were virtually treatments of a philosophical and theological nature, albeit in a pre-modern form. In fact, the term used generally at Telz was not Musar but *Da'at* ('Knowledge'). In his *Sheurey Da'at*, Rabbi Bloch discusses, for instance, the age-old theological problem of divine foreknowledge and human free will and does so, moreover, in true philosophical vein.

To return to the Musar sessions at the Kolel, there we would sit, each in his corner, mournfully reciting the Musar texts. There were no rules regarding which texts we should choose. (There were, in fact, no rules at all in the Kolel. Any attempt at imposing a discipline from without would have been resisted as unbecoming for a college catering to the spiritual needs of mature people, who could be trusted to determine their own code of conduct.) The unspoken assumption was that each would choose a text that would cater to his need and that would help him overcome his particular failing. For instance, one of our members, believing he had been guilty of pride, would chant over and over again the passage calling attention to the folly of pride in the *Ethical Will* of Asher ben Yehiel, a rabbi in Toledo during the fourteenth century. Other popular texts stressed the vanity of worldly things or the destructive power of unbridled lust. I could never acclimatise myself to this public baring of the soul. (To be fair, we were not supposed to overhear one another but that was pretty difficult in view of the loud cries and sobs which attended the exercise.) It all got on my nerves as, no doubt, my sitting there in silence, reading the Telzer *Da'at* booklets (these just about managed to qualify as 'Musar'), must have irritated my colleagues, who nonetheless indulged me and Zusya Waltner as creatures from another world who could not be expected to see the value of 'working on the self'. It was these Musar sessions and the general Musarist tone of the place that got under my skin, so much so that I eventually decided to leave the Kolel and return to Manchester. I am extremely grateful, however, for the instruction the Kolel gave me and shall never forget the generosity, tolerance and sheer goodness with which Rabbi Dessler and his colleagues received into their ranks a raw youngster who was not really a Litvak at all, not even of the Telz variety. I returned to Manchester with their blessing and I guess they were not too sorry to see the back of me. Zusya Waltner stuck it out to the bitter end – or, I imagine, until the bitter became sweet.

Before leaving my account of the Gateshead Kolel, I feel it would be incomplete unless I said something more about Rabbi Dessler, one of the most remarkable men I have ever met. Until he became the spiritual guide of the Ponievezh Yeshivah in B'nai B'rak, near Tel Aviv, Rabbi Dessler was the moving spirit behind the Kolel and his wise counsel was sought by its members even when he had moved to Israel. He was physically small and had a full but neatly trimmed beard until he went to Ponievezh, when he allowed it to grow long. He had studied in his youth at the famed Musar School in Kelm, presided over by the foremost disciple of Reb Israel Salanter, R. Simhah Züssel. He married the daughter of Reb Nahum Zeev, son of Reb Simhah Züssel. Reb Nahum Zeev was also an outstanding Musar teacher. He earned his living as a merchant in Koenigsberg, where he dressed and conducted his life in Western style. His wife and daughters dressed in the latest fashion. He even had a dog. Rabbi Dessler told us of the occasion when a Polish rabbi, in Koenigsberg to consult a physician, was invited by Reb Nahum Zeev to be a guest in his home. Witnessing the Western style in which the home was conducted, the rabbi was careful to eat very little, suspecting that the food was not completely kosher. Late at night, the Polish rabbi was awakened from his sleep by the sound of bitter weeping from a nearby room. Thinking someone needed help, the rabbi went on tiptoe to the room from which the sobs were coming only to hear the 'Westernised gentleman' sobbing his heart out as he chanted the verse from Ecclesiastes: 'Vanity of vanity; all is vanity.' Needless to say, after this experience, the rabbi had no further qualms about eating at Reb Nahum Zeev's table.

On his mother's side, Rabbi Dessler was a great-grandson of Reb Israel Salanter. His maternal grandfather, Reb Eliyahu Eliezer, after whom he was named, was Reb Israel's son-in-law. He had many family traditions about the great Musar teacher, which he shared with us. One of these was that Reb Israel took every Talmudic statement about conduct with the utmost seriousness, including the saying that one has to become so drunk on Purim that one can no longer distinguish between blessing Mordecai and cursing Haman. So, on Purim, the abstemious Reb Israel would drink himself into a stupor out of sheer duty. In his drunken state he would talk to himself, rebuking himself for his failings. His family heard his say: 'Since you have such a subtle mind that can turn this way and that (*vos drayt sich azey und azey*) just think hard of how great is your responsibility.' Another family tradition was that a German official had written on Reb Israel's papers as a means of identification: 'This man is always to be found thoroughly immersed in philosophical thought.'

When Rabbi Dessler first came to England he served as the rabbi of the Montague Road Beth Hamidrash, a small synagogue in Hackney. In my Kolel days, Rabbi Dessler had given up his rabbinic position but refused to take a penny for his own needs from Kolel funds, earning his living by giving private tuition to the sons of wealthy businessmen who, one supposes, paid him quite well. His well-educated pupils would ply him with questions on such topics as the conflict between science and religion. In order to deal adequately with these questions he acquired some knowledge of modern thought. One Sabbath afternoon Pinhas Gard and I paid a visit to the Gateshead Museum where we saw the exhibition on dinosaurs, sabre-toothed tigers and the like. We asked Rabbi Dessler how he managed to reconcile the vast age of the earth as uncovered by modern science with the Biblical account that it is under six thousand years old. He asked us to consider the nature of time. Time, he argued, has no meaning apart from its measurement by humans. God is beyond Time so that a year cannot mean one of God's years but means simply human observation of the earth's revolution around the sun. But motion, as Einstein has shown, is relative. Consequently, it makes no sense to say that the world existed millions of years before man came on to the scene. He also knew something of Freud (not as much as his more fervent admirers thought), whose theories of the unconscious fascinated him, especially since they had (as he saw it) been anticipated by his great-grandfather. After his death, his disciples collected his Musar writings and published them in four volumes under the title *Mikhtav Me-Eliyahu,* from which he emerges as an original religious thinker of much power and depth.

In addition to Musar and various aspects of modern thought, Rabbi Dessler utilised for his fascinating discourses (many of which were first delivered in the Kolel) the Kabbalah and Hasidic literature. For instance, he told us that he had been greatly influenced by the ideas of Rabbi Yitzhak Horowitz (Reb Yitzhak Masmid), a prominent Habad thinker who visited England between the wars. One of the thoughts of this Hasidic thinker which Rabbi Dessler shared with us was in the form of a comment to the Midrashic passage in which it is stated that when the Torah was given the people saw that which is normally heard and they heard that which is normally seen. In our normal experience we have the direct testimony of our senses that the world is real, whereas we are only dimly aware of the reality of the unseen spiritual world which, even when it breaks through to us in moments of great elevation, is gone in a flash. But when God revealed Himself to the people at Sinai the spiritual world became intensely real for them but the world of sense perception receded. At that moment of supreme transcendence, the people 'saw' the spiritual world that is normally hidden and only 'heard' from afar. As for the material world, normally 'seen', this had become so remote that it was only 'heard'. On another occasion Rabbi Dessler delivered a discourse on the Hereafter, a topic that so fascinated him that it became, in a sense, the basis of his religious philosophy. Eternity, he noted, should be understood not as endless duration in time but as beyond time altogether. Eternity is what the mystics call 'the Eternal *Now*', though the rabbi did not actually use this term. This is the deeper meaning of the Rabbinic saying: 'The reward of a good deed is a good deed and the reward of a sin is a sin.' Good deeds are there permanently in Eternity as are evil deeds. It is only in the world of time that the past is buried. In Eternity, all our deeds, good and bad, are ours as if they are all being performed *now*.

Rabbi Dessler was particularly fond of the Kabbalistic idea of *nahama de-kisufa*, 'bread of shame'. He used to refer to the doctrine as found in the Kabbalah but the earliest reference to it that I have been able to discover is in the writings of the eighteenth-century master, Reb Moshe Hayyim Luzzatto. The doctrine runs that God created this world as 'a vale of soul-making'. He rewards us for the good we do on earth with eternal bliss. Since He desires our good, why could He not have given us this eternal bliss without our having to undergo the probationary period on earth? The answer is that God has created man with the most powerful sense of independence and that is man's glory. He prefers to eat the morsel of bread that he has earned and is his own to all the good food and choice wines given to him as a gift at a rich man's table. The independent human spirit rejects unearned bread, 'bread of shame'. In a sense man cannot even enjoy God's gifts to the full unless he earns the nearness of God – the greatest good – through his own efforts.

It was exhilarating to hear ideas such as these expounded by the master. Zusya Waltner, sceptical as ever, used to say that such topics are beyond our ken and should certainly not be discussed in public. Rabbi Dessler was, in fact, very circumspect with regard to those to whom he was willing to impart his ideas, never admitting any of the Yeshivah students or the pious Gateshead householders. This gave us an unworthy sense of belonging to the elitist circle, of being admitted into the ranks of those meriting a discussion of the mysteries of existence.

It will have been seen that Rabbi Dessler was an eclectic in his thinking, drawing on the most diverse sources. Yet he was unable to escape from the sombre atmosphere of the Musar movement to which, for all his originality, he really belonged.

He had a lively disposition and could be very cynical on occasion in a way one would have thought inappropriate for a Musarist who preached the virtues of judging others leniently. Like the school to which he belonged, he would speak of the majority of Mizrahi rabbis, for instance, as opportunists or careerists, people willing to sell their souls in order to curry favour with the ignorant masses. Although he had a highly sophisticated view of Hell, seeing Hell-fire in purely spiritual terms, he believed in Hell, as did his great-grandfather. He once told us, and repeated it in his published work, that Reb Israel, who had an extreme phobia about fire, would place his little finger into the flame of a candle, saying to himself, 'You see, fire burns and hurts.' The result was that all too frequently in Rabbi Dessler's teachings the harshness of the Musar approach would gain the upper hand over the mystical beauty of the Kabbalist, the joy of the Hasidic Jew and the broadness of a mind that could refer with ease to Einstein, Freud, Marx and Darwin. For all his apparent modernism, he was at heart an old-fashioned Musarist. For all his admiration for some aspects of Hasidic doctrine, he remained a Mitnagged. I once heard him tell of a Lithuanian rabbi who was enamoured of Hasidism. 'If you admire Hasidism so much,' he was asked, 'why do you not become a Hasid?' 'Because the Vilna Gaon was against the movement,' the rabbi replied, going on to give this illustration. A beautiful, highly gifted and extremely kind woman was divorced from her husband. A famous rabbi expressed his doubts about the validity of the bill of divorce, the *get*, but the majority of rabbis ruled that the *get* was valid without question. A match for the lady was proposed to a scholar, the *shadchan* (matchmaker) extolling her great virtue and beauty. 'All very true,' said the scholar, 'but how can I marry her when a rabbi of note has raised doubts about her eligibility for marriage?' No matter how much we admire Hasidism, Rabbi Dessler continued, we cannot forget that the Vilna Gaon once declared the movement to be heretical.

It was my impression that the Musarists, of whom Rabbi Dessler was one of the most prominent, tended to see bad in everything. Human nature, in their view, was corrupt. Everyone was tainted by self-interest. The human psyche was sick and unwholesome and could only be made whole again by daily strong doses of the bitter Musar medicine.

For all that, I cannot and do not want to forget what I owe to Rabbi Dessler. Although I was never officially his pupil, he was, in many respects, my teacher *par excellence*. He taught me and so many others to see Judaism in sophisticated terms. He was a great man whose place among the *Gedoley Yisrael* of the twentieth century remains uncontested.

4

SEMICHAH, MARRIAGE
AND MUNK'S SHUL

Back at Manchester Yeshivah, I began to think of taking Semichah (Rabbinic ordination). In the traditional scheme, a candidate for the rabbinate is examined thoroughly for his competence in Jewish law and if he is successful in the examination he is given the certificate of ordination. All this is done by an individual rabbi of renown, not by the Yeshivah, the ideal of the latter being, as we have noted more than once, study for its own sake. Naturally there is nothing to prevent a Yeshivah teacher or Yeshivah head from conferring Semichah on a deserving candidate in his capacity of rabbi. The examination usually tests the candidate on his knowledge of the sections of the *Shulhan Arukh,* the standard Code, which deals with the ritual matters upon which the rabbi will be called to render decisions.

Despite the implicit antagonism in the Lithuanian Yeshivot to the brighter students preparing themselves for the practical Rabbinate, there was an official class at Manchester Yeshivah for the purpose. The existence of such a class was due, evidently, to the appreciation on the part of the Yeshivah administration that it would have been too much to expect students in this country to have no rabbinic ambitions. This class, conducted by the Rosh, was in tractate *Hullin,* the Talmudic tractate dealing with the dietary laws, and the section of the *Shulhan Arukh* dealing with the same subject, *Yoreh Deah.* The traditional role of the rabbi was preserved; he was there solely to render decisions in Jewish ritual law – whether, for instance, a chicken with some defect was kosher or whether and when food cooked in a non-kosher pot is still kosher. The fiction was maintained that the English rabbi too assumes this exclusive role; hence there was no training whatsoever in preaching and pastoral work in a modern congregation. When I organised, unofficially, a class in public speaking (we called on local Jewish ministers to talk to us and give us advice in the art) it was not exactly frowned upon but was not encouraged either.

After the course of study, the Rosh, in his private capacity as a rabbi, not in his official role as head of the Yeshivah, examined four of us and duly ordained us as 'Rabbis in Israel'. The other three were Baruch Steinberg (now a businessman and President of the Yeshivah), Raphael Margolies (now a senior teacher at the Yeshivah) and Isaac Lerner (now Dayan Lerner of the London Beth Din).

As mentioned earlier, I was also examined by Rabbi Rivkin, head of the Manchester Beth Din, and received a further Semichah from him. The Rosh did not exactly stipulate that our Semichah was given on the understanding that we would not study at a University and obtain a University degree, but that was implicit in various observations he made at the time. He hoped, he said, that we would pursue the traditional Rabbinic role and spend all our free time studying the Torah, not wasting time on studies no doubt suitable for those training to be English ministers but not for those who had graduated from a traditional Yeshivah like that of Manchester. Obedient to his wishes, Isaac Lerner and I (the other two remained 'degreeless') did not take our degrees until after the Rosh had passed away.

Playing the innocent but rather futile game, popular with rabbis, of tracing one's spiritual descent, I suppose I can claim to be sixth in line from the Gaon of Vilna in this way. The Rosh, from whom I have Semichah, was himself ordained by the famed Rabbi of Navarodock, R. Yehiel Michel Epstein, author of the Code *Arukh Ha-Shulhan*. Now Rabbi Epstein's son, Baruch (a great Talmudist who earned his living as a bank manager) records in his autobiography (*Mekor Barukh*) that his father (born in 1829) had Semichah from the rabbi of his native town, Babroisk, R. Elijah Goldberg, who, in turn, had Semichah from R. Hayyim of Volozhyn, founder of the Volozhiner Yeshivah and chief disciple of the Vilna Gaon. R. Baruch Epstein informs us that his father also had Semichah from R. Menahem Mendel of Lubavitch, grandson and successor of R. Shneur Zalman of Liady, founder of the Habad movement in Hasidism. R. Menahem Mendel (the *Tzemah Tzedek,* as he is called after his *magnum opus*) was a great authority in Jewish law as well as a Hasidic Rebbe. Tracing my 'descent' in a different line, Rabbi Epstein had Semichah from the *Tzemah Tzedek* who was a pupil of his grandfather who was a disciple of the Maggid of Meseritch, the disciple and successor of the Baal Shem Tov, the founder of Hasidism. For what this show of vanity is worth (not very much), I can thus claim to be linked, as it were, to both the Hasidic and Mitnaggedic leaders, though I suppose my subsequent career has made the links tenuous.

Rabbi Rivkin had studied with Rabbi Joseph Rozin of Dvinsk, the Ragadshover Illui ('Genius'), who knew the whole of the Rabbinic literature by heart and of whom Bialik once said that from one Ragadshover two Einsteins could be carved. The Ragadshover criticised freely all the later commentators, sometimes extending his criticisms even to the mediaeval giants. Any contemporary scholar who had the temerity to take on the Ragadshover in debate only invited abuse as an ignoramus. But this dismissal was only directed against foes worthy of his sword, so that it came to be looked upon as an accolade to be insulted by the Ragadshover. Rabbi Rivkin was proud of the fact that the Ragadshover had once called him an 'ox'.

The Yeshivah organised a small reception for the new ordinands at which all four of us spoke. In my little speech, I referred to the verse from the *sidra* (portion) of that week: 'And Moses and Aaron went into the tent of meeting, and came out, and blessed the people; and the glory of the Lord appeared unto all the people' (Leviticus 9:23). The 'tent of meeting', I said, can be said to represent Eastern Europe where so many millions of Jews met their God. We, however, only knew of that vibrant Jewish life at second hand. Yet the Rosh and Rabbi Dubov, our teachers, who were educated there 'came out' from there to bring us blessings, enabling us to have some slight appreciation of the past glories.

Although I had little formal secular education when I was ordained as a rabbi, I had always been an avid reader of books of every kind: fiction, philosophy, biography, history, anything upon which I could lay my hands at the local lending library. I had no discriminating taste and, no doubt, read a lot of trash, but managed to cover some extremely good material as well.

My particular heroes were H.G. Wells, G.K. Chesterton and G.B. Shaw, of whom I think I can say I read almost everything they had written. It may be evidence of superficiality, but I never went through any *Sturm und Drang* period, whatever religious faith I had remaining undisturbed by my general reading. On the contrary, I found it fairly easy to translate into a Jewish way of looking at things Wells's warnings about human *hubris*, Shaw's celebration of the life force and Chesterton's brilliant paradoxes and defence of traditional religion, even though it was not the Jewish religion and indeed he was rumoured to be a bit anti-Semitic. Problems of faith did not really become pressing in my life until I had been introduced at the University to biblical criticism and, more especially, to the historical approach of the *Jüdische Wissenschaft* school. Of this there was hardly a mention either at the Yeshivah or the Kolel. The whole modern scholarly enterprise was not so much negated as ignored completely. The only occasion on which I can recall, for instance, Rabbi Dessler at the Kolel making any reference to Jewish historical studies was when he was dismissive of Dr Hertz's Humash. 'What can you expect', he remarked, 'of Schechter's disciple?' At the Yeshivah a thick curtain was drawn to shut out any illumination that might come from outside the range of Talmudic studies. Until I had begun to study formally at University even the names of Krochmal, Zunz, Rapoport, Frankel, Shadal, Steinschneider and the other pioneers of historical studies were unknown to me.

Nor did I find sex too much of a problem. From my schoolfriends and from my own reading I had managed to pick up sufficient knowledge to understand the many allusions to sexual matters in the Talmud. I recall Rabbi Dubov reading with us the passage in which it is said that there should be no light in the bedroom on the Sabbath 'because of another matter', a euphemism for sexual intercourse, which, according to the Rabbis, should not be carried out with the light on. Rabbi Dubov simply translated it as 'another matter' and when we quite innocently asked him 'What other matter?' he quickly went on to the next line. None of us at the Yeshivah had much contact with the opposite sex. We had read of the sin of gazing lustfully at women but we hardly saw any women at whom we could gaze lustfully or otherwise. Yet, surprisingly, in view of our almost totally male society, there was no overt homosexuality. Of all the students at the Yeshivah, as I recall, only two young men, little Isaac Mandlestam and his older friend Moshe Cohen (I have changed the names) seem to have had a more than platonic relationship, sometimes walking together in the street holding hands, which the rest of the boys found amusing, calling little Isaac 'Mrs Cohen'. We would not have been normal if we had never had sexual fantasies, but busy as we were with our studies well into the night these rarely became too bothersome. Like Arnold of Rugby, one of the great mediaeval Yeshivah heads used to advise his pupils to take cold baths. This is not to deny that the pages in the holy books we read dealing with explicit sex were well-thumbed. These were perhaps an outlet for young men who never looked at girlie magazines. Without wishing to claim too much, I believe that the purity of the young men at Manchester Yeshivah did confirm the statement of Maimonides that the sex instinct only gets out of control where there is no Torah in the heart.

After taking Semichah, I taught for a while at the Hebrew Classes of the Higher Crumpsall Synagogue (whose Rabbi was the famed Kopul Rosen who, though a young man at the time, was an outstanding orator in both English and Yiddish) and at the *Merkaz Limmud,* a centre for Jewish studies where religious Halutzim, preparing for their *aliyah,* could gain a deeper knowledge of Jewish life and thought. In charge of the *Merkaz Limmud* was Hans Heinemann, a highly gifted refugee from Germany who had studied at the Mir Yeshivah and was writing a thesis for his MA degree at Manchester University. Many years later Hans became the foremost authority in the world on the Rabbinic Aggadah, as Professor Yosef Heinemann of the Hebrew University.

At the *Merkaz Limmud,* I met Shulamit Lisagorska, my wife to be. Shula was on *hachsharah* (preparation for life on a kibbutz) in Bromsgrove near Birmingham. The Yeshivah had no official policy on Zionism but, while the teachers were at best indifferent to the movement, there was no objection to students belonging to such movements as *Bachad,* the religious

Halutzic movement, of which the *Merkaz Limmud* was a kind of educational wing.

Shula's parents, Isser and Jane, were both born in the same little Lithuanian town of Zhetel, coming to London in their teens. They were married there, my father-in-law earning his living as a master cabinet-maker. Just before the outbreak of the First World War, my mother-in-law went off to Lithuania to visit the family, taking with her the little boy Jack and little girl Malka. As luck would have it, they were victims of the vicissitudes of the population movements during and after the war and were away from England for around seven years in all. A year after the family was reunited in London, Jack was Bar Mitzvah, with his mother heavily pregnant with Shula.

Having regard to my Yeshivah background and to the fact that we were both born in England it is not too surprising that our wedding was curious in its blending of Lithuanian Yiddish and Western English customs. For instance, in true English fashion we had fallen in love with one another but our marriage still had to be formally 'arranged'. Shula was also obliged by the custom of the circles in which we moved to wear a *sheitel*, which she continued to wear for several years, to the amusement of her English friends. But English mores were satisfied in that we had bridesmaids and I wore the usual top-hat, black coat and striped trousers. At the wedding reception I simply said a few words in response to the toast to bride and groom, whereas in Lithuanian Yeshivah circles it would have been unthinkable for the groom not to display whatever prowess he possessed in learning by offering the assembled guests a learned discourse in Yiddish on the Talmud. The Talmud states that, in commemoration of the destruction of the Temple, a groom is obliged to place ashes on his head. I had never heard of this being followed in England and I later discovered that very few followed the practice even in the more devout circles of Eastern European Jewry. However, Rabbi Dessler came to Manchester to be present at the wedding and, just before the ceremony proper, he took a tiny amount of cigarette ash, placed it in tissue paper and urged me to wear it under my topper. I was not much of a rebel in those days, so wear it I did.

Shula's parents emigrated to Manchester during the Second World War to set up home there and to be of assistance to their daughter Malka and her husband 'Yank' Levy, a wealthy wine manufacturer and noted Jewish philanthropist. The homes of my parents-in-law and of Yank and Malka offered unbounded hospitality to rabbis and their families who had either arrived in Manchester as refugees from Germany or had come to Manchester to escape for a time the hazards of the London Blitz.

My brother-in-law Yank was a remarkable character. He had qualified as a pharmacist and optician, but when his father died took over his lucrative wine business. Yank's grandfather was the renowned Yiddish preacher, the Kamenitzer Maggid, but I gather that Yank's father, while a fairly observant Jew, was no Jewish scholar and not particularly devout. Yank himself was only introduced to traditional Judaism in its fullness at the Manchester Yeshivah, where he was never actually a student but where he used to attend services regularly. From the day he first began to appreciate the value of the kind of Judaism he had observed at the Yeshivah, Yank was hooked and his adherence to the minutiae tended to border on the fanatical. Malka, a sweet woman with a lovely disposition, indulged her husband in his religious quest. She not only wore a *sheitel* but had dresses with long sleeves which would not have disgraced the modesty of the most pious Eastern European matron.

Helped by Yank, my father-in-law bought us a small house and a Vilna Shas (an edition of the Talmud published by the 'Widow and Brothers Romm', with all the commentaries and super-commentaries), the idea being that I would have no financial worries but would 'sit and learn', quite in the old tradition. For a time that is what I did. In the afternoons I would study the Talmud with Rabbi Judah Segal, son of the Rosh Yeshivah, who later succeeded his father, but who at that time had no salaried position; his father-in-law performing the same service for him that Yank and my father-in-law were providing for me. I also gave a few private lessons to the sons of rabbinic scholars, for which I received a small fee. Every evening I used to teach a page of Talmud, in Yiddish, at the *Mahazikey Hadat* synagogue, composed largely of Hasidic Jews or, at least, Jews from Hasidic backgrounds. The Rabbi of the *Mahazikey*

Hadat was Rabbi David Feldman, author of the Feldman edition of the *Kitzur Shulhan Arukh*. Rabbi Feldman guided his congregation in the way of strict observance. He preferred, at that time, to devote himself entirely to the field in which he was expert, practical Jewish law, but since it was inconceivable that there should be no public Talmud study daily in such a traditional community as the *Mahazikey Hadat,* I was asked to teach the daily '*Blat*' Gemara. I certainly enjoyed it immensely and I believe that they did too, even though I was suspect because I was clean-shaven and worse, wore my hair long in front, which is utterly wrong in Hasidic eyes both because it is said to be evidence of arrogance and vanity and, more especially, because long hair in the place of the head *tefillin* is said to act as an interposition. For all that, I was tolerated because they liked the way I taught and, perhaps, because they were amazed to find an ordinary boy with a working-class background sufficiently familiar with the Talmud to teach it at a Hasidic synagogue and whose wife, born in England, wore a *sheitel.*

This apparently idyllic existence, studying the Talmud and teaching it, happily married and relieved of all financial cares, soon proved unacceptable. My parents were astonished that, instead of pursuing University studies to equip me for a rabbinic career, I was content to be supported by my in-laws without thought at all for the future. My father, in particular, found it contrary to his working-class principles. He called me a lazy bounder (he used a rather stronger word). I, too, had wider ambitions and when I intimated to my father-in-law, an ordinary, unscholarly Jew with an extraordinary stock of common sense, that I would like to obtain a post as a rabbi and make a career for myself, he was overjoyed. He said that he had thought this to be right all along but had not wished to appear interfering. Shula was solidly behind me in all this. My father-in-law had heart trouble and, unfortunately, died very soon after our joint decision. He was not even spared to witness the birth of our son, whom we named Ivor (Isser in Hebrew), after him. The announcement of Ivor's birth, on 30 March 1945, was given by me over the telephone to be inserted in the *Jewish Chronicle.* In those days it was the practice of the paper to give the Hebrew name (in Hebrew characters) as well as the

English name. Due to the name being read over a none-too-clear telephone line, the name appeared in the paper that Friday not as Isser, but as Esau. I received a number of irate letters expressing disgust that a Rabbi should call his son 'Esau'. The next Friday the name appeared correctly with apologies from the paper for the error.

I was slowly moving away from the world of the Yeshivah to seek wider horizons. A further distancing from the Yeshivah came about when, rather stupidly, I took part in the correspondence that was going on in the columns of the *Jewish Chronicle* regarding the role of the Jews' College. In my very immature letter I was critical of Jews' College for the absence of the kind of intense Talmud study found in the Yeshivot and of the Yeshivot for failing to provide its students with adequate preparation for a career in rabbinics in the modern world. What was required, I suggested, was an institution that would combine the virtues of Jews' College and the Yeshivah with the faults of neither. The letter was ridiculous. As soon as I saw it in print I realised how wrong I had been to write it. But it did reflect what I sincerely believed at the time – the tremendous problem of how to combine the modern and traditional approaches to Jewish learning being quite beyond my awareness. At any rate, this letter was my first contact in print with the problems of Jews' College, to be followed, many years later, by contacts fraught with far greater significance for me, as I shall relate in due course.

This episode, combined with the fact that I now had a wife and child to support, made me more eager than ever to obtain a rabbinic position, preferably in London, where I could also enrol as a student at London University. The opportunity came when I was invited by the synagogue in Golders Green, headed by Rabbi Dr E. Munk, to become assistant rabbi. After a number of trial lectures and various discussions I was appointed to the post. There could not have been a better position for me at that stage in my career. The work at 'Munk's Shul' was interesting and highly congenial, Rabbi Munk was easy to get on with, the salary, though not excessive, was adequate and I was to be allowed time off to study for my BA at the University. The happy years I spent at 'Munk's', few though they were, introduced me to the world of German Jewish Orthodoxy, the world of Samson Raphael Hirsch and Frankfurt where a valiant attempt was made to combine the riches of the Jewish tradition with Western life and culture – Torah and Derekh Eretz.

The Golders Green Beth Hamedrash, as Munk's was officially called, had a fine Hebrew School attached to it. The Principal of the school was Rabbi Dr Alexander Carlebach and it often happened that the baby carriages of his infant girl, Tirza, and my infant boy, Ivor, would be left side by side when Marga Carlebach and Shula were attending some communal function. The ladies of the community, cooing over the two infants, loved to forecast that one day the two would marry. In adolescence, Ivor and Tirza were members of the Jewish Youth Study Group. Knowing nothing of the prognostications of the good ladies of Munk's, they did fall in love with one another, eventually to marry and fulfil the prophecies in true fairy-tale fashion.

My main job was to teach the advanced class at the Hebrew School and conduct a Talmud class for the congregants every Sunday morning, very occasionally to preach, and to act generally as Rabbi Munk's assistant. When Dr Munk was given absence from the congregation in order to stay for about six months to help succour the survivors of the Holocaust, I acted, raw though I was to the position, as a rabbi of the congregation while he was away.

There was great respect for Dr Munk in the congregation for his fine personal qualities; in any case it was a part of the German tradition that special tokens of respect be paid to a rabbi by his congregants. Only the rabbi, for instance, was allowed to wear his *tallit* over his head during prayer. The rest of the congregation wore hats – not, incidentally, *yarmulkas*. When I was appointed, I was informed that I, too, if I wished, could wear my *tallit* over my head. They used to tell of a Jew in the Frankfurt synagogue who, without a by your leave, was observed praying with his *tallit* covering his head. The *shamash* said to the man: 'If you wear your *tallit* over your head you must be a *talmid hakham*. But if you are a *talmid hakham* you must be aware of the rule that an *'am ha-aretz* (ignoramus) must not wear his *tallit* over his head. So why do you wear your *tallit* over your head?'

The congregation was very Germanic. They were all very Jewish and strictly observant but the observance sometimes had a neo-Prussian emphasis on doing this or that exactly right. The services were conducted with the utmost decorum. No one dared to engage in conversation during the services and not a line of the most insignificant liturgical poem was ever skipped. Many of the congregants were Frankfurtians, bringing Hirschean ideals to Britain. A favourite word in the congregation was 'discipline'. Whenever I was questioned as to why they were expected to do one thing or refrain from doing another, all I had to do was to murmur something about it being part of the Jewish discipline, and that was the end of the matter. The Frankfurters in the congregation were fond of telling, against themselves, the story of a visit to Frankfurt by the great rabbi and preacher of Lublin, Rabbi Meir Shapira. Rabbi Shapira was both impressed and dismayed at the manner of Jewish observance; impressed at the organisation of the Frankfurt community and dismayed that it tended to override the kind of fervour he knew as a Hasid. As he was being shown around a kosher ice-cream emporium, Rabbi Shapira saw a large notice stating: 'All our products are frozen under the supervision of the Rabbinate.' 'True', he could not help saying, 'of the whole of your Judaism.'

Yet there were few congregations in the Jewish world then, and even fewer now, to compare with Munk's in its successful combination of loyalty to Orthodox Judaism in all its ramifications and the adoption of Western culture and values. Many of the members had been prominent in Germany, some also in Britain, as university professors, bankers, scientists, physicians, musicians, artists, philosophers and literary figures. Rabbi Munk himself had obtained his doctorate in Germany for a dissertation on Wordsworth! Every Sunday afternoon, the congregation's intelligentsia would meet for philosophical discussions on Judaism at the home of Abba Horowitz, a lawyer of distinction, son of Rabbi Markus Horowitz and grandson of the greatest of the nineteenth-century German Talmudists, Rabbi Jacob Ettlinger, author of the *Arukh Le-Ner* and the first Orthodox rabbi to study at a university. (The Hasidim used to say of Ettlinger's university period that it was Satan's work, showing that it was possible to study at a modern university and yet remain, like Rabbi Ettlinger, a very pious and extremely learned Jew!) The discussions ranged far and wide. I did not know at what to be more astonished and admiring: their erudition, their simple faith or their thorough acquaintance with Western mores. It was an experience for Shula and me in beautiful homes to be served tea poured from silver tea-pots and delicious kosher pastries from exquisite china services.

The congregation spared no expense on education. Soon after my arrival, a large church building was purchased by a neighbouring synagogue body and in some of the rooms a part-time Yeshivah was established at which I taught Talmud. I was only a few years older than my students and got along very well with them, teaching them (in addition to Talmud) how to master the niceties of ping-pong, a skill I had acquired at Balkind's Cheder. The most promising of the students was Abba Horowitz's son, Felix (now R. Baruch Horowitz, head of the Dvar Yerushalayim Yeshivah in Jerusalem). At the formal opening of the Yeshivah, young Horowitz delivered a Talmudic discourse worthy of his Rabbinic forebears. Later on, when I had become the subject of controversy, R. Baruch wrote a fundamentalist tract under the pen-name of Ben Levi attacking my views. It is typical of the man that he came to my house to assure me that there was nothing personal in it. I had to tell him that I, for my part, found his fundamentalism detrimental to Judaism. In the tract he adopts the worst excesses of the fundamentalists, stating for example that the Bible foretells in a magical way the events of our day. We have remained friends from afar, but it is a great pity that he and many of his contemporaries have swung so far to the right theologically.

I tried to introduce my students at the Yeshivah into the type of analysis of concepts I had learned at Gateshead and from my reading in the material produced in the Lithuanian Yeshivot. It is well-known that ever since the Middle Ages, Yeshivah circles have created riddles and logical puzzles designed to sharpen the mind. I shared some of these, which I had myself heard in Manchester and Gateshead, with my students at Munk's.

For instance many are the illustrations of how the way a text is 'sung' can alter its meaning. Professor Lauterbach at the Reform College in Cincinnati saw some young people with tennis rackets turning sorrowfully away from the tennis court at the College because of a notice which read: 'Private. No Visitors Allowed.' You should read this as a Talmudic text, said Lauterbach, to which you bring your own intonation. This notice means: 'Private? No! Visitors Allowed.'

Rabbi Aaron Kotler, the famous Rosh Yeshivah, used to set puzzles for prospective students at his Yeshivah to test what we today call their IQ. One of these was: prove which of the following two statements is true and which is false. (1) No two people on earth have exactly the same number of hairs on their head. (2) There are people on earth with exactly the same number of hairs. The proof that (1) is false is, of course, that since there are billions of people on earth it is impossible for everyone to have a different number of hairs – that would mean that there are people with millions of hairs on their head and clearly there are no such people.

A similar puzzle which I heard had been set by R. Aaron Kotler to test his students' ability to deal with problems was already familiar to me from the 'Japes and wheezes' column in my boyhood comics. A lily pond doubles itself each day and in 28 days the pond is full. How long does it take for the pond to be a quarter full? The answer is, of course, 26 days, not, as most people reply, seven days.

Another Yeshivah puzzle: why is it that someone who has to have an operation will first make exhaustive enquiries regarding the competence of the surgeon and yet will fly in an aeroplane even though he knows nothing about the competence of the pilot? The answer is that the pilot himself flies with the plane and if anything untoward happens it will happen to him as well.

Numerous are the tales about the detection abilities of the great rabbis. A rabbi (the story is told of more than one) was sent a chicken for his decision as to whether it was kosher or terefa. The rabbi said to the girl who had brought the chicken: 'This chicken is kosher. But please go home and tell your mother to send the other chicken for my decision.' The girl went home and told her mother what the rabbi had said and, indeed, there was another chicken with something peculiar about its innards. That chicken was terefa. How did the rabbi know? The chicken the girl had brought him was so perfectly wholesome-looking that the rabbi guessed there must have been another chicken about which a decision as to its kashrut was required.

My students at the Yeshivah took to their studies eagerly. Only one of them, Baruch Horowitz, became a rabbi but so far as I know the others have also remained observant and good Jews and keep up their Talmudic studies as good Jews should.

In the Memorial Volume for Rabbi Munk (*The Blessing of Eliyahu*, London, 1982), his biography (written after I had become very controversial) does not ignore my contribution to the Golders Green Beth Hamedrash, although naturally there is disapproval of my views. With a nice blend of appreciation and implied condemnation (some of the facts are not quite as I recall them) the biography states (pp.47–48):

Among the applicants for the position of Rosh Yeshivah was Rabbi Louis Jacobs, then of Manchester, who was unknown to Rabbi Munk. Although Rabbi Jacobs withdrew his application at one stage, preferring to stay in Manchester, Rabbi Munk met him and persuaded him to accept the leadership of the Yeshivah, which opened on *Rosh Chodesh* Ellul, 1946 (*sic*). It was known as *Yeshivat Sha'arey Tzion* and met in the hall of the Shomrei Adath Synagogue in Hampstead.

But the venture proved ill-fated. Already at the opening ceremony, Dayan Abramsky had a difference of opinion with the new Rosh Yeshivah. Recruits from outside the area did not come forward and the principal beneficiaries of the scheme were members of the Golders Green Beth Hamedrash who had the benefit of stimulating and popular *shiurim* delivered by Rabbi Jacobs. The Yeshivah closed after the second course and Rabbi Jacobs left the Golders Green Beth Hamedrash. Great was Rabbi Munk's concern in 1959 when he read Rabbi Jacobs' writings, challenging the traditional basis of the *Halakhah*. He wrote to Rabbi

73

Jacobs explaining to him how his views contradicted traditional teachings and pleaded with him to withdraw, but to no avail.

It should be said that the reference to Dayan Abramsky's disagreement with me at the opening meeting of the Yeshivah had to do with some remarks I had made about teaching the Talmud in English and had nothing to do, as might be said to be implied in the above passage, with my later theological views. It might also be of interest to note that when Rabbi Munk retired to live in Israel, he taught Jewish thought at the Yeshivah *Dvar Yerushalayim* headed by his (and my) former pupil, Baruch Horowitz.

5

UNIVERSITY COLLEGE

While I was at the Golders Green Beth Hamedrash, I had enough time off from my duties there to study for a degree at University College. The College, then recovering from severe bomb damage, was engaged in heavy reconstruction work with the result that accommodation for classes was in very short supply. Since, however, I was the only undergraduate student for the BA Hons. course and since Dr (later Professor) Siegfried Stein was the only tutor for the course, we managed to find a tiny room vacant for the occasions when we needed it.

In preparation for the course, in those days, one had to take what was known as the 'Intermediate' examination, consisting in my case of papers on Logic, Ethics, German and English literature. Whenever I could I attended courses in Greek and Latin at the College, though these were voluntary.

The course itself was a pretty stiff one. An Honours degree in Semitics involved a thorough knowledge of the whole of the Hebrew Bible, the Targumim, Aramaic and Syriac, Hebrew poetry, mediaeval Jewish philosophy, Jewish history, from the earliest period down to the present day, and comparative Semitic grammar, as well as the ability to translate accurately from English into classical Hebrew. It was rumoured that, in the old days when Dr Büchler, Principal of Jews' College, was the examiner, he would require the candidates to translate the third leader of *The Times* into classical Hebrew. I was rather more fortunate in that all I was required to translate were a few of Byron's *Hebrew Melodies*.

I thought I had done well in the final examination and expected to receive a first. Alas, when the results came through, all I managed to get was a lower second, a very disappointing result. I resisted the temptation to blame either my teacher or the examiners. The latter were, in addition to Dr Stein, Dr I. Epstein, Principal of Jews' College and editor of the justly-famed *Soncino Talmud*, and Professor Danby, a non-Jewish scholar who translated single-handed the whole of the Mishnah into English, with, it should be said, many mistakes. (When some of the mistakes were pointed out to him, Danby retorted: 'What can you expect from a *goy*?') I must be wrong but I seemed to have made a good impression on the examiners at the *viva* and am still puzzled. Be that as it may, Dr Stein still welcomed me as his assistant at University College, in which capacity I served for a short time.

As a lecturer at the College, I shared a room with Dr Stein. This room was next to that of Professor Alfred Ayer, then a young philosopher who had created a tremendous stir with his book *Language, Truth and Logic*, in which, influenced by the Vienna Circle, he espoused the verification principle, according to which all statements other than tautologies and those capable of verification are neither true nor false but logically meaningless, so that both theism and atheism are logically meaningless. Ayer later modified his approach considerably. Although we had adjacent rooms at University College, Ayer and I taught at different hours of the day and week so that we never actually met until years later. Then, at a dinner party, Ayer showed some interest in my book *Studies in Talmudic Logic*, especially in my contention that the Talmudic rabbis knew of a form of inductive logic similar to that of John Stuart Mill's 'Method of Agreement'.

Since only the two of us were present while I was studying for my degree, Dr Stein felt free to discuss with me many subjects of Jewish interest other than those strictly covered by the course. Stein had studied in Germany under Elbogen and others at the Hochschule in Berlin, where, as in the famous Bresslau Seminary, critical scholarship was seen as in no way incompatible with Jewish observance. Dr Stein was an observant Jew who had managed to reconcile his totally observant life with a knowledge and acceptance of Biblical and historical criticism. Stein warned me before the course that I must expect to be disturbed by the facts we would be uncovering, though it is my impression that he had not thought through the problem in any convincing way.

Neither, for that matter, had any other observant (I refrain from using the term 'Orthodox' in this context as question-begging) Jew who taught Semitics or who had graduated in the subject. There was, and still is, among many observant Jewish scholars a good deal of compartmentalism, almost as if the world of critical scholarship and that of Jewish observance were really incompatible only one had somehow to meet the demands of both. I was never able to accept this 'two truths' approach or, rather, lack of approach.

The particular problem was, of course, the Pentateuch. Like the students at Jews' College who took the same course, it seemed evident to me that both the Higher and Lower Criticism of the Old Testament required a revision of the usual interpretation of the doctrine 'Torah min Ha-Shamayim' ('The Torah is from Heaven'). On the basis of Jewish dogma it is generally understood that every single word of our present text of the Pentateuch was dictated by God to Moses. Again and again in our studies we came across variant readings in the Septuagint and the other ancient versions (the Kittel Bible, listing these, was our mainstay) and it quickly became apparent that the versions, while not always correct, were certainly not always to be rejected in favour of the Masoretic text. In fact, our studies of the Higher Criticism seemed abundantly to demonstrate that – even if the 'Documentary Hypothesis' could be disproved – the Pentateuch is plainly a composite work produced at different periods in the history of ancient Israel. The Jews' College students had to face the same problem. I know that one of my most brilliant contemporaries, a student at Jews' College, was bothered by the problem but more especially by the implication by his teachers there that all criticism was irrelevant (even though one had to mug it up in order to get a good degree in Semitics). This man left the Orthodox ministry to become a noted Reform rabbi. Reform, he used to say, has at least faced up to the implications of Biblical Criticism and is not content either to ignore it completely or dismiss it as a game. There appeared to be a conspiracy of silence on the subject at Jews' College. It was rumoured that Dr Büchler, at the meetings he used to attend of the London Society for the Study of Religion, would calmly let drop such expressions as 'Maccabean Psalms' and other expressions showing his complete familiarity with (and acceptance of) critical theories, but never a word of this was conveyed to his students at the College. Dr Stein told me that another very distinguished teacher at Jews' College, Dr Arthur Marmorstein, once said to him, 'It *is* difficult to believe in the Mosaic authorship of the book of Deuteronomy', or words to that effect, meaning perhaps that difficult though it is it still has to be accepted on faith.

Dr Stein introduced me to the need for accuracy and objectivity in the study of Jewish sources. He himself wrote comparatively little but whatever he did write was polished, completely honest and supported by impeccable proof from his sources. His essay on the influence of the Greek Symposia on the Passover Haggadah has been accepted by the majority of scholars as the final word on the subject. 'Before you do any research', he used to advise, 'become familiar with everything that has been written on the subject.' He was fond of quoting the great Steinschneider, the prince of Jewish bibliographers, as saying, 'The beginning of wisdom is bibliography.' I was aware, of course, that the verse in Proverbs from which this saying was adapted, says: 'The beginning of wisdom is the fear of the Lord.' Evidently there were two kinds of 'wisdom'. Here was I teaching at the Golders Green Beth Hamedrash the wisdom of Torah, yet learning at University College that other wisdom of objective scholarship applied to the same texts. Could the two be reconciled? I had a sufficient sense of responsibility to refrain from even hinting at my uncertainties to the young boys of the Yeshivah.

Though I was living in two worlds – that of traditional Jewish learning and that of critical, historical scholarship – this did not cause me to deviate in any way from my religious observances. The Yeshivah and Kolel background was too strong for that. And to this day, I see no reason why following the ideal of critical investigation into the Jewish classical sources need prevent acceptance of the Halakhah, albeit with a sense that Jewish law has had a history and did not drop down ready-made from Heaven. While studying with Dr Stein, I came to see that this was the problem considered by the forerunners and subsequent leaders of Conservative Judaism – Zecharias Frankel, Solomon Schechter, Louis Finkelstein and, especially, Louis Ginzberg who spoke of the 'genetic fallacy' of assuming that because an institution can be shown to have had base origins, the institution is itself debased; whereas the question we should ask concerning the Sabbath and the dietary laws is not about their origin, but rather what they have become through the historical experiences of the Jewish people.

My Yeshivah and Kolel background also prevented me from being attracted to Mordecai Kaplan's naturalistic views, that God is the name we give to the power in the universe that makes for righteousness and that the *mitzvot* are vehicles for the enrichment of the Jewish soul. Reductionist philosophies of that kind made no sense of the intense religious commitment of my teachers who saw the *mitzvot* as the very word of the living God. To be sure I had come to appreciate that the whole process had to be seen in dynamic rather than in static terms – here the voice of historical investigation could not be silenced, even though my teachers had never heard it at all – but, in traditional Theism, God alone is the Lord of history. The adjustment that was called for was not on the question of the divine nature but with regard to the meaning of Torah and *mitzvot*. There had to be a different concept of revelation from that which obtained before the rise of critical scholarship, but revelation itself could not be denied without depriving Judaism of its spiritual power and distorting the truths it taught. I was, and remain, an unabashed supernaturalist. Of all this I intend to say something more when looking at the 'Jacobs affair'.

Dr Stein was also my supervisor for the London University Ph.D. degree but, although he taught me a good deal about modern, scholarly research methods, I had to do all the actual work for my thesis on my own, only beginning the task at University College and completing it after I had moved to Manchester. The subject of my thesis was 'The Business Life of the Jews in Babylon 200–500 CE'. My main source was the Babylonian Talmud but I utilised any available extra-Talmudic material. For instance, I discovered that in the excavations at Doura-Europas, shops were uncovered dating from the same period as that of my thesis and not too distant from the home of the Babylonian Amoraim. These shops still had prices of goods for sale marked on the walls. It was startling to discover that these prices tallied, more or less exactly, with those recorded in the Talmud for the same goods.

My double life resulted in another interest I have tried to pursue. In my reading of elementary introductions to logic, I saw at once that the Aristotelian syllogism was a totally different form of reference from the Talmudic *kal va-homer*, even though the great Viennese scholar, Adolf Schwartz, had written a celebrated monograph in which he treated the two methods as virtually identical. I wrote two articles, one on this subject and another on Talmudic induction, for the *Journal of Jewish Studies*, then edited by J.L. Teicher. Dr Teicher liked my articles sufficiently to publish them virtually without alteration and I have since done further work on Talmudic reasoning.

Modern Talmudic scholarship has had enormous successes in discussing such matters as correct Talmudic and Rabbinic texts, the historical development of the Talmud, the form-criticism of the Talmud and so forth, leaving the analysis of what the Talmudic arguments mean to Talmudists of the old school. These latter, especially in the Lithuanian Yeshivot, have done excellent work on what might be termed internal analysis, but this work is vitiated by a total lack of historical perspective. They used to boast in the Yeshivot that 'while people like Zunz can tell you what kind of trousers Abbaye wore, we can tell you what Abbaye said!'

Nowadays there are some slight indications that the two worlds are beginning to meet, at least with regard to acceptance by the Yeshivah world of textual criticism of rabbinic literature (not, Heaven forbid, of the Bible where the dogma still prevails of a divinely guaranteed textual accuracy). In my books on Talmudic reasoning I have tried to combine the Yeshivah methods with modern critical method – whether successfully or not is for others to say. But, successful or unsuccessful in my particular case, I am convinced that sooner or later scholars will produce important work in which the two methodologies are combined.

Dr Stein wanted me to remain with him as part-time lecturer at University College. I was sorely tempted at the prospect of an academic career but the lure of the practical rabbinate was too strong. I was extremely reluctant, having spent so much time studying for the rabbinate, to swap horses in mid-stream. Moreover, I had become interested in Jewish theology and realised that the best place for me to think things out in this direction was a pulpit – an Orthodox pulpit, to be sure, but one hospitable to theological probings. Luckily I found such a pulpit in my home town of Manchester.

Another link with University College was forged many years later. I have tried to avoid influencing my children in deciding which course of studies they should pursue at university or, indeed, whether they should go to university at all. But my daughter Naomi did follow me in studying under Dr Stein at University College, eventually taking a degree in Jewish Studies. After her marriage, when she had settled in Israel, Naomi studied at the Hebrew University from which she obtained an MA degree. During her time at University College, Naomi was the first woman chairman of the Jewish Society of the College, her term of office coinciding with my term as President of the Society. It was extremely gratifying for me to be introduced by Naomi when I delivered the presidential address at the annual dinner.

My son, Ivor, took a degree in economics and business management at Manchester University where he was secretary of the Students' Union and chairman of the Jewish Society. Like my father, Ivor is a good organiser. He was the students' representative on the Manchester Communal Council where he rubbed shoulders with the communal leaders, some of them my contemporaries at school or Balkind's Cheder.

A much later association with the Hebrew University was when my friends established there, on my 60th Birthday, a Scholarship in Jewish Mysticism, in my name.

6

MANCHESTER, CENTRAL SYNAGOGUE

My old teacher, the Manchester Rosh Yeshivah, died after a short illness at the end of 1947. On hearing the news, I took the midnight train to Manchester so as to be there for the funeral on the next day. From all over the country, pupils of the Rosh came to pay their respects to the master. A great scholar's coffin is taken into the synagogue so that eulogies may be offered over it, and in obedience to this tradition the Rosh was afforded this honour. The synagogue in the Yeshivah building being too small to accommodate the huge assembly expected there, the synagogue chosen was the Central Synagogue, where the Rosh's son, the Rev. Aaron Segal, had officiated as Second Reader from the age of eighteen. The eulogies in the synagogue were delivered by Rabbi Dr A. Altmann, the Communal Rabbi of Manchester, and by Dayan Abramsky of the London Beth Din, who took as his text Psalm 92 verse 14, 'Planted in the house of the Lord they shall blossom in the courts of our God.' The righteous, he said, when they die, are securely planted in Heaven, in the house of the Lord, but their influence persists in this world, the courtyard, as the Rabbis say, of the after-life, where they continue to blossom and bear fruit. Although the Rosh had gone to his eternal home, his memory would continue to inspire his many disciples.

After the funeral, I was approached by the Honorary Officers of the Central Synagogue to ascertain whether I would be interested in applying for the vacant position of rabbi of the congregation. It seemed a heaven-sent opportunity and I declared my interest at once. To satisfy the constitutional requirements of the synagogue, I sent in a formal application for the post, after which I was invited to deliver two trial sermons, one in English, another in Yiddish. After various deliberations with the Executive and Council of the Central Synagogue I was duly appointed rabbi of the congregation, at the age of 27, in 1948.

The Central Synagogue was founded towards the end of the last century by Jews of Lithuanian extraction. At first, the synagogue was situated in the old Jewish district of Cheetham Hill, near to the city, but a splendid new building was later erected in Heywood Street, just around the corner from my childhood home in Penrose Street. I recall as a boy playing cricket on the open ground on which the synagogue was to be built and hearing the older members grumbling, 'Fancy building a Shul away from the centre of Jewish life!' It is ironic that by the sixties the Jewish population had moved so far northwards across Manchester that the Central Synagogue was again central no longer, but now it was on the southern border of the Jewish population. Eventually, the congregation merged with another congregation in Salford and the fine building had to be sold for use as a mosque. (It was, I believe, sold formally to a private owner who then sold it to be used as a mosque, in obedience to an alleged rule that a synagogue building should not be sold directly to be used for other than Jewish worship – although it is somewhat doubtful whether there is, in fact, any such rule.)

I knew the synagogue well from my boyhood. In fact, I served in its choir; surprisingly, since my musical ability leaves much to be desired. In my induction address as rabbi, I expressed the hope that the notes I would sound in the pulpit would be less discordant than those I sounded in the choir. I remember vividly from my boyhood days attending a service at the Central one Friday evening when the family of a young Jewish man who had been executed that morning at the Strangeways prison for the murder of a prostitute were greeted in the customary manner of greeting and comforting mourners on the advent of the Sabbath. The choirboys used to give nicknames to the members of the synagogue. One elderly gentleman was the spitting image, as we delightedly remarked, of King George V; small beard, dignified gait and all. Naturally we called him 'King George'. The poor man could never understand why the choirboys treated him with such particular deference, bowing from the waist whenever he came into the synagogue.

The first rabbi of the Central Synagogue was Rabbi Yossele Yoffey, a distinguished Lithuanian scholar who wrote a book long before the Balfour Declaration urging Jews to help settle Palestine as a Jewish homeland. The rabbi's daughter married a young man who had studied in Telz Yeshivah (Telz again) with the same name of Yoffey (probably he adopted his father-in-law's name). Rabbi Israel Yoffey at the age of 23 succeeded his father-in-law as rabbi of the Central Synagogue, in which position he remained for the rest of his life. (His son, J.M. Yoffey, born in Manchester, studied medicine and became Professor of Anatomy at Bristol University and Dean of the Medical School.) Rabbi Israel Yoffey wrote a number of books containing excellent sermonic material in Hebrew and still widely used by preachers, especially those of the old school. Full of ideas for sermons, as his books testify, Rabbi Yoffey was an indifferent preacher in English, the language he was obliged to use when addressing a Bar Mitzvah boy. The choirboys used to fall about hilariously whenever the rabbi performed this unwelcome task. He once used the illustration of a motor car which he called, in his Yiddish pronunciation, 'han hoto mobil', providing the choir with a catchword for months afterwards. 'How's your hoto mobil?' we used to ask one another. Rabbi Yoffey dressed and conducted himself as a Lithuanian rabbi. He was a good Talmudist and also served for many years as a member of the Manchester Beth Din. Naturally, he did not wear canonicals but these were worn by the Cantor, the Second Reader, the Bass and Tenor of the choir. The choirboys, too, were fitted out with black robes and little velvet caps. A choir containing female voices was unheard of in Orthodox circles in Manchester. That was reserved for the *goyim* of the south.

Rabbi Yoffey, a staunch Zionist, died in Alexandria on the way to Palestine, a land he had longed to visit all his life. This was some years before the outbreak of the Second World War and no successor was appointed until well after the end of the war. The reason for the congregation's tardiness in appointing a successor was the strong internal divisions over the type of rabbi they wanted. The older Yiddish-speaking members wanted someone like Rabbi Yoffey, who could serve as an old-time rabbi, whereas the younger members wanted someone who could speak eloquently in English, had a university degree and could compare with the English ministers in some of the other Manchester synagogues.

My appointment was accepted without dissenting voice by both parties in the congregation. I was, after all, a child of the congregation in a sense. Moreover, it was understood that I would preach regularly in English but would speak in Yiddish whenever this would be required. During my years at the Central I delivered the traditional *derashah* in Yiddish on *Shabbat Ha-Gadol* and *Shabbat Shuvah*, consisting of an Halakhic discourse followed by a homily. I cannot pretend that I was eloquent in Yiddish but I got by, concentrating on the Halakhic part of the *derashah* with which I could cope fairly easily through my studies at the Yeshivah and the Kolel.

Each night I taught the *Blat* (a page of the Talmud) in Yiddish for the older members, many of whom used to frequent Rabbi Yoffey's *Blat* years before. The *Blat* was taught in the Beth Hamedrash adjacent to the synagogue. This was a large oblong hall with book-lined walls and long wooden tables, around which the participants sat with copies of the Talmud while I expounded the passage we were studying, quite in the old style. A visitor from London, coming in one evening and seeing all this activity, remarked that for a moment he imagined he had wandered into a Lithuanian conventicle, as, indeed, he had. I delivered my weekly sermon in English and in the Western style of preaching though even the younger members liked me to introduce into the sermon an occasional Yiddishism or a Yiddish quote.

This blend of Lithuanian-style rabbinic conduct and English-style formality and decorum took some getting used to. It was made more difficult by the presence in the congregation of a number of people who remembered upbraiding me, together with the rest of the choir, for unruly behaviour.

My daughter, Naomi, was born in 1947. When the day came for us to go to Manchester, Shula and I arrived at the railway station, together with my mother-in-law (who lived with us after the death of her husband), Ivor aged almost three and Naomi aged nine months. To our astonishment we were met at the station by a welcoming party comprising the President

85

and Honorary Officers of the Central Synagogue, including Mr Abraham Gadian, an elderly Lithuanian gentleman with whom I became good friends. Seeing that I was carrying Naomi in my arms, Mr Gadian quietly intimated that it was inappropriate for the 'Rov' to carry a child, even his own child, in public. (I never understood why. Perhaps it was because a Lithuanian rabbi must never be seen to be acting like a nursemaid.) We were all whisked away to the President's house where a repast was waiting for us and where we drank to our future as rabbi and congregation.

They never referred to me as 'Rabbi' or used my first name. I was always the 'Rov' and Shula always the 'Rebbetzin'. Noticing that, after all those years, the congregation thought it had a rabbi like my predecessor, I soon gave up sporting my flashy University College scarf. I could not play rugby anyway, and appreciated that a rabbi who even remotely resembled a rugger player was the last thing the members of the Central Synagogue wanted.

On Sunday, 18 April 1948, the day of my Induction by Dr Altmann, I arrived at the synagogue with Shula in a taxi to find a huge crowd making their way into the building. It was an alarming experience for the erstwhile choirboy, who tried to steel himself to appear calm and collected. Lithuanian rabbis, I told myself, do not suffer from the jitters.

In his address, Dr Altmann spoke of the discussion among political theorists on whether an MP is the agent or the representative of his constituents. Was he obliged to think only of their opinions, since he represented them, or was he entitled to have his own opinions and to voice them, even in Parliament? A rabbi, said Dr Altmann, has to have his own opinions or rather, opinions based on the Jewish traditional teachings. He has to be something more than a mere mouthpiece of his congregation.

In my induction sermon I quoted Rabbi Israel Salanter who once declared that both the Hasidim and the Mitnaggedim are in error – the Hasidim because they imagine they have a rebbe, the Mitnaggedim because they imagine they can get along without a rebbe. I said to the congregation, 'You are of Mitnaggedic stock and have appointed me as your rabbi. Please do not imagine that I am here to teach without you teaching me. Give me your helpful criticism when needed.' This was a rash thing to say, but I was young and inexperienced. I could hardly complain when, afterwards, one or two congregants took me at my word and were all too fulsome in their criticism.

Inexperienced though I was, I still had enough common sense not to quote another saying of Rabbi Israel Salanter, 'A rabbi his community does not wish to get rid of is no rabbi. But if they succeed in getting rid of him he is no *mensch*.' Why ask for trouble? Indeed, I have never been at all sure that this saying is either sound or wise. To be sure, a rabbi should not be prepared to sacrifice his principles on the altar of popularity, but it seems perverse to suggest that a popular rabbi is thereby a failure as a rabbi. Self-denigration on the part of a rabbi can be disastrous. The Manchester Rosh Yeshivah told me that when the renowned Rabbi Simeon Skopf came to Manchester in order to raise funds for his Yeshivah in Grodno, he was accompanied by another rabbi who was an eloquent speaker. This rabbi would first praise Rabbi Skopf to the skies and then go on to appeal for funds. Rabbi Skopf was then expected to add his few words, during which he, in his humility, invariably replied, 'Please disregard my colleague's too fulsome praise. I can learn a little but am not the great scholar he makes me out to be.' When the Manchester Rosh Yeshivah approached a wealthy businessman to support Rabbi Skopf's Yeshivah, the man retorted, 'Why should I give any of my cash to the Yeshivah of a man who publicly admits that he is not a great scholar?' In other words, as the Gateshead Rov said when Rabbi Dessler was as self-denigrating as Rabbi Skopf, if you repeat often enough that you are unworthy, it will not take very long for people to believe it to be true.

My colleagues at the Central Synagogue were Moshele Price, the Chazan (Cantor), and Aaron Segal, the Chazan Sheni (Second Cantor). Moshele Price, then still a very young man, had already acquired an enviable reputation as the Chazan of the major Orthodox synagogue in Budapest. His virtuoso rendering of the prayers in his marvellous tenor voice held the congregation spellbound. On the second night of Passover, the synagogue was filled to capacity by people who came from all over Manchester to hear Price sing the prayer for *Sefirat Ha-Omer, Ribbono shel Olam.* Aaron Segal was, as the saying goes, a first-class Second Reader. He read the Torah and conducted the services in a manner that would have made him qualify for the post of Chazan in the most prestigious congregation, yet he was quite happy in his secondary role in his home town.

All three of us got along splendidly with an absence of friction resulting, in good measure, from clear demarcation lines. My colleagues never sought to preach, which I imagine they could have done if they had put their mind to it, and I never sought to act as Chazan or Chazan Sheni, which I could not do anyway, as shown by my career in the choir. In any event there prevailed in the congregation the view, a hangover from Lithuania, that it was somehow *infra dig.* for the rabbi to take the service or read the Torah. I attended services in the Beth Hamedrash each morning and evening – not because this was laid down as part of my duties and not because I had any duties to perform there (except for the teaching of the *Blat* in the evening to which I have referred), but because it was quite unthinkable that the 'Rov' should not be present at every service of the day. In short, I was less a minister doubling as a 'Rov' than a 'Rov' who carried out occasional ministerial duties.

Manchester was a hive of Jewish activity. In addition to my work at the Central Synagogue, I took part in the activities of the various communal organisations. I also found time to take some courses at Manchester University and to work on my PhD thesis. Among the bodies to which I and most of my rabbinic colleagues belonged was B'nai B'rith. In Manchester this was an elitist group, almost a secret society. One was required to be proposed for membership by at least two members and it was not unknown for a candidate to be 'blackballed' in a secret ballot. All the members of the society were prominent in communal endeavours. At the meetings discussions were held ranging over all the problems facing Jewry in the post-war world. It reminded me of Abba Horowitz's 'salon' in Golders Green, except that this had a more English tone. Not long after my arrival in Manchester and, I believe, in Shula's merit, I was elected chairman of the Manchester Torah Va-Avodah ('Torah

Opening of Golders Green Yeshiva in 1947. From left to right: Dr E. Munk, Dayan Lazarus, Dayan Abramsky (speaking), author, Mr Y. Zimmer, President of the Congregation

Association of Manchester Rabbis, summer 1951. Rabbi Dr A. Altmann middle, author second from left

Consecration of the new Federation Synagogue, Wanstead and Woodford, May 1954 (*Jewish Chronicle*)

and Work'), a branch of the religious Zionist movement. I was also elected to the chairmanship of the Manchester Association of Rabbis, with Dr Altmann as President. And thereby hangs a tale.

A meeting of the Association took place shortly before the High Holy Days at which there was considerable discussion regarding what the assembled rabbis could do to improve decorum in the various synagogues, always crowded during this time of the year. It was decided by all the rabbis present to make some very minor changes in the service with a view to achieving, to some extent at least, the greater spirit of decorum that seemed so urgently to be needed. The 'reforms' suggested were very minor ones: the omission of some of the more laborious and meaningless *piyutim*; the omission of *Hineni,* the private prayer in which the Chazan expresses his unworthiness (which unworthiness Chazanim tended to express with full musical virtuosity); one blessing (*Mi Sheberakh*) for all those called up to read from the Torah, instead of a lengthy one for each person; and one or two other small adjustments. It was all quite innocent. In fact, all that was suggested was that Manchester synagogues follow the pattern of the synagogues in London under the jurisdiction of the Chief Rabbi. These synagogues, under the general heading of the United Synagogue, had long used the Routledge *mahzor,* in which the proposed changes had been taken for granted. A vociferous group of religious extremists, however, had been 'gunning' for Dr Altmann because of his modernising tendencies, as they saw them, and seized the opportunity to get even with him. These men sent letters to some prominent rabbis in Israel and in the USA asking whether it was permitted to make innovations in the synagogue services. Unfortunately, instead of taking the elementary step of first inquiring from Dr Altmann what was really happening, these rabbis allowed themselves to believe that Manchester was liberalising its attitude and turning 'Reform', and it issued a decision (*pesak din*) forbidding the innovations. One bright morning Manchester Jewry awoke to find copies of the rabbis' ban liberally distributed among all the Manchester synagogues, where they had been pasted under cover of darkness in conspiratorial haste.

The whole thing was ridiculous in the extreme. But Dr Altmann was deeply hurt and did not feel he could dismiss it as a sorry joke. Consequently, when Dr Trude Weiss-Rosmarin, editor of *The Jewish Spectator*, published in the USA, asked him to clarify the position, he requested me, as chairman of the Association, to write an article in defence of our position. This article was duly published by Dr Weiss-Rosmarin. In it, I pointed out that the changes were very minor and totally acceptable to Orthodoxy but that in fact the Halakhah had always been tolerant of changes within its own framework – and I gave a number of examples. (Years later, when I was under attack by Chief Rabbi Dr Brodie and the London Beth Din, Dr Weiss-Rosmarin republished the article exactly as it had appeared in *The Jewish Spectator* the first time round.) The affair got into the Israeli papers where one correspondent made the not unpenetrating remark that if Anglo-Jewry could become so agitated over minor changes in the prayer-book, this went some way to show that its Judaism was less life-centred or Torah-centred than prayer-book-centred.

The regular meetings of the Manchester Association of Rabbis, held at Dr Altmann's house, were stimulating and often intellectually exciting. Dr Altmann himself and some of the other members in turn read papers on whatever aspect of Jewish thought, literature or history they happened to be researching at the time. Whenever a distinguished Jewish scholar happened to be visiting Manchester he would be invited to share some of his insights with us.

Dr Brodie, on a pastoral visit to Manchester, came to one of our meetings and Dayan Weiss of the Manchester Beth Din, though not a member of the Association, was also invited. Shortly before the Chief Rabbi's visit, a prominent member of the Manchester Jewish community, Mr Joseph Mamlock, had died. Mamlock had been a leading figure in the Masonic Order and, after the formal, traditional Jewish service, a number of Jewish Masons took over, reciting Masonic texts and throwing sprigs of acacia into the grave. In a spirit of mischief, I am afraid, some of us egged on Dayan Weiss in his innocence to take up with the Chief Rabbi, himself a senior member of the Masonic movement, why these and similar Masonic rituals did not fall under the heading of *avodah zarah* ('idolatry'), severely condemned in Jewish law and teaching. Dayan Weiss, horrified at the thought that there should be traces of idolatry in his community, duly raised the matter with the Chief Rabbi at our meeting, implying that in the light of the latter rituals it was difficult to see how the Chief Rabbi could belong to the Masonic Order. The embarrassed Chief Rabbi could only mumble something about the Masonic rituals being based on ignorance of some of the Jewish sources, but denying that there was anything smacking of idolatry in the Masonic play-acting.

Manchester Jewry was organised in a Communal Council. The function of this body was to pool resources in the community and help along Jewish life in Manchester in all its ramifications. The dynamic Secretary of the Council was the Reverend Nathaniel Jacobs, formerly Minister to the Jewish community of Jamaica. Nathaniel Jacobs' father was a graduate of the Volozhyn Yeshivah but Nathaniel himself, educated at Jews' College, was a typical English Minister, fluent in impeccable English, urbane, very broad-minded and extremely knowledgeable about English literature, music, Jewish history and Jewish thought in general. Nathaniel told me that after his graduation from Jews' College, he had toyed with the idea of becoming a Reform rabbi and consulted his father, who made the acute observation, 'If you become an Orthodox rabbi very little will be demanded of you personally other than to keep the laws. But if you become a Reform rabbi, your congregants may not expect you to keep all the laws but they will expect you to be a man of God. Are you capable of being a man of God?'

It was Nathaniel who urged me to take part in the lectures, organised by the Communal Council, to small non-Jewish groups in and around Manchester. On visiting these groups (generally but not always Free Church) I came across the solid virtues of northern Nonconformism for the first time. The men and women who attended the lectures, as I could see from the printed programmes, had wide interests; they were eager to hear talks on economics, politics, ethics and, especially, the religions of the world. The lectures on Judaism were always well-attended, though some of the questions put during question-time were incredible. 'Why do the Jews bury their dead in an upright position?' was a question I was asked time and again. It is still a puzzle to me how the belief that Jews bury their dead standing up managed to gain such a hold in the north of England. Often these good people were astonished to learn that the New Testament is not part of the Bible for Jews as it is for Christians. The chairman at these lectures would usually offer an extemporary prayer before the meeting began. An example of the *genre* I remember ran 'Dear Lord, as Thou knowest, a young rabbi, like Jesus, has come to talk to us. Grant that we listen carefully to what he has to say and benefit from it.' It is probably apocryphal, but I heard of a chairman at one of these meetings whose prayer began, 'Dear Lord, as Thou hast read in the newspaper this morning . . .'!

There were good Jewish–Christian relations in Manchester. I made friends with a number of Christian clergymen in Manchester and recall sharing a platform with Dr Greer, the Bishop of Manchester, at the Jewish Waterpark Club where I served as voluntary Chaplain. The Bishop's Chaplain told me that the Bishop, who lived in a Jewish district, was once asked, to his astonishment, to switch off the electric lights on the Sabbath because the time-switch had failed to work. To have a Bishop as the Sabbath *goy* must have been a novelty, even for Manchester.

After the death of Rabbi Rivkin, from whom, as mentioned earlier, I had Semichah, a new Av Beth Din was sought. The choice fell on Rabbi J.J. Weiss, mentioned above, an international authority on practical Jewish law even then, and formerly rabbi of Grosswardein in Hungary. Dayan Weiss published the first volume of his Responsa, *Minhat Yitzhak*, in Manchester. Since then he has authored seven more volumes, accepted today as classical statements of the Orthodox understanding of the Halakhah. When, years later, there was talk of my becoming Principal of Jews' College, Dayan Weiss is reported to have said that on the day such a terrible event happened, he would proclaim a public fast. My friend Rabbi Wolfe Kelman remarked that it was a pity that this did not happen. Not everyone can claim the honour of having a public fast proclaimed against him.

MANCHESTER, CENTRAL SYNAGOGUE

Dayan Weiss, a gentle scholar, is considered to be extremist in his decisions in Jewish law. In one of his Responsa he discusses, in reply to a questioner, whether a woman may wear ski-pants or whether this offends against the Deuteronomic law against a woman wearing the garment of a man. He remarks that one might ask whether a good Jewish woman should go skiing at all. In another Responsum, in reply to a question by a Yeshivah student whether it is permitted to play chess on the Sabbath, he expresses doubts whether a Yeshivah student should play chess even on a week-day since his time is better spent studying the Torah. On his retirement from the Manchester Beth Din, Dayan Weiss was appointed Head of the *Edah Haredit* in Jerusalem, a group who were far to the right of the Israeli Chief Rabbinate and whose mentor was the Sotmarer Rebbe. It is ironic that the man so eminently suitable for this position could have been seen as suitable for the position in Manchester with its tradition of the Lithuanian rabbis, who usually tried to make things as easy as they possibly could without negating the *din*.

The Manchester Beth Din was composed of Dr Altmann, the Communal Rabbi, Dayan Weiss and Dayan Golditch, my teacher at the Yeshivah. When Dr Altmann was unable to be present at the writing and delivery of a *get*, I was called in to serve as the third Dayan, a Beth Din of three being required for the purpose. At that time Dayan Weiss had no cause to be suspicious of me. He was an authority on *gittin* and it was an education to witness the care he took to get all the details correct. It was from Dayan Weiss that I gained a little practical experience in these matters, something we had never done in the Yeshivah, even though we had studied the whole of tractate *Gittin* from a purely theoretical point of view. According to Jewish law, for identification purposes a *get* can only be written in a town situated by a river and the name of the river or rivers must be recorded in the *get*. The formula for Manchester was: 'situated on the rivers Irk and Irwell and on conduits from the reservoirs.'

A character in Manchester was Mr Abraham Gadian, mentioned earlier, an elder statesman of the Central Synagogue. Gadian came to Manchester from Lithuania and was the typical Lithuanian *Maskil*, well-versed in the Bible and fluent in

Hebrew, admiring but somewhat aloof from Talmudic learning, staunchly Zionist and a keen student of general works of European thought. He was a great admirer of the Hebrew essayist, Ahad Ha-Am. Gadian told me how he had heard that the famous Zionist thinker had acquired an office in Mincing Lane, in London, where he worked as the London representative of Wissotsky, the Russian tea firm. The young Gadian, anxious to meet his hero, made an appointment and journeyed especially to London, expecting to see the tall, imposing figure of a philosopher with flowing locks and an absent-minded air. Instead, as Gadian put it, he was confronted with 'a little *yidel*' engaged in the sale of tea. But Gadian's disappointment evaporated as soon as Ahad Ha-Am, seeing a young enthusiast, began to explain lucidly his ideas about Judaism as an ethical religion and Palestine as the spiritual centre out of which the Jewish ideas would spread for the benefit of all men.

Sir Leon Simon, another disciple of Ahad Ha-Am and translator of the master's essays into English, told me that his teacher was a real connoisseur often capable of telling the home of any particular brew merely by tasting it. Although not particularly observant, Gadian attended all the synagogue services and anything else that was going on in the congregation. His advice was sought by the management of the synagogue in matters great and small. He was a shrewd man with a dry sense of humour. He used to tell how he once made a call at a house while collecting funds for the Zionist cause. The woman who opened the door willingly gave him sixpence even though she had refused to give a penny to a previous collector. Gadian asked her, 'Please tell me why you refused him and yet contributed so willingly when I asked you?' The woman replied, 'He said a million pounds is required for the settlement of Eretz Yisrael, so I said: "If you want a million pounds do not come here. Go to Rothschild." But you ask for sixpence. Here's sixpence.' Another Gadian story was about Rabbi Dr Herzog, when the latter was Rabbi of Dublin. The Irish half-penny had embossed on it the figure of a little pig (a *chazerle* in Yiddish). A pious Jew, known for his miserliness, asked Rabbi Herzog whether it was permitted to put such a coin into a Jewish collection box. 'Don't be a *chazerle*,' replied Rabbi Herzog, 'Put a penny in the box.'

I only preached occasionally at the Golders Green Beth Hamedrash, either when invited by Dr Munk or during his absence in Germany. At the Central Synagogue, it was my duty to deliver a sermon every Sabbath and festival morning; to deliver a eulogy at every funeral and speak words of comfort at the house of mourning; and to address every bride and groom under the *chuppah*. (Very often I was called upon to speak again at the wedding dinner, when I was expected to be anecdotal and humorous.) With little homiletical experience behind me and with no training in the subject at all in the Yeshivah, I was plunged into an orgy of public speaking, seeking material from books of Jewish sermons in English (I.H. Levinthal's books were a constant standby or, at least, a springboard for my own ideas) and trying to acquire a measure of voice-control by attending a course in elocution and voice production given by a Mr Harrison. This elocution teacher, a non-Jew, made me do exercises in breathing and I had to recite poems for him such as Robert Southey's 'The Cataract of Lodore'. Mr Harrison's favourite expression was, 'Get a ring, a resonance in your voice.' This became a catch-word in our family circle. My children would with mock innocence ask me, 'Daddy, do you have a ring, a resonance in your voice today?' These exercises were boring, but necessary, since there were always to be found one or two congregants who would say, 'Rebbe, what you say is fine, so we are told, but we cannot hear you at the back of the synagogue.' I decided it would be more beneficial to me to learn how to send my voice out to the back of the synagogue than to tell them bluntly to sit nearer the front.

The congregation at the Central Synagogue was composed largely of small traders and workers from the numerous raincoat and waterproof factories in the city. These people were the salt of the earth: pious, hard-working, respectful of Jewish learning, regular in their synagogue attendance. They did not want any high-faluting sermons. On the other hand, they hated, and rightly so, to be talked down to, so my sermons had to be homely, practical and down-to-earth but with the necessary degree of quotation from Jewish and general literature. I learned to adjust to the needs of the congregation. Like most young rabbis, however, I was astonished to realise that they liked to be admonished, provided it was done in not too pointed a way. 'Did he give it to them!' was a cry frequently heard to express the delight of the congregation at a sermon with a sufficient degree of castigation, though I myself have never really been able to 'let them have it'. At the best this is self-indulgent. At the worst it panders to the need of some congregants to get a masochistic kick out of castigation directed against themselves, as well as more than a dollop of Schadenfreude out of the admonishment of others for faults to which they themselves were not prone. The Hafetz Hayim used to say, 'I am not referring to anyone in particular, but if there is anyone here who thinks I mean him, I do mean him!' Shunning admonitory sermons all my preaching life, I confess to many occasions when I should have been out-spoken but failed to be, out of false modesty and unwillingness to hurt good people rather than out of sheer cowardice. The price a rabbi pays for making his sermons expository rather than exhortatory is that he inevitably misses out when there are real abuses for him to correct. Nevertheless I would prefer to err on the side of indulgence. After all, Jewish synagogue-goers are worthy people with no one compelling them to regular attendance.

Funeral services were a trial, not so much when an elderly man or woman died but when I had to speak at the funeral of a young boy or girl and try to offer words of comfort to the bereaved family at the house of mourning. I soon realised the futility of turning the address into a theological exercise, of trying to explain the mysterious ways of God. All that a sympathetic rabbi could be expected to do on such tragic occasions was to dwell on the virtues of the deceased and the care given by the devoted family during the months or years of sickness, and to explain that God is with those who mourn. As for the rest, silence is best. The Talmud states that, when confronted with tragedy, one should not ask 'What can I do?' as if questioning the divine benevolence. By implication, it is proper to say 'What can I *say* that will be of comfort to you?' Again like every young rabbi, I tended at first to become too personally involved when tragedy befell one of my congregants; coming to realise, however, that while a rabbi must never be anything but sympathetic he should not take all the cares of the world on his poor shoulders and treat every tragedy as if it had happened to him personally, otherwise the weight of pain and grief could exact their cost in a nervous breakdown. In this respect the rabbi has to acquire a degree of professionalism, in the same way that a doctor could never achieve anything if he were to look upon every one of his patients as a member of his own family.

Of the distinguished preachers who visited Manchester none was more popular than Kopul Rosen. I had taught in the Hebrew classes of his Manchester synagogue, the Higher Crumpsall Synagogue, whence he had gone to become Communal Rabbi of Glasgow and later Principal Rabbi of the Federation of Synagogues in London. During his time in London and Glasgow, Kopul had grown a beard. His opening remarks in his sermon at the Higher Crumpsall on his visit to Manchester were, 'It is good to see the old familiar faces even though I present a very unfamiliar one.' When Dr Hertz died and a successor as Chief Rabbi was being sought, Kopul was one of the three candidates on the shortlist. He was rejected, however, not because of any inadequacies but because it was felt that such a position should not go to a young man who was only 33 years of age. Kopul was one of the most gifted speakers I have ever heard – learned, witty, eloquent in both English and Yiddish and quite fearless in expressing what he felt and believed to be true. He was a capable defender of traditional Judaism to Jew and non-Jew alike. Kopul's name will also live on as the founder and Principal of the Jewish Public School, Carmel College.

Kopul's passing in his forties was a severe blow to world Jewry. During his last illness, only a fortnight before he died, I visited him at Carmel where we talked for hours about the spot of bother that had then begun concerning my candidature for the principalship of Jews' College. Kopul was on my side in the affair, albeit with some reservations. It was not this that impressed me, but rather the fact that a man who knew his days were numbered could talk brilliantly and with keen interest and sympathy about a problem which would not be resolved in his lifetime.

A few of us used to meet at Kopul Rosen's house during my earlier period in Manchester in order to listen to Talmudic discourses from another "Koppel", Rabbi Koppel Kahana. Rabbi Kahana was a typical Lithuanian *illui* ('genius'). He had studied in his youth under the famed Lithuanian analytical scholar Rabbi Itzel Ponievezher and in the Yeshivah of the Hafetz Hayim in Radin. When in Radin, Rabbi Kahana told me, he was sitting late one night in the hall of the Yeshivah puzzling over the meaning of an extremely difficult passage in the Tosafists. Suddenly the door opened to admit the Hafetz Hayim, who went straight over to Kahana and, without even looking at the page, proceeded to explain the Tosafists, thus removing Kahana's difficulties. Rabbi Kahana observed that at the time he believed this episode to confirm what the Hafetz Hayim's disciples had long attested, that the saint had the gift of the holy spirit (*ruah ha-kodesh*). When he told me the story, Rabbi Kahana stressed that he had *then* believed it, perhaps to imply that now he was not so sure.

Rabbi Kahana resolved to obtain a good university degree and was at that time busy studying English and Latin for the Cambridge University Entrance Examination. Before he began his Talmudic discourses at Kopul Rosen's home, he would startle us with a show of his knowledge of English. I recall him asking us, 'What is the difference between an "agglomeration" and a "conglomeration"?' We gave up, whereupon, with a triumphant smile, he proceeded to explain the difference and then said, 'You are all English and I am a foreigner and yet my English is better than yours.'

Rabbi Kahana had a photographic memory. He not only knew most of the Talmud by heart but could actually see the pages in his mind's eye. One Purim he exhibited his prowess by performing a feat popular with Lithuanian Talmudists of his ability. We placed a pin through a page of the Talmud, taken at random, and he was able to recite by heart the lines of the page at the spot where the point of the pin came through. As an illustration of Rabbi Kahana's analytical skills, I quote here a subtle distinction he made in following the ideas of his teacher. If *terefa* food is inadvertently cooked in the same pot together with kosher food, the whole mixture is permitted to be eaten provided there is sixty times as much kosher as terefa food. This is the principle of *battel be-shishim* ('neutralisation in a ratio of one to sixty'.) If there is less than sixty times as much kosher food the whole mixture is forbidden. Similarly, meat and milk cooked together is forbidden, but if a drop of milk falls into a meat dish and there is sixty times as much meat as milk, the whole mixture is permitted because the milk has been neutralised. So far, the principle of neutralisation is the same in both cases. However, supposing there is less than sixty times as much kosher than terefa food (in the first instance) but then a further amount of kosher food is added so that *now* there is a ratio of one to sixty. The rule here is that the neutralisation principle still obtains since, after all, there is now sixty times more kosher than terefa. In the second instance, of the milk and the meat, the rule is different. Here if, at first, there is less than sixty times as much meat as milk the whole dish becomes forbidden even if more meat is later added until there is a ratio of one to sixty. Why the difference? The difference, said Kahana, is this. Since it is forbidden to eat meat and milk cooked together and since, at first, there was less than sixty times as much meat than milk, then the whole mixture – the meat as well as the milk – is meat cooked together with milk. The meat is meat and milk and the milk is meat and milk. Here it cannot suffice that later on a further amount of meat is added, since it is not the milk alone that has to be neutralised, but the original quantity of meat as well. In the case of the terefa meat, on the other hand, the kosher meat remains kosher even if there is less than sixty times as much kosher as terefa. The mixture is only forbidden because there is an amount of terefa food that has not been neutralised. It follows that once further kosher food has been added the principle of neutralisation can still come into operation.

Rabbi Kahana eventually obtained a Master's degree in Roman Law at Cambridge University, where he took on successfully all the experts in the field by applying the methods he had learnt to use in his Talmudic analysis. He wrote a number of learned articles and books on Jewish, Roman and English law, especially from the comparative point of view. These works suffer from what is basically an unhistorical approach but are rewarding for the brilliant insights they afford into the principles of the Halakhah. Later on, Rabbi Kahana conducted the Semichah class at Jews' College, where he trained two generations of rabbis. Generally he tended to fight shy of giving practical decisions, claiming that he was a theoretician. During the period in which I had the privilege of being a colleague of Rabbi Kahana at Jews' College, he encouraged me in my work and sincerely looked forward to my appointment as Principal of the College. His admiration for the Chief Rabbi, who was blocking my appointment, was less than whole-hearted and he loved the intrigues that were going on behind the scenes. He often chided me for making things difficult by my interest in theology. Religion, he said to me, is chiefly a matter of psychology, so why create disturbances by introducing theological mystery? Like many Lithuanian Talmudists, Rabbi Kahana could see little point in studying theology or, indeed, in having any theological concern. He once told me that he had heard the Rosh Yeshivah at Radin, Rabbi Moshe Landinsky, say that if it were true that the soul survives bodily death, it would have been mentioned in the Torah. When I visited Rabbi Kahana in hospital before he was due to have an operation, he said, 'What if the operation is unsuccessful? To go to sleep for ever . . .'

Rabbi Kahana was a great man, with a noble if somewhat naive character, looked upon by his peers as one of the most distinguished Talmudists of his day. He was essentially a very humble man but was not averse to an occasional declaration of his own worth. He once said, 'There are only three good Talmudists in England: Rabbi Rabbinov, Dayan Abramsky and myself. And not necessarily in that order.'

The name of Rabbi Israel Brodie (later Sir Israel) will be met frequently in this story. He was installed in his high office as Chief Rabbi in 1948 at the New Synagogue in Stamford Hill when he was 56 years of age, after a distinguished career as a rabbi in Australia and as Chaplain-in-Chief to the Jewish forces. The three candidates considered in the final count were Rabbi Kopul Rosen, Dr Altmann, Communal Rabbi of Manchester, and Rabbi Brodie. As was noted earlier, Kopul Rosen was rejected as too young for the office despite his many talents. It was widely rumoured that Sir Robert Waley-Cohen, President of the United Synagogue and Chairman of the Chief Rabbinate Council, dismissed Dr Altmann's candidature on the absurd grounds that a 'German' rabbi could not serve as the spiritual head of a community so recently at war with Germany! Rabbi Brodie, as English as they came, was therefore favoured. (It is worth noting that no rabbis ever had a say in the appointment of a British Chief Rabbi, even though his authority when he is appointed may weigh heavily on rabbinic colleagues under his jurisdiction.) It was also rumoured that Sir Robert, a powerful personality who insisted on having his own way, was tired of the constant struggle he had had to engage in with the equally strong and self-willed Dr Hertz. Sir Robert, it was widely held at the time, favoured Rabbi Brodie as a more tolerant, not to say more pliant, leader.

Rabbi Brodie, after becoming Chief Rabbi, expressed an interest in my future. He remarked that I had promise, as he put it, when he paid a visit to the Central Synagogue. One fine day, in a rather roundabout way, it was intimated that the Chief Rabbi wished me to come to London to serve as the Minister of the Brondesbury Synagogue and as a *Dayan* of the London Beth Din, both positions having been held by Rabbi Moshe Swift who had resigned from them in order to accept a call to South Africa. A month or two before this, I had been invited over the telephone by Dayan Abramsky to visit him at his home in London and found the learned Dayan discoursing generally on the politics of Anglo-Jewry and remarking that Rabbi Brodie was a really Orthodox Chief Rabbi. Why the Dayan wished to see me was never clearly stated, but in the light of the invitation to succeed Rabbi Swift, it was clear that he felt it only right to meet me before I was offered the position.

I had only been at the Central Synagogue a short time, and was happy there. Yet the offer of the joint position in London was not without its attraction. I took the President of the Central Synagogue, Mr Harry Leigh, into my confidence and he strongly urged me to accept. In his blunt northern way Harry Leigh said, 'Take it. I like to see a young man get on.' What I failed in my naivety to see was the unfortunate hole-in-the-corner way in which such appointments were made. Why, for instance, was there neither any official application on my part, nor any official invitation on the part of the Chief Rabbi? In any event, off I went to London where I met with the Board of Management of the Brondesbury Synagogue at the home of the Chairman, a Mr Williams. We got along well, as I recall. I was asked to telephone Rabbi Swift, who told me that the two positions were quite prestigious, even though he had received a better offer in South Africa. This, too, I found odd. Having to discuss the two positions over the telephone with the previous holder seemed far too cloak-and-dagger for my liking. To cap it all, I then had an appointment with the Executive of the United Synagogue at the headquarters of their organisation in Woburn House. They seemed satisfied with my credentials but the President, Mr Frank Samuel, let slip a remark to the effect that the final nature of the position at the Beth Din would have to be determined by the Chief Rabbi. Evidently, I thought, someone had had second thoughts. This was confirmed when I eventually met the Chief Rabbi. He said that he could not offer me the position Rabbi Swift had occupied of Dayan but only that of Registrar to the Beth Din, since I was still a very young man, but that would grow into the superior position. I felt very distressed. After all I had not taken any initiative in the matter and, if the truth be told, did not want to leave the Central Synagogue. On my return from the alarming series of interviews, I consulted Mr Abraham ('Abse') Moss (later Sir Abraham), a Lord Mayor of Manchester and a member of my congregation. He advised me in no circumstances to accept the position offered, warning me that if I did Rabbi Brodie would never allow me to proceed to the office of Dayan and would keep me in subordination. 'He is not Moses,' said Abse Moss. Consequently, I decided to remain at the Central Synagogue. With hindsight I can see how disastrous it would have been to have become associated with the London Beth Din, a body with which I later engaged in battle several times. The views of the Beth Din on Judaism were not my views even then, and nothing could have so effectively killed off my theological quest as to have become a member of a body with no confidence at all in free inquiry.

Not long after my abortive attempt to leave the Central Synagogue for London, overtures were made from the Jewish community in Holland to ascertain whether I was willing to visit Holland to explore the possibility of becoming Chief Rabbi of the Orthodox Community. Again with Harry Leigh's encouragement to 'get on', I took a plane to Amsterdam. I had never travelled by air but Harry Leigh said, 'Don't worry. I have been up in a plane at Blackpool. There's nothing to it!' I spent ten hectic days in Amsterdam delivering lectures in English and Yiddish and meeting with the leaders of the Dutch community. The Dutch Jews could not have been more charming and welcoming, but my experience during these ten days convinced me that the language barrier would prove insurmountable. I could learn Dutch but felt I would never acquire the fluency a Dutch Chief Rabbi should have in the language. In addition, I sensed that my appointment would be an affront to the Orthodox rabbis in Holland who would be far better suited to the position than myself, if only because of their greater knowledge of Dutch life. Most of all, I had begun my quest for a 'middle way' and felt it dishonest to take up a position in an at least nominally Orthodox community, subscribing evidently to a fundamentalist approach that I could not share. Unfortunately, that approach eventually became an obstacle to my continuing at the Central Synagogue, much as I was otherwise hugely contented with my position there. Maybe I had too many scruples, since no one at the Central appeared at all bothered by any views I held. Yet so it was. I resolved to seek a position in a synagogue where I could do my work freely without the burden of double-think. The opportunity came in an unexpected way and will be related in the next chapter.

My congregation were as sorry to see me go, I think, as I was to leave these good people who could not have been more considerate. I delivered my farewell sermon, Shula was given an inscribed pair of Sabbath candlesticks and I was presented with a complete set of the Soncino Talmud, and together with Shula and my three children (David, the youngest, was born in 1952) set off for London in 1954 to take up the position of Minister-Preacher to the New West End Synagogue.

7

THE NEW WEST END
SYNAGOGUE

The New West End Synagogue in St Petersburg Place, Kensington, was the Anglicised synagogue *par excellence*. It was founded by Sir Samuel Montagu (later the first Lord Swaythling) and other prominent figures in the West End Jewish community who had broken away for some reason from the Bayswater Synagogue, although both the New West End and Bayswater remained constituents of the United Synagogue. The services were almost completely traditional in practice except for a few innovations introduced with the approval of Chief Rabbi Hermann Adler, evidently in order to stem the Reform tide which exercised a powerful pull among West End Jewry.

The result was typical Anglo-Jewish compromise. While men and women were seated separately (the latter in the special ladies' gallery) there was a mixed choir, situated in the choir-loft built over the Ark. The part of the Musaf prayer calling for the restoration of the sacrificial system was not recited aloud by the Cantor, but silently by those who wished to recite it. In this connection, it is appropriate to refer to the case of the Rev. Morris Joseph, author of *Judaism as Creed and Life*, who was 'inhibited' by Chief Rabbi Adler from serving as minister of the Hampstead Synagogue because of his refusal to pray for the restoration of sacrifices. (Joseph became instead the minister of the Reform Synagogue in Upper Berkeley Street.) Many years later, Chief Rabbi Hertz wrote in his Commentary to the Prayer Book:

This portion of the Musaf Prayer has been much assailed in modern times. 'References to the sacrificial Service, and especially prayers for its restoration, are disliked by some', wrote the Principal of Jews' College, the saintly Dr M.

104

Friedlander, over fifty years ago. In view of the later origin of this prayer and in view, furthermore, that for a long time the whole Musaf Prayer was deemed to be voluntary for the individual worshipper, we can quite endorse his decision, 'Let him whose heart is not with his fellow-worshippers in any of their supplications silently substitute his own prayers for them; but let him not interfere with the devotion of those to whom "the statutes of the Lord are right, rejoicing the heart; the commandments of the Lord pure, enlightening the eyes; the judgments of the Lord true and righteous altogether" (Ps.19.9.10), and who yearn for the opportunity of fulfilling Divine commandments which they cannot observe at present.'

And so it was at the New West End (and some other synagogues belonging to the United Synagogue). After the Chazan and the choir had led the congregation in the Musaf *kedushah*, some of the congregation recited the section dealing with the restoration of sacrifices while others could be observed remaining respectfully silent but clearly determined to demonstrate by that silence, 'You won't catch us praying for the restoration of sacrifices.'

The first minister of the New West End was the Rev. Simeon Singer, translator of the Authorised Daily Prayer Book (the 'Singer' Prayer Book) in which, incidentally, he collaborated with Claude Montefiore, the founder of Liberal Judaism in this country. (The sentence in Singer's preface, in which he acknowledges his indebtedness to Montefiore, has been excised in the new edition published under the jurisdiction of Chief Rabbi Brodie.) Singer's son-in-law, Israel Abrahams, was also a prominent founder member of the Liberal movement. Singer himself was hardly Orthodox in theory, though so far as I know he was observant in practice. He had studied in Vienna under the famed historian of Jewish law, I.H. Weiss, hardly a champion of fundamentalist Orthodoxy. (Chief Rabbi Hermann Adler had been sent by his father, his predecessor as Chief Rabbi, to study in Prague with S.J. Rapoport, like Weiss one of the foremost representatives of the *Jüdische Wissenschaft* school.) Singer obtained his Semichah from Weiss but was not allowed by the Chief Rabbi to use the title 'Rabbi'. There was only one rabbi in Anglo-Jewry and that was the Chief Rabbi! All the others, including those with impeccable rabbinic credentials, were the Chief Rabbi's 'Ministers'. In one of his published addresses, Singer approves of J.L. Gordon's attack on those rabbinic laws of marriage and divorce unfair to women.

Singer's successor, Dr Hochman, was a brilliant young scholar with a fair measure of eccentricity. I was told that he would go riding in Hyde Park in the afternoon, where he would gallop to the synagogue, tether his horse to a lamppost while he took the afternoon service and then ride off home on the horse, trailing clouds of glory, as it were. He was editor of the *Jewish Review*, where, during the interregnum between Chief Rabbis Adler and Hertz, he wrote to a number of community leaders questioning the wisdom of the whole institution of Chief Rabbi, an office, he believed, that exerted far too strong an influence on individual rabbis, depriving them of the independence the Jewish tradition gave them. After a few years Hochman left the New West End to pursue a career in law, later becoming legal adviser to the King of Siam. In later life he returned to England where he became a member of the New West End.

My immediate predecessor at the New West End was the Rev. Ephraim Levine, serving as minister there for forty years until his retirement. Ephraim Levine was acknowledged as the most outstanding preacher in the 'English' style. The fact that he was born in Scotland and spoke with a delightful Scottish accent only enhanced his reputation. His book of sermons, *The Faith of a Jewish Preacher*, published in 1935, is still used by preachers as a guide to preaching in this style at its best. He was a sort of Jewish Sydney Smith, popular as an after-dinner speaker and renowned for his wit, which, it must be said, could be wounding at times. In his youth, after taking his BA Hons. degree at Jews' College, he studied for his Master's at Cambridge. Another minister, whose family were in the furniture business, was a rival candidate to Levine for a London pulpit. When the other man was appointed, Levine wryly remarked that the congregation evidently preferred furniture polish to Cambridge polish. Levine was interested in horse racing and in sport of all kinds. After my appointment to the pulpit of the New West End, he and his

wife Annie came to dinner at our home in Manchester when my
parents were also present, Levine spending a good deal of the
time discussing the rival merits of soccer and rugby with my
father. On this occasion he took out three huge cigars, giving
one to my father and one to me. I had never smoked a cigar
but, wishing to appear a man of the world, accepted and began
to puff away. A good cigar it certainly was but it was far too
rich for my untutored palate and I had to leave the dinner-table
in haste to be sick in the bathroom.

Ephraim Levine was in Manchester on that occasion to
help raise funds for Jews' College. Speaking at a meeting of
communal leaders he discussed rabbis who officiated in South
Africa, Australia and New Zealand and said, 'A Rov in the Rand
is worth two in the Bush.' He also remarked that the title of a
New Zealand rabbi ought to be 'Maori Morenu' ('Our Maori
Teacher'). There were two Chief Rabbis in South Africa at the
time, one in Johannesburg, the other in Cape Town. Levine
quoted Dr Hertz as saying, when he set out on a pastoral tour
of South Africa, 'I am going to visit the African chiefs.'

I cannot claim that my relations with Ephraim Levine were
always cordial. He had been too long in the congregation to
relinquish his hold easily and gracefully. He would sit there
in the synagogue week after week glowering, tut-tutting or
gnashing his teeth (sometimes all three) whenever something I
said in the pulpit was not to his liking, which was very often.
In my later struggle with the Chief Rabbi he seemed to waver
between supporting him and supporting me. In any event our
backgrounds were totally different and I realised from the start
how fatal it would be to try to model myself on him, though I
did try – perhaps unsuccessfully – not to be too much of a new
broom.

The New West End, with its background of tolerance, broadmindedness and love of tradition, seemed the ideal congregation, one in which I could express my views freely and yet live
a traditional Jewish life. The Chazan (Minister-Reader was the
official title, in contradistinction to Minister-Preacher) of the
New West End was the Rev. Raphael Levy, a cultured man
who was probably the leading practitioner of Chazanut in the

Anglo-Jewish mode. Raphael Levy had served as Minister to the Preston Hebrew Congregation. While at Preston he travelled frequently to Manchester where he took his Master's degree at the University. I met Raphael Levy and his wife, Celia (both, alas, no longer in the land of the living), while lecturing at a Torah Va-Avodah summer school in Deal. We became friends with a good deal in common and it was Raphael who suggested that I apply for the vacant position of Minister-Preacher of the New West End. This I did and eventually delivered my trial sermon which must have gone down well. After another trial sermon (but by this time my appointment was more or less a foregone conclusion) and a rather daunting interview with the board of management of the synagogue, I was duly elected. I was inducted into office on 13 February 1954 by Chief Rabbi Brodie. At the *kiddush* after the service I met the congregation, which numbered among its members some of the most illustrious names in Anglo-Jewry.

Chief Rabbi Brodie, I have in honesty to say, could not have been more friendly and encouraging. His induction address welcomed me as a new recruit to the ranks of the London Jewish Ministry and he treated me more as a colleague than a subordinate. Ephraim Levine, speaking at the *kiddush*, said that the large congregation had come to hear its new Minister with 'Great Expectations', which, he hoped, would be realised. In my reply I said that since Dickens was being quoted, as a former citizen of Manchester mine was 'A Tale of Two Cities' and that, like my former congregation, I could only hope that my new congregation would do an Oliver Twist and ask for more.

In my introduction sermon I took as my text the prayer of the Reader of the Morning Service on Rosh Hashanah: 'O my Creator, give me understanding that I may transmit thine inheritance; strengthen and uphold me that I may be far from weakness and fear.' Speaking of the Anglo-Jewish tradition represented by the New West End, I said:

> This Anglo-Jewish tradition is a great and glorious one, which never falters in spurning the superficial tinsel attrac-tions of the *Zeitgeist* out of loyalty to the perennial ideals

of our eternal faith. At its best it is a worthwhile blending of all that is good in the Jewish and British character. It is conservative but not hidebound; firm and consistent but not fanatical; proud of its origins but not insular; sober but not unimaginative; acutely conscious of the significance and importance of Jewish law but not formalistic; it has a love of learning but is not pedantic. The philanthropic achievements, in particular, of those who have followed this tradition have won the admiration of the whole world.

Ephraim Levine, in his few words at the *kiddush*, implied that I was busy buttering up the congregation and I have to admit that I did pile it on a bit. But I really did believe at the time, and still believe today, that the Anglo-Jewish ideal, with all its faults (more than I realised when I gave that sermon), does have the unique blend of which I spoke all that time ago, and it is a pity that there are those in the community who would be only too glad to see it vanish.

On my appointment to the pulpit of the New West End I received a number of welcoming letters from members of the congregation. It was typical, however, of the extreme formality with which the United Synagogue conducted its affairs that the official notification of my appointment was cold and curt:

18th October 1953

Dear Rabbi Jacobs,
    I have pleasure in informing you that, at a meeting of the members of this Synagogue held to-day, you were elected Minister-Preacher.

With best wishes,
Yours sincerely,
Isaac Kaska,
Secretary

The Rev. Ephraim Levine's letter of welcome was not unfriendly but, with hindsight, I was able to detect a slight patronising note and what perhaps amounted to a warning of things to come.

From   24 Palace Court, W.2
The Rev. Ephraim Levine, MA,
Minister of
The New West End Synagogue

19th October, 1953

Dear Mr Jacobs,

Let me be amongst the first to congratulate you on your election to the Ministry of the New West End Synagogue. I have not the pleasure of knowing you, except by your writings which I have enjoyed reading from time to time in the Jewish press, and from talks I have had with Manchester friends who speak in appreciative terms of you. Having occupied the position, to which you will soon succeed, for 38 years, I can speak of the honour bestowed upon you and of the responsibility which will be yours. The New West End Synagogue has come to be regarded as the premier London synagogue; Simeon Singer was its first Minister who raised its pulpit to a supreme height and I have striven to maintain its reputation. I may have helped to keep it high, and throughout the many years I do not think its prestige has suffered. I am sure that you will treasure the heritage and add lustre to our beloved synagogue.

When you are in London I shall be glad to see you and tell you much that you will like to know of the work that lies ahead of you. If I can befriend you in any way, and keep 'your feet from stumbling on the dark mountains' I shall be happy.

For the present accept my good wishes and those of my wife for your future happiness in London.

Yours sincerely,
Ephraim Levine

I thought the reference to Ephraim Levine keeping my feet from stumbling on the dark mountains a little ominous, but in due course Shula and I paid a visit to the Levine home where he again assured me of his willingness to help, adding only that he would still like to officiate at weddings and funerals when asked to do so by the family concerned.

Among the members of the New West End was the first Viscount Samuel who as a boy of eight had been made a member by his father at the time of the Synagogue's inception. All his life Herbert Samuel occupied the seat towards the rear of the synagogue that had been allotted to him in his boyhood. He was getting on in years when I came to the New West End and was a little hard of hearing so a hearing-aid was attached to his seat, the other end attached to a small microphone in the pulpit. Ephraim Levine said to me, 'You don't have to worry whether you are doing all right in the pulpit until you see Lord Samuel switch off his hearing aid.' Like all the members of the New West End, Ephraim Levine had great respect for Lord Samuel, but I was told that on one occasion when Samuel was critical of remarks Levine had made in the pulpit, Levine said to him, 'I do not tell you what to say in the House of Lords and I do not want you to tell me what to say in the pulpit.'

Lord and Lady Samuel were very welcoming to Shula and me. We used to go to their home for afternoon tea when Lady Samuel would discuss the weekly *sidra* with me. It appeared that she never missed reading the weekly portion in the Hertz Humash. We were also invited to the Samuel home on the occasion of their diamond wedding, Lady Samuel wearing the dress she wore at her wedding. The speech at the reception was to have been given by Lord Trevelyan, the historian, who had been best man at their wedding, but he was in his 80s and too frail to attend. Lady Trevelyan, a few years younger, read out her husband's speech. A few elderly ladies were to be seen walking around proudly telling everyone that they had been bridesmaids at the wedding sixty years before. I am afraid I have been guilty of name-dropping but it is difficult to avoid this when writing about the New West End; the list of members I was given when I came to the congregation contained the names of peers and knights of the realm, judges, scientists, physicians and surgeons, musicians, artists and well-known figures in the business life of the community such as Sir Simon Marks of Marks and Spencer.

The Rev. Dr Abraham Cohen, scholar, preacher, communal leader and author of several books on Jewish thought (among them *Everyman's Talmud* in the Everyman Series published by Dent) had been elected President of the Board of Deputies of British Jews on his retirement from the Singers Hill pulpit in Birmingham, where he had served with great distinction for forty years. This was the first time in its history that the Board had had a clergyman for its head. Dr Cohen lived in London not too far away from the New West End, where he became a regular worshipper. He must have shuddered at some of the things this young preacher uttered in the pulpit but he never allowed himself a word of criticism and was unfailing in his encouragement. Mrs Cohen, a vivacious lady with a biting wit, used to sit next to Shula in the Ladies Gallery, where she would offer good advice from her experience on how a minister's wife should get along with her congregation. 'Pretend to be looking at the prayer book,' she would say, 'and no one will guess that we are talking instead of davening.' In most of the 'Anglicised' congregations the priestly blessing was not said by the *kohanim*, there was no *duchaning*, as part of the 'reforms' introduced during the last century – why I do not know, unless it was because the congregations could not see why some members, as a result of birth, should have been considered especially worthy to bless others. At the New West End, long before I came there, Mr Elkan Adler, son of Chief Rabbi Nathan Marcus Adler and brother of Chief Rabbi Hermann Adler, a noted bibliophile (his collection is now housed in the Jewish Theological Seminary Library in New York) insisted as a Cohen on his right to *duchan*, this then becoming the normal practice on the festivals. (Sir Robert Waley-Cohen always insisted on *duchaning* together with his sons at the Central Synagogue.) Dr Abraham Cohen had never *duchaned* in Birmingham but led the *kohanim* in *duchaning* at the New West End.

This matter of *duchaning* is a typical illustration of the love of tradition on the part of leading members of the Anglo-Jewish community, in public life at least. In their private life they were not all so observant. On my very first Kol Nidre eve at the New

West End, as I was changing before the service into my white robes – not so much a *kittel* as a minister's gown in white satin with a white, large minister's hat – a sarcastic member of the congregation exclaimed, 'When does the baking start?' I then had a brief conversation with the third Lord Swaythling whom I had just met. Time was pressing and I suggested that we go into the synagogue for Kol Nidre. Swaythling remarked that he did not want to enter the synagogue for a while and that he would explain why after the service. His explanation was that his grandfather, the first Lord Swaythling, although a very observant Jew, did not hold with the Kol Nidre formula and used to wait patiently and quietly in the foyer of the synagogue until this part of the service was over. His son, the second Lord, less observant and more than a little indifferent to the whole question, would still wait outside because his father had done so. The third Lord explained that he personally did not understand what it was all about, but felt obliged to carry on the family tradition!

The first Lord Swaythling's daughter, the Hon. Lily Montagu, who had rebelled against her father's Orthodoxy to become co-founder, together with Claude Montefiore, of the Liberal Synagogue, thought the festival of Purim and the reading of the Megillah (the book of Esther) to be very unfortunate. It was far too particularistic and vindictive for her and Montefiore's liberal taste. As luck would have it, the Hon. Lily had *Yahrzeit* for her father on Purim and was torn between her wish to say *kaddish* for her father and her Liberal conviction that it was wrong to listen to the reading of the Megillah. Her duty to her father won out. On Purim eve, Lily and her sister Marion consequently attended the service at the New West End where they sat, ill at ease, during the reading of the Megillah, so that they could recite *kaddish* when the ordeal was over. Tradition again!

Another son of the first Lord Swaythling, the Hon. Gerald Montagu, was also a member of the New West End. Gerald was a gentle soul, never excited or agitated, not even when he had to take his sisters, Lily and Marion, mad about cricket, regularly to Lord's cricket ground to watch a game for which he had no fondness whatsoever. Gerald's wife, Firenza, a Sephardi, was a deeply religious lady who never paraded her piety. Shula and I became close friends of Gerald and Firenza. Firenza became President of the Women's Mizrahi movement, not, as she explained to me, because she was such a strong Zionist but because she believed that if you have to follow Zionism, it should be in a religious form. She would often entertain young Mizrahists in her lovely home where, surrounded by things of great beauty and interest she and her husband had collected over the years, she would instruct them casually in the art of gracious living. She was once heard to say, 'Really, Mr Halpern. Not *that* glass for sherry!'

Another member of the Montagu clan who was a member of the New West End was the Hon. Ewen Montagu, son of the second Lord Swaything, distinguished lawyer, sailor and intelligence officer during the Second World War, who devised the spoofing of the Germans and the saving of many Allied lives by his plan known as 'The Man Who Never Was'. (Ewen's book on the subject was a bestseller and was made into a film starring Clifton Webb.) Ewen and his wife, Iris, befriended me from the beginning and played a leading part in the events to be related in the following chapters of this book. Ewen was a wonderful man but he never claimed to be an observant Jew or even a regular synagogue-goer. (This did not prevent him from becoming Treasurer and later President of the United Synagogue.) Yet, after his death, a letter appeared in the *Jewish Chronicle* from his tailor in which he stated that Ewen, when ordering an overcoat, would instruct him to see that it was free of *shaatnez*. Tradition yet again!

At the New West End I soon became acquainted with the facts of life for employees of the United Synagogue. The United Synagogue, the largest synagogue body in the world, believed in what one can only describe as socialised religion. I have always had socialist leanings – my father was a working man – but the way this operated in the United Synagogue, run, incidentally, by people hardly any of whom voted Labour, was unbelievable. All funds and all resources of the constituent synagogues were pooled and the whole organisation was run, with a central bureaucracy, from the head office. Ministers were not, in fact, employed by their own synagogue at all but by the United Synagogue. For instance, I discovered that part of my duties was to be Jewish Chaplain to one of the large hospitals (at first the Middlesex and later St Mary's, Paddington, where Alexander Fleming discovered penicillin). This was over and above visiting sick people belonging to my own congregation. I recall feeling very aggrieved that I had to send weekly reports of my visits to a Miss Rosenbaum at head office who had nothing to do with my own congregation. The advantage of the system for ministers was that it made them independent, in a sense, of the members of their own congregation, who were not their employers and to whom they were not beholden. Provided a man did his job properly, no matter how much he quarrelled with his congregation and how unsatisfactory his sermonising, nothing could be done to get rid of him. Carrying out the duties laid down in his contract with the United Synagogue was all that was required of him and he had tenure for life.

One disadvantage of the system was the remoteness of head office. More serious, however, was the fact that, according to the Constitution of the United Synagogue, the Chief Rabbi's word was law. It was the Chief Rabbi, the rabbi of the organisation as a whole, who was, in fact, the rabbi of the local congregation as well. No innovations in the service, for example, were tolerated, even if desired by the local minister and his congregation, unless sanctioned by the Chief Rabbi. I was fully conscious of this severe disadvantage in the system when, later, the Chief Rabbi exercised his veto against my appointment, even though it had the full approval of the whole congregation.

Furthermore, the very bricks and mortar of the synagogue building belonged not to the local congregation, the members of which had paid for them, but to the overall body. During my term of office, I, together with Donald Samuel, Lord Samuel's nephew, and Lawrence Jacobs, collected a considerable sum of money for the erection of the Herbert Samuel Hall, adjacent to the synagogue, in honour of Lord Samuel's eighty-fifth birthday. Yet when the members of the New West End, including Donald Samuel and Lawrence Jacobs, broke away from the United Synagogue to form their own congregation, the New London Synagogue, they were obliged to relinquish both this magnificent hall and the beautiful synagogue itself to start again from the beginning.

By this time, I was able to live with the tensions caused by my traditional background and my growing awareness of the implications of modern historical scholarship. My tentative approach was to see Judaism as a 'quest', finding solace in the idea that the search for Torah is itself part of the Torah. Together with a young idealist in the congregation, Alan Jacobs, son of Lawrence, a sincere God-seeker if ever I saw one, I edited a synagogue magazine with the appropriate title, I thought, of *Venture*. Here and in study groups, as well as at the meetings of the excellent Centre Society, attached to the synagogue but catering to young men and women from all over London, we tried to explore the meaning of Judaism as a quest. I cannot pretend that we came up with many solutions but we all did come to value the idea of the quest as itself a solution.

No doubt my very appointment to the pulpit of the New West End had distanced me even more from Gateshead and the Manchester Yeshivah, but there was no overt criticism from these quarters. My former friends at the Kolel and the Yeshivah had become quite indifferent to my career as a minister, as they had every right to be towards one who had, in their eyes, forsaken the green pastures of exclusive Talmudic studies. Apart from that, the United Synagogue and all its works were of no concern at all to the totally dedicated students of the Torah in its traditional understanding.

In the United Synagogue itself I was not viewed, at that time, with the slightest degree of suspicion. As I have said, Chief Rabbi Brodie was friendly and encouraging from the start. Not long after my appointment, he invited me to deliver the sermon at the service of dedication for London teachers (in his presence) at the Central Synagogue on 8 May 1955. On 7 September 1955, when he was convalescing from an illness, I deputised for him to consecrate the Slough and Windsor Synagogue and install the minister, the Rev. B. Greenberg. On 14 March 1955, the Chief Rabbi was the Guest of Honour at the dinner to celebrate the first anniversary of the study group I led at the New West End. He delivered the sermon at the special Girls' Consecration and Chanukah Service (the title was his) at the New West End on Thursday, 15 December 1955. The neighbouring congregations of Bayswater and Hammersmith had joined with the New West End in the venture of a class for girls which I conducted, the culmination being the service (with a mixed choir!). These facts are not without bearing on the story which unfolded later.

Also relevant to the story is the attitude taken by the organ of the Mizrahi Movement, *The Jewish Review*. In the issue of the paper dated 11 June 1954, there appeared an article by Norman Cohen, later one of the main publicists supporting the Chief Rabbi's stand, in fierce opposition to mine. The article, under the heading 'The United Synagogue, Progressive Conservatism', purported to show that the United Synagogue was moving determinedly to the right, despite the claim of its president, Ewen Montagu, that its religious position was still that of 'progressive conservatism'. Cohen concluded:

> Nowhere has this change of outlook manifested itself more remarkably than at the New West End Synagogue, the congregation of which the Hon. Ewen Montagu is himself a member. Who, a few years back, would have dreamed that the successor of the Rev. Ephraim Levine would be an alumnus of the Gateshead Yeshivah! While Mr Montagu was nailing the colours of progressive conservatism defiantly to the mast at Woburn House, his own synagogue was springing a leak.

Leaving aside the inaccuracy about my being an alumnus of the Gateshead Yeshivah (I was never at the Yeshivah but at the Kolel in Gateshead) Cohen was correct in detecting the swing to the right. He was quite wrong in seeing my appointment as evidence of this tendency. On the contrary, both the congregation and I saw the appointment as furthering the 'progressive conservatism' of which Mr Montagu had spoken. Sad to say, most of us realised – even at that time – that we were fighting a losing battle.

Neither then nor subsequently did I try to hide my views. On Monday, 6 September 1954, in an address to the London Jewish Graduates' Association on the flexibility of Jewish law, I said that given liberal interpreters the law could be workable. Speaking at the Hampstead Jewish Literary Society on

Sunday, 9 January 1955, I expressed regret that any attempt to treat certain practices in a different fashion from that of the old Halakhah evoked immediate cries of heresy. Certainly, I said, the earlier Halakhic authorities were not afraid of free discussion.

To be sure, views I later held were only incipient at the time. One of my reasons for wishing to serve in the pulpit of the New West End was that I saw there a congenial atmosphere for a quest in which we were all engaged. It came as a tremendous relief to find that one could try to work out one's ideas about traditional Judaism in a free and unfettered pulpit. It was never my intention to sail under false colours, to use Norman Cohen's nautical metaphor.

Another forum for the discussion of ideas was the Association of Anglo-Jewish Preachers. This extraordinary body was composed of both Orthodox and Reform/Liberal ministers and rabbis. After a year or two, I became vice-president of this organisation. At that time there was no objection to Orthodox ministers 'fraternising' with non-Orthodox colleagues but, increasingly, some of the younger Orthodox men became extremely reluctant to co-operate with Reform or Liberal rabbis, even to discuss such matters as preaching, pastoral work and the like which they had in common. Consequently, in the present less tolerant age, the Association of Anglo-Jewish Preachers is now virtually defunct.

I tried to record my thoughts in my first controversial book, *We Have Reason to Believe*, published in 1957. (I had previously published three smaller books, *Jewish Prayer*, and guides to Rosh Hashanah and Yom Kippur.) The title was suggested to me by a dear friend, Dr Ian Gordon, after I had addressed a meeting of the Centre Society on the theme of reason and its role in religious life. The book was fairly innocent (Professor H.H. Rowley applied to it the words of Robertson Smith: 'Should such a faith offend?'), and no notice was taken of it until my acceptance in the book of Biblical Criticism was brought to the attention of the Chief Rabbi in order to influence his decision to block my appointment as Principal of Jews' College. After thirty years I still fail to see how the book could have been considered heretical in the tepid Orthodoxy typical of Anglo-Jewry. It was pointed out at the time, and later, that the term 'Orthodoxy' is not to be found in the Constitution of the United Synagogue, where the religious position of that body is described as 'Progressive conservatism'. Every author and author's agent knows that the best way to sell a book is to have it attacked by a bishop. In the case of *We Have Reason to Believe*, the Chief Rabbi's ban was even more helpful. No sooner did he mention the book as a cause of offence than it sold out, necessitating a second edition and later a third, in which I replied in an Epilogue to my critics. But more of this later.

Little time though there was for them in a busy ministry, I tried to pursue my scholarly interests, translating, with an introduction and notes, Cordovero's *Palm Tree of Deborah* and Dov Baer of Lubavitch's essay on contemplative prayer *Tract on Ecstasy*. I also published a study of the early *Habad* thinker Aron of Starosselje, which I called *Seeker of Unity*. On a more popular level I contributed articles to the *Jewish Chronicle* on all kinds of subjects.

For a time I was the anonymous 'religious consultant' to the *Jewish Chronicle*, being called upon to state the position in Jewish law of questions under discussion in the community. I remember Mr Norman Cohen writing in the *Chronicle* that only rabbis and ministers expert in the laws of Jewish marriage and divorce should be allowed to officiate at a Jewish marriage ceremony, quoting tractate *Kiddushin* , page 6a, where it is stated that anyone who is inexpert in the laws of marriage and divorce should have nothing to do with these matters. Rashi understands this to mean that he should not act as a judge rendering decisions on these topics, but the Soncino translation, followed by Cohen, understands it as 'to celebrate a marriage'. The *Chronicle* asked me to reply in my anonymous capacity and · I could not resist producing the limerick:

If with Rashi Mr Cohen were au fait,
He would see he'd been led astray
By the Soncino, with deference,
To a judge is the reference
In tractate Kiddushin 6a.

When the Institute for Jewish Studies, founded by Dr Altmann in Manchester, moved to London, there to be headed by the profound scholar of Jewish mysticism, J.G. Weiss, I was enabled to give further expression to my venture into the world of Jewish scholarship. A few of us met regularly to hear and to read papers on various aspects of Jewish thought. Here I became more familiar with the important work being done in the field of Jewish mysticism. Professor Gershom Scholem, the supreme master in the field, came to London to deliver a lecture on 'The Historical Ba'al Shem Tov', a classic treatment of the problem of how to discover what the founder of Hasidism was really like. Among other evidence, Scholem adduced that of the Ba'al Shem's disciple, the Maggid ('Preacher') of Pulnoyye. When called upon to propose the vote of thanks, I said that many of us knew Professor Scholem from his works but we wanted to know what this legend in his own lifetime was really like. It was my privilege as the 'Maggid' of the New West End Synagogue to state that the scholar we had just heard, the 'historical' Gershom Scholem, was even greater than the legend.

For all the generosity and kindnesses I had received at the hands of the New West End members, I could not help being attracted by an offer I received from Professor Louis Finkelstein, Chancellor of the Jewish Theological Seminary in New York, to become a full-time member of the Faculty of the Seminary. A few of my friends, however, were kind enough to wish to keep me in this country and they explored the possibility of obtaining for me a similar academic post in London.

Rabbi Dr I. Epstein, the then Principal of Jews' College, had an international reputation as a Jewish scholar and theologian. He had edited the superb Soncino translation of the Babylonian Talmud, had done important and original work on the Responsa literature, and, above all, had no scruples about doing theology at a time when it was decidedly unpopular. His book, *Judaism*, has sold in enormous quantities (and is still the best succinct survey of the religion from the Orthodox point of view) and his *Faith of Judaism* is the best work of Jewish apologetics, despite the fact that he was a foe of Biblical Criticism as was

Dr Hertz; however, as a Professor of Semitics he knew far more about the subject than did Hertz. Dr Epstein had been a rabbi in Middlesborough before his appointment, first as lecturer, then as Principal of Jews' College. During his stay in Middlesborough, the lights in his study were seen burning late into the night. At a meeting of the board of management of the synagogue, someone complained that the rabbi was guilty of wasting electricity and that the synagogue had to foot the bill. 'But the rabbi is studying at night,' the president of the congregation patiently explained. 'Studying?' members of the Board protested, 'we thought we had engaged a fully-qualified rabbi who had no need for further studies'! How very different from the case of the rabbi of Vilna in the eighteenth century. The rabbi was deposed because people saw that there were *no* lights in his study at midnight!

Dr Epstein, after years of distinguished service, was due to retire shortly as Principal of Jews' College and the search was already on for a successor. My friends thought that I would be a suitable candidate for the post and it would be one that would allow me to remain in London. The Executive of the College, with Sir Alan Mocatta as Chairman and Lawrence Jacobs as Treasurer, favoured my eventual appointment. The Haham of the Sephardi Community, Dr Solomon Gaon, an alumnus of the College and its Vice-President, agreed with the Executive that I would be a suitable candidate. The snag was, as Dr Gaon pointed out, that the Chief Rabbi, Dr Brodie, was President of the College. As Chief Rabbi he had (according to the Constitution of the College) the power of veto, and his attitude with regard to my appointment was very uncertain. My close friend, William Frankel, editor of the *Jewish Chronicle*, took a leading part in the whole affair right from the beginning and he arranged a meeting between Dr Gaon and me at which he was present. As a result of this meeting I agreed, very reluctantly I must say, not to force the issue of the principalship for the time being but to leave the New West End to take up the position of Moral Tutor to the College. Dr Gaon was insistent that to confront the Chief Rabbi head on at that stage would be to court disaster. On the other hand, the Chief Rabbi would have no objection to my appointment to the lesser post and in due course I would so fit in with the work of the College that I would be bound to be given the post of Principal, this time with the full approval of the Chief Rabbi. Dr Gaon's argument convinced the Executive and I agreed.

Unaware of these deliberations, not to say intrigues, my friends in Manchester and elsewhere thought I had gone completely off my head to leave the most prestigious pulpit in Anglo-Jewry for the very unusual and vague position of Moral Tutor to an institution that was then beginning to show signs of decay. With hindsight I see how misguided I was. I should have stayed on at the New West End, where I had found my feet, until Dr Epstein's retirement. Then, if the Chief Rabbi had concurred, I could have gone to Jews' College as its Principal but, if not, I would hardly have been badly done by since I had the New West End pulpit. All this sounds very calculating, and no doubt I did not lack the itch of ambition. Yet in my defence I can only say that I sincerely wished to immerse myself in the kind of academic work that would fit in with my career as a rabbi and honestly wished to see what could be done to prevent the much-debated decline of Jews' College, which seemed to be failing to attract students for the Anglo-Jewish ministry. It was simply not true, as my opponents later hinted, that I was only bent on using the principalship of Jews' College as a stepping-stone to the Chief Rabbinate, a position which would become vacant on Rabbi Brodie's retirement. I may have been calculating, but if to that extent and with the aim of eventually securing the office of Chief Rabbi, I would have been far better advised to remain at the New West End, then the premier synagogue in the United Synagogue movement. When Rabbi Brodie did retire, the Israeli paper *Panim el Panim* ('Face to Face') ran a feature on the possible candidates for the position of Chief Rabbi, together with their photographs and comments on their prospects: 'good prospect', 'little prospect', 'some prospect' and the like. My photograph appeared with the comment: 'Not the slightest prospect'!

Why it should have gone in sixes I do not know, but I left the Central Synagogue in Manchester for the New West End after six years and after six years at the New West End I left there, in a divided state of mind, to become Moral Tutor at

Chief Rabbi's Ministers' Conference 1959, Westcliffe. Seated: Rabbi Koppel Kahana, third from left; Rabbi Dr A. Altmann, third from right; Chief Rabbi Brodie, middle. Author standing between Rabbi Kahana and Chief Rabbi

Professor Louis Finkelstein, Chancellor of the Jewish Theological Seminary of America, taken at a reception for him at the New West End Synagogue, July 1959

Author speaking at Inaugural Meeting of Society for Study of Jewish Theology. Seated front Mr Ellis Franklin; Chairman of the Society Sir Alan Mocatta, first right; the Rev. Ephraim Levine, second left (*Jewish Chronicle*)

Jews' College. Shula was solidly behind me in this move into unknown territory.

Before going on to describe the events at Jews' College that led to the 'Jacobs Affair', I must refer to another event that took place while I served in the pulpit of the New West End – the founding of the Littman Library. Mr Louis Littman, a successful solicitor and owner of a large dairy farm in Dorset, had a dream of endowing a library of translations and original works of Jewish scholarship in memory of his father, Joseph Littman. (Louis has told elsewhere how his dream was realised.) When he began to plan the Library, he consulted me (and others) as a friend and as his rabbi on the feasibility of the project. I became an editor of the Library, the other editors being Dr Lionel Kochan (later on his place was taken by Dr Vivian Lipman) and, as editor-in-chief, Dr David Goldstein, whose marvellous translation of mediaeval Hebrew poetry was the first book to be published in the series. The present publishers of the Littman Library are Oxford University Press. The Library now has a list of over thirty titles of real substance and has made a lasting contribution to Jewish learning, thanks to the generosity of a great patron of Jewish scholarship.

Sad to relate, both Louis Littman and David Goldstein died in 1987. A Memorial Service was held for Louis in the New London Synagogue on 31 January 1988, where I paid a deserved tribute to Louis's remarkable achievement.

8

JEWS' COLLEGE

Jews' College had been the sole college for the training of ministers of the Anglo-Jewish community for over a hundred years. The usual procedure for a young man wishing to have a career as a minister was to take the course in Semitics at the College, leading to a London University Honours degree, while supplementing these studies with those required for him to function satisfactorily as a minister. The college course was thus an amalgam of university studies and training for the practical Jewish ministry. The trouble was that the two sets of studies were often in conflict with one another. For example, a student who had acquired a sound knowledge of Biblical Criticism, which he had to do if he was to obtain good results for his university degree, was bound to ask himself how this could be reconciled with what he was being taught in the courses preparing him for the Jewish ministry. This was the traditional doctrine that the whole of the Pentateuch had been dictated by God to Moses during the forty years' stay in the wilderness, word for word and letter by letter. Somehow, in spite of the problem, the College, in typical Anglo-Jewish fashion, managed to muddle through. In any event, the graduates of the College would be neither rabbis nor theologians but ministers whose chief functions would be to preach and to engage in pastoral work and for whom, consequently, the theoretical question did not loom particularly large.

All this changed when the College began to place greater emphasis on training for the rabbinate rather than the ministry. Rabbi Koppel Kahana took a class in Rabbinics (although this was mainly a graduate course for men already serving congregations as ministers). A new pattern began to emerge in Anglo-Jewry in which the usual type of spiritual leader was no longer the minister but the rabbi. Young men were also admitted to the special class for Chazanim at the college. This class pursued a less rigorous course of studies at the completion of which the student was awarded a diploma in Chazanut. Young men and women could also enter the College for a teacher's training programme.

The Yeshivot and Orthodoxy's right wing generally looked askance at Jews' College as an institution which taught heresy or, at least, one in which the study of Talmud, supreme in the Yeshivah, had been relegated to very much a second place. A Yeshivah student who decided to further his studies at Jews' College was seen as a traitor to the ideal of Torah study for its own sake, and as an unscrupulous careerist ready to sell his soul for financial gain and a better position than could be obtained by a Yeshivah student.

This was the situation I found at Jews' College when I came there to occupy the position that had been created especially for me, Moral Tutor and lecturer in Pastoral Theology. Because my appointment was, in reality, no more than a subterfuge to get me into the College without awakening the Chief Rabbi's suspicions, my duties were ill-defined. The students did consult me, as Moral Tutor, about their problems and I tried to help as best as I could. I persuaded myself that even where I could offer no help it was good for them to have a sympathetic ear. What was meant by 'Pastoral Theology' was even more obscure. It chiefly involved sharing my experiences in the practical ministry with the students, who were about to graduate as ministers. We discussed such matters as how to fill in a *ketubah*; how to officiate at weddings and funerals; what to say when visiting the sick; what to wear on various occasions (no brown shoes or red ties at funerals) and how to get on with awkward congregants. My brief did not cover preaching; for this there was a special class given by senior ministers in rotation. Dr Abraham Cohen put his lectures on homiletics into a book, still the only comprehensive guide to the art of Jewish preaching. Otherwise, I was allowed to take a class in elementary Talmud and one, for the prospective teachers, in Rashi on the Pentateuch.

Both Dr Epstein and the Chief Rabbi seemed to treat my appearance at the College as something of an intrusion – for Dr Epstein a not too unwelcome one, for the Chief Rabbi a decidedly unwelcome one. By this time my views were more or less known in the College circle. Consequently, I felt far less inhibited about airing them with the students about to graduate. Most of these were staunch traditionalists who eagerly crossed swords with me, which I enjoyed. The very last thing I wished to do was to destroy the students' faith with critical theories. On the contrary, I tried to show them that their knowledge of Judaism as a developing religion – knowledge they were gaining all the time from their College studies – was perfectly compatible with Jewish piety and observance. It was all great fun, I must confess, and it is possible that I had some slight influence in making some of the students appreciate that a non-fundamentalist approach is perfectly respectable, both Jewishly and intellectually.

The College faculty were all scholars with an international reputation in their respective fields. Dr Naftali Wieder was probably the foremost authority in the world on the Jewish liturgy. Dr H.J. Zimmels was the author of a number of learned works in which he illumined Jewish history through his massive researches into the Responsa literature. Mr Eli Cashdan, a remarkable polymath and exciting teacher, taught Bible and Hebrew Grammar. In all their courses modern scholarly method was the norm, as it was in the days of their predecessors, Dr Büchler, Dr Marmorstein and Dr Daiches. Theology, however, was never presented as a serious scholarly discipline and, except by Dr Epstein occasionally, the kinds of issue I was raising – about revelation, fundamentalism and a philosophy of the Halakhah – were never mentioned. Nevertheless, I felt it to be neither incongruous nor dishonest for me to have the ambition of becoming Principal of the College. My intended policy, if I did become Principal, was not to promote 'heresy' in an institution strongly committed to fundamentalism – Jews' College was never that – but to try to make more explicit that which had long been implicit in all that was taught there: that modern scholarship has shown the developing nature of Jewish thought and practice. Moreover, right-wing Orthodoxy had always considered the College to be a non-Orthodox institution, so that whatever the official theological position of the College, its very existence would be taboo to the right wing. I believed that the College could only hope to enjoy success if it firmly nailed its colours to the mast. For the College to be constantly looking over its right shoulder could only result in dislocation of the neck and the head resting on it.

In this connection, painful though it might be, I want to quote two right-wing rabbis, hitherto never mentioned in the controversy over my role there.

The first quote is from a letter by Rabbi E.E. Dessler published in the third volume of his *Mikhtav Me-Eliyahu* ('Letter from Elijah'). (In the book dots are substituted for the words 'Jews' College' but the words appear in the same letter published in an Israeli journal and it is obvious, in any event, from the context that the reference is to Jews' College.) Rabbi Dessler, discussing the dangers of an Orthodox Seminary in Gateshead for the training of teachers, argues that while Jews' College affords no temptation to Yeshivah students the proposed Seminary, at which secular subjects would be taught, might well lure Yeshivah students to forsake their Talmudic studies. Rabbi Dessler writes:

> It is essential to know that in this generation an Institution such as Jews' College will not be as detrimental to the Yeshivah as an academic institution together with *yirat shamayim* ('the fear of Heaven'). The reason is obvious since a young man connected with a Yeshivah, nowadays, is already sufficiently God-fearing not to contemplate going to Jews' College.

The second and far more pungent critique is that of Rabbi Shalom Moskovitz, the Shotzer Rebbe, doyen of the Hasidic Rebbes in England. This critique is found in Rabbi Moskovitz's 'Ethical Will' as an 'Addendum' to the will and is printed at the end of the work *Mayyim Rabbim* by his ancestor, Rabbi Yehiel Michel of Zlotchow, published by the Moskovitz family in Brooklyn in 1979. The passage reads (in my translation):

> When a physician visits someone who is ill he tries hard to discover the roots of the disease so that he can proceed to

127

a cure. One of the root causes of the disease from which
the Anglo-Jewish community suffers is the existence of
Jews' College, where are trained rabbis, reverends, ministers, – that is to say, ignoramuses, and with an acceptance
of false beliefs, opposed to the tradition of our holy sages,
of blessed memory, by whose mouth we, the people who
are old Israel's children, live. They should not say, 'after all
a minister is not a rabbi'. This is not so, for such a person
has a great influence on the laymen, who respect him as if
he were a rabbi. When he preaches, what does he preach?
Not the fear of Heaven and the wholehearted observance
of the Torah. All his preaching is external since he knows
himself that, for our many sins, he is not God-fearing in
private as in public. They [the Anglo-Jewish ministers]
should be judged in the scale of merit. For after all, he has
never seen the light, never spent years in a Yeshivah for
his soul to be sated with Gemara, Tosafists and the fear of
Heaven. It is at Jews' College that he receives the final tap
of the hammer that makes him one of the most indifferent
to piety. For who are the teachers there, for our many
sins, and what further subjects to a *goy* and an assembly
of *goyim* ... I know for certain that the Chief Rabbi
himself, long may he live, spoke adversely of Jews' College
to someone, declaring that the College was no good. 'Woe
to the dough against which its baker testifies.' This house
has leprosy in it. It is absolutely unclean. 'The house shall
be torn down – its stones and timber and all the coating on
the house – and taken to an unclean place' (Lev. 14:45).
But if other stones are taken and other earth, the plague will
revert to the house for it is accursed leprosy, it is unclean.
No reforms are possible by bringing in new teachers.

I have omitted the Shotzer Rebbe's bitter attack on Rabbi
Kahana whom he accuses of betraying the Torah by giving an
air of rabbinic respectability to the College.

During my time at Jews' College, I continued to officiate as a
rabbi when called upon to do so. For a while I served as acting
rabbi of the Western Synagogue. I preached at the Marble Arch,

Central and Hammersmith Synagogues and, on Rosh Hashanah and Yom Kippur, at the United Synagogue in Leeds. It might be necessary to add that I lived an observant Jewish life, and still do, since my whole contention was that to keep the *mitzvot* did not depend on a fundamentalist understanding of the doctrine 'The Torah is from Heaven'.

However, I became restless in contemplating the uncertainty of my future at Jews' College. Meetings were held with Sir Alan Mocatta and my other supporters, who counselled patience. '*Festina lente,*' Sir Alan repeated, implying that all would turn out well in the near future, but my patience was fast running out. Repeated overtures were made to the Chief Rabbi who, as if unaware of my supporters' hopes, loudly proclaimed that he was busy looking for a suitable successor to Dr Epstein. Whenever my name was mentioned as a candidate for the position, the Chief Rabbi rejected it out of hand, giving different reasons for his opposition to the different people who approached him. To some he said that I lacked the scholarship such a position required. To others he declared that, whatever my scholarship or lack of it, my beliefs were not those that a Principal of Jews' College should hold. I was left, in the Talmudic phrase, 'bald on this side and on that'.

In the meantime Dr Epstein had retired, Dr Zimmels serving as Director of Studies and the Chief Rabbi himself as Acting Principal. It had become obvious that the Chief Rabbi was determined to pursue his quest for a Principal and that whoever it would be it would not be me. Sir Alan and the others were still counselling patience, but by this time the whole matter had become public and I told Sir Alan that I could no longer continue in this state of uncertainty and had no recourse but to resign from the College. Sir Alan agreed that a meeting should be arranged with the Chief Rabbi, and it duly took place with Dr Gaon also present. Even at this late hour, the Chief Rabbi declared himself to be adamant in refusing even to consider me for the position of Principal. Seeing that there was no hope of persuading the Chief Rabbi to budge, I wrote to Sir Alan resigning from my position at the College.

The *Jewish Chronicle* published my letter of resignation to the Chairman of the College, dated 14 November 1961:

Dear Sir Alan,

It is with the deepest feelings of regret that I tender my resignation from the staff of Jews' College.

You will recall that two and a half years ago I was invited by you and your colleagues to come to the College as Tutor. You pointed out at the time that it was the intention of the Hon. Officers that I should be appointed Principal after the retirement of Dr Epstein, though there could be no definite promise on their part since the appointment depended, under the Constitution, on the Chief Rabbi's approval.

Since Dr Epstein's retirement last July, the Chief Rabbi had been asked to give his approval for the appointment, but has failed to do so on various grounds, the one recurring most often being that views I have expressed in writing render me unsuitable for the position. These views are contained in my books *We Have Reason to Believe* and *Jewish Values*. I remain firmly convinced that the approach to traditional Judaism I have sketched in these books is one that must commend itself to all who are aware of modern thought and scholarship. I have tried to show that intense loyalty to Jewish tradition and observance need not be synonymous with reaction and fundamentalism. Furthermore, I would claim that no reputable scholar in the world has an approach that is basically different from mine.

What I had hoped to do at Jews' College was to help train men able to hold their own in the field of objective scholarship and, at the same time, imbued with the spirit of *yirat shamayim*; men who would realise, in some measure, at least, the implications of the verse: 'For this is your wisdom and your understanding in the sight of the peoples' (Deut. iv, 6). In this task intelligent Jews everywhere are engaged. It would be sad if Anglo-Jewry, with its traditional breadth of vision, were not to participate in such a presentation of Judaism.

I want to express my thanks to you and your colleagues for your confidence in me.

* * *

The present Chief Rabbi, Lord Jakobovits, writing from his pulpit in America (he later published the letter in his *Journal of a Rabbi*) accused me of being bombastic in my claim that 'no reputable scholar in the world has an approach that is basically different from mine'. This claim, he wrote, is 'as patently absurd as it is immodest'. I no doubt have my full share of immodesty but the claim is not an immodest one. I did not say that the scholars agree with me but that I was simply agreeing with them. Why such a claim is 'absurd' I do not understand. Of course, not all scholars are prepared to draw theological conclusions from their own or their colleagues' research. But the scholarly enterprise itself does not and cannot proceed if objective investigation is to be ruled out or prejudged by what tradition says or is understood as saying.

After my resignation a meeting of the Council of Jews' College was held at which the Chief Rabbi was present. Sir Alan, as Chairman, put forward the resolution: 'That this meeting of the Council of the College respectfully requests the Chief Rabbi to give his consent to Rabbi Dr Louis Jacobs being appointed Principal of the College as from 1 October 1962, with Dr H.J. Zimmels as Director of Studies.'

The Chief Rabbi requested that this item on the agenda be not discussed that evening. He said, 'I have many reasons for making this request but I will only say this. As I look round the table I know that opinions will be divided, and it will be most unfortunate for the College if this particular motion is discussed and decided upon. It has been put on the agenda against my wishes and since, in a few days' time, I shall be away from the country for a while, I consider that it would not be right to have the matter considered at present.' When Sir Alan stated that he did not see how the matter could be further postponed, the Chief Rabbi declared, 'I want to state it clearly that Dr Jacobs will not have my consent to becoming the Principal of Jews' College. There are many matters in connection with this but I will not mention them to avoid creating divisiveness.' However, after further discussion, the Chief Rabbi said: 'I made a statement a little while ago and it was a very categorical one. I asked the Chairman to defer the whole thing until my return to avoid the creation of an atmosphere of divisiveness and contention which would reflect itself in the College. The College is to me more important than any personality and that is something I have been insisting upon the whole time. I will now say this – I climb down. This letter of resignation and even this meeting should be deferred until such time as I return. For the time being I do not give my consent to the appointment of Dr Jacobs as Principal.'

The Council finally passed a resolution to request me to withdraw, or at least withhold, my resignation, and three of its members, Mr R.N. Carvalho, Mr (later Judge) Israel Finestein and Mr Bruno Marmorstein were selected to call on me to present this resolution. I had a very cordial discussion with the members of the Council whom I met at Jews' College, but could not see how it would be of any use to accede to the Council's request. In a statement I gave to the *Jewish Chronicle* (at the paper's request) I said:

I have been asked to withhold my resignation until the return of the Chief Rabbi from Australia in April. The Chief Rabbi has been aware of my intention to resign on this issue for some weeks. But ever since I came to the College, two and a half years ago, the Chief Rabbi has had the opportunity of considering whether or not I would be a suitable Principal.

During the last few months particularly, the Chief Rabbi has had many and lengthy discussions with me and others on the subject. The facts of the matter are therefore all within his knowledge. The only answers the Chief Rabbi has given to requests that my appointment should be made have been that he would 'consider the matter' or that he hoped I would change my views. Latterly, and at last Monday's meeting, he said that he would consider the matter again in three months' time. This has introduced nothing new and still gives no indication when or indeed whether finality can be achieved. Nor does it commit the Chief Rabbi to anything that cannot be other than a delaying tactic which will lead to further delays.

The appointment of a Principal to such an institution as Jews' College cannot be made in this undignified fashion.

Moreover, self-respect and my regard for the College prevent me from accepting an offer if it could only be made after elaborate deliberations as to my alleged suitability. I was therefore unable to withdraw my resignation.

After this, Sir Alan, Mr Lawrence Jacobs and Mr Felix Levy, the joint Treasurers of the College, and the Rev. Dr I. H. Levy, minister of the Hampstead Synagogue (a colleague and friend who taught Homiletics at the College and who, despite his position in one of the foremost congregations belonging to the United Synagogue, declared where he stood with typical courage and forthrightness), resigned together with other members of the Jews' College Council.

Felix Levy, twenty-five years later, wrote a letter to the *Jewish Chronicle* protesting against the abolition of the mixed choir at the Hampstead Synagogue, seeing this as further evidence of the swing to the right in Anglo-Jewry (*Jewish Chronicle*, 18 July 1986). In the letter he recalled the part he and his colleagues had played:

> In company with the other honorary officers, I resigned from the Council of Jews' College over the last catastrophic manifestation of intolerance, the 'Jacobs Affair'. Its result has been nearly a quarter of a century of a paucity of adequately trained ministers.

By the time the Honorary Officers of the College had resigned, the whole affair had reached the Press, including the general Press, and the fat was in the fire. The first stage of the 'Jacobs Affair' had begun.

9

THE JACOBS AFFAIR, STAGE I

From the day the controversy in which I became involved erupted until it was all over, the *Jewish Chronicle* was solidly on my side; as a result, the paper was accused of bias and even seen as a foe of traditional Judaism. William Frankel, the editor of the *Chronicle*, was Chairman of the Education Committee of the New West End when I arrived there. He had been instrumental in my introduction to Jews' College in the first instance, and was a close personal friend. Nonetheless he really had a firm grasp of the issues involved and I believe that he would have sided with me, knowing all the facts, even if we had never met. William eventually became a founder-member of the New London Synagogue. The reporting of the *Chronicle* throughout the affair was scrupulously even-handed, letting both sides enjoy the hospitality of its letters column. It was only in the editorials that William thundered against the Chief Rabbi and the London Beth Din, the latter having taken a hand in the conflict, and, it was widely believed, being behind the Chief Rabbi's obdurate stand. Some cynics suggested that William Frankel's true motive was to provide the sensationalism that sells newspapers. There was, in fact, very little sensationalism. It is the business of a newspaper to obtain the widest possible readership, but the *Jewish Chronicle* was not doing badly at all before the controversy and certainly had no need to whip up excitement in the community in order to increase sales. Since William was responsible for arranging the *shidduch* between me and Jews' College, he can hardly have wished for it to break down in order to provide a selling point for his paper.

The Times, on Saturday, 30 December 1961, quoted 'a leading member of the Jewish community in London' as saying to the paper,

134

> There is no real rift in the Anglo-Jewish community but a number of Jewish scholars who have come to Britain from abroad in recent years now occupy positions of authority. Their outlook is very different from what we regard as the more tolerant Anglo-Jewish outlook and it would seem that the present crisis was brought to a head because of the influence which some of these scholars have been able to bring to bear on the Chief Rabbi.

The reference to recently-arrived foreign scholars was a nasty one, especially when appearing in *The Times*, and I would not have been party to it had I known and had I been consulted. I was told on good authority that the 'leading member of the Jewish community in London' was the Rev. Ephraim Levine, at that time, if not subsequently, on my side in the controversy. Whether he should have given it to *The Times* is another matter, but Levine's sentiment was sound and he had long deplored the ascendency of the right wing in Anglo-Jewry.

In reply, *The Times* published an interview with Rabbi Myer Berman, former Chairman of the Association of Ministers of the United Synagogue and a past President of the Anglo-Jewish Preachers' Association (this was the body mentioned earlier comprising Reform and Liberal rabbis as well as Orthodox). Rabbi Berman was reported to have said:

> Dr Brodie was not a fanatical obscurantist but a modern cultured broadminded and tolerant traditional Jew of deep and sincere religious feeling. He had acted within the highest traditions of the Chief Rabbinate in the stand he had taken. If he was not completely satisfied with the religious attitude of any potential principal of the College it was his solemn duty to withhold his sanction for the appointment of such a person. The lay and other personalities who were attempting to bring a pressure on Dr Brodie to change his mind were entirely wrong. The Chief Rabbi required no prompting by 'foreign scholars'. He was motivated by the principles of his religious convictions and he had the support of the whole of traditional Jewry.

Rabbi Berman was undoubtedly correct that the Chief Rabbi was all he said he was. But to deny that pressure was brought to bear on him, especially by the London Beth Din, is contrary to the facts. The London Beth Din took part in the controversy from the beginning, even though its members had always been indifferent, if not positively hostile, to Jews' College. In a statement to the *Jewish Chronicle*, published in the paper's issue of 5 January 1962, the Dayanim of the Beth Din declared:

> The question of the proposed appointment at Jews' College having now been brought into the open, and in response to many inquiries received at the Beth Din, the Dayanim find it necessary to state: considerations of special scholarship and other qualifications apart, some of the views expressed in recent years in publications and articles by the proposed candidate are in conflict with authentic Jewish belief and render him unacceptable.

Dayan Dr Grunfeld, an author and lawyer and a man of culture and wide learning, and at that time a member of London Beth Din, confessed to me that he had approached the Chief Rabbi and set the whole process in motion. He explained that he had found it unthinkable to appoint a man who had expressed in his book doubts about the traditional doctrine 'The Torah is from Heaven'. However, Dr Grunfeld expressed his remorse for having done so, and on more than one occasion came close to directly apologising to me. After the affair had begun and he had retired from the Beth Din, Dayan Grunfeld invited William Frankel and me to his home for a discussion on the theological question. He tried to convince us that the problems raised by Biblical Criticism could be solved on the basis of the Kantian distinction between the *phenomena* and the *noumena,* i.e. that Biblical Criticism operated on the level of that which is perceived and could not therefore, be applied to the Torah which was not a human production but a divine communication. I pointed out that if this distinction makes any sense when applied to the Torah, it would follow that no one has ever understood or can understand the Torah, hardly a position a devout Jew can hold. Incidentally, when our visit to Dayan Grunfeld's home was discovered, the learned Dayan received an anonymous letter (which he showed me) accusing him of fraternising with heretics.

It was the *Jewish Chronicle* that first brought into the open the influence of the right. In a Leader entitled 'The Community's Future' (29 December 1961) the writer stated:

It is no secret that in this, as in other issues, the Chief Rabbi allows himself to be guided by the extremists of the right. Our right-wing, like all other sections of the community, is entitled to its own views. But their opinions are neither in theory nor practice acceptable to the majority of thinking Jews. They are, moreover, opinions at variance with the benevolent Anglo-Jewish traditions of tolerance and reasonableness. From *Kulturkampf* against Reform, our extremists have passed to heresy hunting with Orthodoxy, hence the opposition to Dr Jacobs' appointment.

This question of my 'Orthodoxy' was to be raised again and again during the following years. The one thing I did not want to do was pull wool over people's eyes. I said repeatedly that if Orthodoxy denotes fundamentalism, I was not Orthodox and did not want to be Orthodox. But if Orthodoxy meant, as it had in Anglo-Jewry, an adherence to traditional practice, then I could claim to be Orthodox. In its issue of 3 January, 1962, the *Jewish Chronicle*, in a 'box', quoted the remark of Chief Rabbi Hertz, when preaching at a service at the Great Synagogue to mark the beginning of joint celebrations on the occasion of the 75th anniversary of Jews' College, the 70th anniversary of the Jewish Religious Education Board and the 60th anniversary of the United Synagogue. On that occasion Dr Hertz said:

The United Synagogue has given its distinctive character to English Judaism. By its example and influence it has made Progressive Conservatism – i.e. religious advance without

loss of traditional Jewish values and without estrange-
ment from the collective consciousness of the House of
Israel – the Anglo-Jewish position in theology.

It is only fair to say, however, that Dr Hertz, a determined
foe of the Higher Criticism, would certainly have taken violent
exception to my acceptance of the view that the Pentateuch is
a composite work. Whether this would have been sufficient
for him to exercise his veto against my appointment to the
principalship of Jews' College, had he been Chief Rabbi, is
another matter.

The word 'fundamentalism' has been bandied about a good
deal. If my memory serves me correctly, I think that, on the
Anglo-Jewish scene, I may have been responsible for the use
of this term to describe what seem to have been the views of
the London Beth Din. Perhaps the use of the term was a little
unfortunate. Repeatedly, I was informed that no traditional Jew
could be a 'fundamentalist' since the tradition does not insist on
a literal reading of the Bible. On the contrary, to take the Bible
literally was the offence of the Karaites, against which Rabbinic
Judaism struggled. This is a manoeuvre that does not work. The
fact that the 'traditional' interpretation is not the literal one
aggravates the problem, in that it involves a more extensive
fundamentalism – namely that the traditional understanding
is inerrant, not only the actual Biblical text. Through the years
there has not been the slightest attempt on the part of my
opponents to deal with the real issue. This is that modern
scholarship has shown the developing nature of the tradition
itself. For instance, the statement that the doctrine 'The Torah
is from Heaven' means that the present text of the whole of the
Pentateuch was dictated by God to Moses, is itself the result
of a development within Jewish thought. The Pentateuch itself
makes no such claim. On the contrary, it is hard to believe
that, for instance, the words, 'And the Lord spoke unto Moses,
saying' were intended to convey the thought that these words,
too, were spoken by God to Moses! I doubt whether many
members of the United Synagogue believed that then or believe
it now.

Time and again when I tried to defend my views, I was told, 'But everyone believes as you do. Surely the Chief Rabbi does not believe *that*.' The result was that I frequently found myself having to go over extremely well-trodden ground, as if we were all living in Dayton, Ohio at the time of the 'Monkey Trial'. I remember seeing the film 'Inherit the Wind', based on the trial, three times, each time feeling a sense of bewilderment that we in Anglo-Jewry were still debating such a dead issue. I had become a 'controversial figure' in a controversy that was strictly a non-event, at least on the level of theory.

On Monday, 7 May 1962, at the Annual General Meeting of Jews' College, the Chief Rabbi made his first public statement since the controversy began. He stated that he had found himself unable to accept my appointment as Principal because of 'his published views and having regard to the standards of outstanding scholarship and other qualifications required for the office of Principal'; again the implication that, quite apart from my views, I was unsuitable for the position on other grounds. This made it extremely difficult for me. I could defend my views but could hardly protest that I was otherwise the best candidate, particularly since I was only too well aware of my scholarly limitations. I had agreed to put myself forward as a candidate because I did not believe that great scholarship was required for the position. The chief qualification, as I saw it, that a principal of a theological college should have was some knowledge of and interest in theology; something the majority of scholars who might have been considered did not possess. Nor did they have any practical experience, as I had, in the Anglo-Jewish ministry. The sober fact is that no great scholar with anything like an international reputation was ever appointed to the position. Of course, the Chief Rabbi could not have left it that it was my views that prevented him agreeing to my appointment since, knowing my views, he had agreed to my appointment as Moral Tutor to the College.

Dr Epstein had passed away in the meantime, and the Chief Rabbi first rightly paid a tribute to him at the Annual General Meeting. He then went on to deplore the attacks (by the *Jewish Chronicle*) on the London Beth Din (*Jewish Chronicle*, 11 May 1962):

At the same time, I deplore the attitude which has been taken up in certain quarters regarding the Ecclesiastical Court [sic], the London Beth Din. I wish to stress the loyalty and respect which are due to the Beth Din in the interests of religious well-being, communal discipline, and unity. The members of the Beth Din are *talmidei hakhamim* who have the responsibility of faithfully administrating Jewish law, and whose reputation stands high among rabbinic authorities throughout the world.

Why men whose job it was to administer Jewish law should have intervened in a dispute about theology, in which subject they had no expertise whatsoever, and regarding the appointment of a Principal of Jews' College, an institution to which they had, at the most, a very luke-warm attitude, the Chief Rabbi did not say. It had been, in fact, the first time that the Beth Din had ever intervened in a matter of this sort, lending credence to the view that the Chief Rabbi was not uninfluenced by men who had hitherto been content to remain 'backroom boys'.

I felt that the time had come for me to make a public statement. To continue to refuse to say anything at all was not, I felt, to preserve a dignified silence but would be construed as an admission of guilt. I addressed a public meeting, at the Herbert Samuel Hall of the New West End Synagogue, on Monday, 19 June 1962, on the subject 'We Have Reason To Believe', the title of the book that had caused all the bother in the first place. More than a thousand people attended the meeting and many were turned away because of lack of space. I stated the obvious – that Judaism is not frightened of reason and that faith need not be shaken through coping with the problems raised by modern Biblical scholarship. I was still in employment at Jews' College when I addressed this meeting but my term of office was nearing its end. Mr Ellis Franklin, who presided at the meeting, remarked in his forthright manner, 'Dr Jacobs stuck to his faith and lost his job.'

Who were the Dayanim of the London Beth Din who became my chief opponents in the controversy? They were Rabbi Laib

Grossnass (my former study-partner at the Gateshead Kolel); Rabbi Abraham Rapoport; Rabbi Dr Myer Lew; Rabbi Meir Steinberg; and Rabbi Morris Swift. (Rabbi Dr Grunfeld, as I have said, had retired due to ill-health.) With the exception of Rabbi Swift the Dayanim were mild-mannered men, who in the main, kept their peace, leaving the vituperation to Rabbi Swift who was very good at it. It was also an open secret that on the theological pronouncement of the Dayanim advice was given by Rabbi Dr Grunfeld. Rabbi Swift's brother, Rabbi Harris Swift, at that time Rabbi of the independbent Western Synagogue, expressed himself publicly and privately as being solidly on my side.

Rabbi Morris Swift was born in Liverpool. He had studied for several years at the Mir Yeshivah in Poland. He was a powerful orator in English and Yiddish but could come out with the most outrageous attacks on individuals and groups that did not meet with his approval. A journalist who interviewed him on the subject of women's rights in Judaism described him as 'an amiable bigot'. Amiable he could certainly be on occasion and he was not so much a bigot as a man carried away by his eloquence to express opinions on matters of which he knew very little and to which he had given no thought. I had crossed swords with him before at a conference of rabbis and ministers called by the Chief Rabbi, to which Swift, who was not a member of the Conference, had been invited to make an appeal on behalf of Gateshead Yeshivah. I was minister of the New West End at the time and was conducting a study group on Cordovero's *Palm Tree of Deborah,* an essay on Kabbalistic ethics, later published in my book of that name. Quite out of the blue, and totally irrelevant to the appeal he was supposed to be making, Swift attacked me for teaching the Kabbalah in public. A *Jewish Chronicle* reporter at the meeting said to me, 'You seem to be in hot water'. I could only reply, in the words of Chesterton, that the advantage of being in hot water is that one keeps clean.

While the controversy was raging, I undertook a lecture tour of the United States under the auspices of the B'nai B'rith Adult Education Department. This was followed over the years by a number of such engagements in that great country, far more hospitable to the quest in which many of us were engaged. My thinking, for what it is worth, was very close to that of the thinkers of the Conservative movement in the USA. I was invited to address the students at the Jewish Theological Seminary, the College (far more influential than Jews' College) for the training of Conservative rabbis. In fact, the basic issue on which the Conservatives differed from the Orthodox in the USA was precisely on the understanding of the doctrine, 'The Torah is from Heaven', the Conservatives refusing to interpret the doctrine in a fundamentalist manner. My friends, Professor Seymour Siegel and Rabbi Wolfe Kelman, Executive Vice-President of the Rabbinical Assembly, the Conservative body of rabbis, had arranged for me to deliver the address, which was attended by a number of the distinguished Faculty members of the Seminary, including Professor Abraham Joshua Heschel. I spoke on the problems raised by critical scholarship, practised and accepted automatically at the Seminary, arguing that once the methods of this kind of scholarship are applied, successfully, to the rest of the Bible, the Rabbinic literature, and Jewish thought in general, it is illogical to give up the use of these methods when it comes to the Pentateuch. I was told later that one of the Professors at the Seminary argued against me that a nose, ear and throat man who had achieved great success in the operations he had performed would still be extremely cautious in performing a brain operation lest it kill the patient. This attitude still prevails in some circles, but it is obviously untenable. If faith is to be invoked to prejudge scholarly investigation, then scholarship is stifled even when applied to any work on which the 'tradition' has spoken, to say nothing of the fact that modern scholarship has demonstrated that the 'tradition' has itself had a history. Your nose, ear and throat man may not be prepared himself to perform brain operations but he will have sufficient confidence in the methods he uses to be convinced that people are capable of using the same methods for brain operations and that these may have to be performed if the patient is to survive.

Over the years, my association with Conservative Judaism in the USA became stronger. I became a member of the Rabbinical Assembly (the thousandth member, I was informed, though I suspect the number owed something to the manipulation of my good friend Rabbi Kelman) and a Vice-President of the World

Council of Synagogues, the Conservative body of lay-leaders to which my synagogue, the New London Synagogue also became affiliated soon after its foundation. For all that, I have never believed that the pattern of synagogal life prevailing in Conservative synagogues in the USA should or could be successfully transported to Anglo-Jewry. We have our own traditions and what is suitable there can be very unsuitable over here.

For the sake of honesty I have always felt bound to declare where I stood in this matter. In theory I was solidly on the side of Conservative thought. Professor Elliot Dorf, in his excellent book on *Conservative Judaism*, does me the honour of counting me as one of the contemporary Conservative 'thinkers'. Furthermore, the Anglo-Jewish tradition was 'Conservative', a position that was equated with Orthodoxy in Anglo-Jewry, and when Solomon Schechter helped to found in the USA the Conservative Synagogal body he adopted the name of the major 'Orthodox' body over here to call it the United Synagogue of America. Yet, repeatedly, I have been accused of misleading people by trying to foist an 'alien philosophy of Judaism' on the unsuspecting public, who, nominally at least, subscribe to Orthodoxy.

I now had to face the sober fact that, at the age of forty, with a wife and three children to support, I was out of a job. I did not suppose that I could not find a rabbinic or academic position in another country and had, in fact, received a number of invitations, including one or two from Reform and Liberal congregations in this country. However, I was extremely reluctant to leave the country in which I was born and educated and I was neither Reform nor Liberal by conviction. I wanted to stay on to continue the fight within the traditional community. My supporters, headed by Mr Ellis Franklin, who had taken the chair at the public meeting, and William Frankel, loyal and supportive as ever, decided to form the Society for the Study of Jewish Theology with me as Director. Miss Maisie Sampson was appointed Secretary of the Society, we acquired headquarters in Wigmore Street, and we launched our new venture with a mixture of confidence and trepidation. The Society continued to function until the second 'Jacobs Affair', when it merged with the Society for Jewish Study.

143

10

THE SOCIETY FOR THE STUDY OF JEWISH THEOLOGY .

The Inaugural Meeting of the Society for the Study of Jewish Theology took place on Monday, 26 September 1962 at Kensington Town Hall with Mr Ellis Franklin in the chair. Around 700 people were present at the meeting. Ellis Franklin referred to my address at the public meeting in June at the Herbert Samuel Hall, and went on to say:

> Some of us felt that these thoughts and this thinking should not just stop at this one address. We had to act quickly. If the matter was to be carried further urgent steps had to be taken, as Rabbi Jacobs, then excluded because of his views from a post in which he could have done most for the community, was receiving offers of appointment in America, South Africa and Australia. We felt that the object of advancing this point of view could best be carried out by the formation of the Society for the Study of Jewish Theology, a title that had been scoffed at by someone who should have known better. Its aim is to encourage the study based on sound scholarship of the teaching of traditional Judaism. We appointed Rabbi Jacobs as Director. We collected funds and now we stand before you at this inaugural meeting. We shall need members – we already have some – and in due course need more funds.

My memory fails me as to whom Ellis Franklin was referring to when he spoke of 'someone who should know better' but, aware of the fact that many did pour scorn not only on a Society for the Study of Jewish Theology but on the whole notion of

Jewish theology, I tried in my address to answer the question, 'Is There a Jewish Theology?'

It had been suggested, I said, that Jews have no theology, that they ought not to discuss such a topic, still less have a society to further the topic. I remarked that I found myself with a degree of sympathy with those who argued that, on the whole, Jews had not been over-fond of systematic thinking about theological questions. But to state baldly that there was no such thing as Jewish theology was to completely misread the history of Jewish thought. Jews today, I went on to say, want to know not only what they should do but what they are expected to believe. In referring to the controversy, I may have succumbed to the temptation that I had tried hard to avoid of yielding to feelings of personal bitterness. In any event I thought fit to add, 'The day may come when there may be increasing rigidity in the community, that there will be more heresy hunting and a greater clamping down of freedom of thought. If that day ever comes, then God help the Anglo-Jewish community.' Twenty-five years later, there are sufficient indications that my prophecy – according to the Talmud, after the destruction of the Temple, the prerogative of fools – has come to pass.

The Society organised study groups and public meetings, for which we were fortunate to be able to call upon some very distinguished scholars and thinkers. We wanted, in particular, to invite speakers who held the fundamentalist view, but when we offered our hospitality there were no takers.

Under the aegis of the Society, I undertook a number of speaking engagements in the provinces, addressing meetings in Manchester, Glasgow, Birmingham, Leeds, Liverpool and some of the smaller centres of Jewish life. Also as part of my work as Director of the Society I used to visit regularly the Jewish Societies at Oxford, Cambridge, London and other universities, where I was often attacked for my views by the more traditionalist students, and I must say I enjoyed this immensely. I have always found the study of theology fascinating and theological controversy stimulating. The opportunity to engage in these without any of the rancour that often attended my parries with the London Beth Din was very attractive. I tried at these meetings (not always too successfully) to avoid giving the impression

145

that I was apologising for living. I urged my audiences to think the issues through with me as objectively as possible; an ideal, it must be admitted difficult to attain in theology, where personal conviction, background and experience are hard to transcend.

I became increasingly outspoken at these meetings. A favourite illustration I would use was the institution of Yom Kippur, the holiest and most solemn day in the Jewish calendar. The fundamentalists believe that the institution of Yom Kippur and most of its details were directly ordained by the word of God spoken to Moses in the wilderness at a particular and definite date, and that if this belief were to be rejected there would be no point in keeping Yom Kippur. Our point of view, I used to say, is that Yom Kippur, like other Jewish institutions, has had a history. If modern scholarship is to be trusted, Yom Kippur did not just drop down from Heaven all at once, as it were, but developed gradually, growing over the centuries into the day of spiritual power we now know it to be. Thus someone who agrees with our approach will feel completely free to investigate – if he is historically minded – the origin of Yom Kippur and may even discover at the end of his researches that it contains some primitive elements. But if he is at all spiritually sensitive, he will not fail to see that this day is so much a part of his people's mode of worship, providing Jews with a direct encounter with their God, that, whatever its origins, the observance of this day will remain a divine command. Such an approach does require one to give up the doctrine of verbal inspiration. But it can without too much difficulty be accommodated to the doctrine, 'The Torah is from Heaven.'

In a sense this approach was very old-hat, even in Anglo-Jewry. Herbert Loewe, for instance, expounded something very much like it in his debates with Claude Montefiore, in their joint *A Rabbinic Anthology*, as Herbert's son, Professor Raphael Loewe, pointed out in his preface to the new, American edition of *A Rabbinic Anthology*. Raphael Loewe, who, it should be said, was constant in my support and a source of great encouragement to me, once gave the illustration of a nuclear explosion, radioactive for long afterwards. The spiritual energy released at Sinai is having its effect down the centuries of

Jewish living to this day. But Herbert Loewe, though a strictly observant Jew, was a teacher at a university, a layman whose views could be tolerated by the rabbinic establishment; I was a rabbi, a graduate of a Yeshivah and a Kolel to boot, and I, it was implied, should have known better.

Over the week-end of January 11th–13th 1963, I travelled to my home town, Manchester, to address two meetings under the aegis of the Society: one at the South Manchester Synagogue Hall on 'Judaism in the Twentieth Century', the other at the Reform Synagogue Hall on 'The Problem of Pain'. (By this time, there was only a muted 'I told you so' when I spoke at a Reform synagogue.) My mother having passed away and my aging father with enough to do looking after himself, I did not stay with him over the Sabbath but at a Jewish hotel, Fulda's. My successor at the Central Synagogue in Manchester was my old pupil from Golders Green Yeshivah days, Baruch Horowitz, who had written a pamphlet under the pen-name of Ben Levi in which he attacked my views as heresy. I felt that, in the circumstances, it would have been embarrassing all round for me to have attended the Sabbath services at the Central Synagogue. Alderman (later Sir) Sidney Hamburger, an old friend from Torah Va-Avodah days and a leading member of the Orthodox community, and his wife, Gertrude, invited me to their home for the Sabbath meal on Friday night, where, in a relaxed atmosphere, I was able to discuss my views with them and the members of their family, all observant Jews.

I would not wish to imply that Sidney Hamburger agreed with all my views but, despite differences, I found him then and always to have a keen sense of fair play and tolerance. He worshipped at the Holy Law Synagogue, whose rabbi was Rabbi Julius Unsdorfer, another old friend from my Manchester Yeshivah days, who was also very welcoming. The wardens of the Holy Law, on the other hand, were extremely reluctant to appear to be siding in any way with me in my quarrel with the Chief Rabbi. The result was that I was not given an *aliyah*, as is usual for a visiting rabbi. The invitation would no doubt have been offered had I – as a local apologist for both me and the Chief Rabbi inelegantly expressed it – kept my 'big mouth shut'. The local Jewish press took the matter up. The President of the synagogue, in an interview, in which no one was taken in, patiently assured them that no slight was intended. There was a Bar Mitzvah in the synagogue that day, he explained, and there were simply not enough *aliyot* to go round!

The meeting on the Saturday night in South Manchester was under the auspices of the Northenden and Gatley Literary and Zionist Society. The reason for this was to avoid any official invitation by the South Manchester Synagogue, in whose hall the meeting was held and which was under the jurisdiction of the Chief Rabbi. Nevertheless, the minister of the synagogue, Rabbi Felix Carlebach, and the minister of the Sephardi congregation, the Rev. Maurice Gaguine, both former colleagues of mine in the Manchester Rabbinate, were courageous enough to attend the meeting, as did other prominent members of the Orthodox community. The chair was taken by Mr M. Landau, President of the South Manchester Synagogue, thereby making it clear to all that the Literary and Zionist Society was only a front.

At this and at my other meetings I spoke bare-headed, that is without a *yarmulka* (as we called it in Manchester; in London it is referred to as a *coppel* – 'cappel', little cap, in Cockney pronunciation), which was remarked upon by the Jewish press in Manchester. It was perhaps foolhardy to throw down the gauntlet in this way but I wished by the gesture to make two things clear: first, that I no longer wished to be seen as an 'Orthodox' rabbi in the new, fundamentalist, understanding of the term, and second, that here, too, there had been a departure from the older Anglo-Jewish tradition. This is not the place to rehearse the pros and cons of bareheadedness, upon which so much has been written. The point is that even the spiritual leaders of Anglo-Jewry in former times such as Chief Rabbi Hertz and Dr Büchler, Principal of Jews' College, frequently appeared in public with their heads uncovered. I realise with hindsight that it was a rather petty gesture of defiance which harmed my cause and gave unnecessary offence to the traditionalists.

My lecture in South Manchester covered more or less the same ground as my lectures in London. Around five hundred people were present. Alderman (later Sir) Abraham Moss proposed the vote of thanks to me, which was seconded by Alderman Leslie

SOCIETY FOR THE STUDY OF JEWISH THEOLOGY

(later Lord) Lever; both men belonged to Orthodox synagogues and were squarely rooted in the Orthodox tradition.

Rabbi Felix Carlebach and Rev. Maurice Gaguine were certainly not alone in their readiness at least to be seen associating with me. Among other colleagues who were prepared to stick their necks out were the Rev. Dr I.H. Levy, of course (he was on my side from the beginning, as I have said), Rabbi Isaac Newman, the Rev. Leslie Hardman, the Rev. Saul Amias, Rabbi Dr Simon Lehrman and the Rev. Dr Chaim Pearl, my successor at the New West End Synagogue – all of them serving in prominent synagogues belonging to the United Synagogue. Dr Lehrman, addressing a meeting of the Society for the Study of Jewish Theology, prefaced his remarks by saying that his presence at a meeting of the Society did not necessarily mean his complete endorsement of all the views I had expressed but was meant primarily to show his rooted dislike of any attempt made at what has been called 'ecclesiastical heresy-hunting'. For his attendance Dr Lehrman was attacked by a warden of his synagogue. The meeting was to have been held in the hall attached to Dr Lehrman's synagogue, the New Synagogue in Stamford Hill, but the same warden had stepped in to prevent the hiring of the hall for the purpose. Another meeting of the Society was to have been held in the Edgware Synagogue Hall to be addressed by Dr Pearl, with the full approval of the minister of the synagogue, the Rev. Saul Amias. Dayan Swift, a regular worshipper at the Edgware Synagogue, brought extreme pressure to bear on the wardens to close their hall to the Society. In the event, the meeting had to be held in another hall, although the invitations had already gone out stating that it was to be held in the Edgware Hall.

Two letters appeared in the *Jewish Chronicle* (18 January 1963) a week after my lecture at the South Manchester Synagogue Hall. I think it useful to record these two letters here as indications of the different kinds of response I had been receiving from intelligent members of the Orthodox community on the other side in the controversy.

The first of these letters came, oddly enough, from Mr M. Landau, President of the South Manchester Synagogue, who

HWI—F*   149

had taken the chair at the meeting. Evidently in the few days since the meeting Mr Landau had suffered pangs of remorse. He wrote (and I quote it as a typical response I have had over the years):

Sir, – I had the honour of presiding over a crowded meeting in our Steel Memorial Hall, where Rabbi Dr Louis Jacobs delivered a lecture on 'Judaism in the Twentieth Century'.

The central theme of his lecture was a plea to the Jewish community to accept the historical findings of Biblical criticism. I would like to ask the distinguished rabbi whether those who attended the meeting – if they had all accepted his thesis of Bible criticism when they left the meeting and went home – would they then have been better Jews and Jewesses, better fathers and mothers, better sons and daughters? Would it make them into greater lovers of the people of Israel, and the land of Israel; lovers of peace and haters of violence, bloodshed and falsehood?

Does it really matter who wrote the Psalm 'By the rivers of Babylon, there we sat down, yea, we wept, when we remembered Zion', apart from the fact that it has helped us in our age to return to the land of Israel? In the same way, is it so terribly important for us to know who was the author of Shakespeare's works, Bacon or anyone else?

Is it really so important whether certain items in the Biblical narrative are historically true or myths – is it not sufficient that these 'myths' have fashioned countless millions of Jews over the ages into saintly and civilised beings with a record of family life?

Ought not a rabbi, being the religious guide and teacher to his flock, to leave all these comparative inessentials to the critics, historians and professors, and address himself to the moral issues which *do* trouble the Jewish people and Judaism in the twentieth century?

M. Landau
Pinewood, 23 Pine Road, Manchester 208

I have often been confronted with this type of argument – that it makes no difference whether one is a fundamentalist or not so far as loyalty to Judaism is concerned. That is exactly what I myself had been saying. Mr Landau's question does require an answer. Questions of faith and its meaning are the province of every intelligent Jew. I believe that we need to pursue the implications of what the 'critics, historians and professors' have been saying for the past 150 years. Otherwise we are left with a situation, destructive of faith, in which intelligent youngsters become familiar with, say, Biblical Criticism, in the sixth form at the latest, only to find their Jewish mentors either dismissing it all entirely as 'un-Jewish' or else preserving a conspiracy of silence on the whole question. A prominent Orthodox rabbi was asked by one of my staunch supporters, the Rev. Dr I.K. Cosgrove of Glasgow, 'What would you say if a young man asked you whether Moses wrote the whole of the Pentateuch?' The rabbi replied, 'I would tell him to mind his own bloody business!' I would not dream of introducing Wellhausen and the like to a pious Jew of simple, uncomplicated faith, secure in his religion. But my remarks were never addressed to a Jew of that kind. There were enough Jews bothered by such questions to warrant an attempt to consider them honestly. In any event, the matter was brought into the public forum by rabbis who had been saying, in contrast to Mr Landau, that it is essential to adopt the fundamentalist view as the only one which guarantees Jewish observance. When that happens it is surely necessary to state the obvious – as Mr Landau seemed to admit – that Jewish observance is possible for those with unblinkered minds. The whole controversy had erupted through people using extracts from books I had written *in defence* of Jewish observance exhibiting them to the public gaze as an *attack* on Jewish observance.

The other letter in the *Jewish Chronicle* contained a far more sophisticated argument. The author, Mr Shlomo Reich, a very learned Manchester businessman, had been a younger contemporary of mine at the Manchester Yeshivah and an occasional pupil of mine. I quote from this letter not only for its intrinsic value and to be fair to those opposing my views, but also as indicative of arguments I have had to face over the years. Mr Reich wrote:

Sir, – Now that the controversy raging round the person of Dr Louis Jacobs has abated, it is perhaps the right moment for a calm appraisal of his teachings and their consequence for Anglo-Jewry.

In recent weeks his numerous appearances on the platform as an exponent to the public at large of his particular brand of Jewish Modernism and his dynamic personality present a most serious challenge to those who cherish our spiritual legacy and find it as meaningful and valid in our contemporary life as it was to our ancestors.

I have just had the opportunity of hearing Rabbi Dr Jacobs elaborating his point of view in a lecture entitled 'Judaism in the Twentieth Century'.

It was admittedly a remarkable *tour de force* and was expressed with a sincerity and honesty which may have carried conviction to those who perhaps have not realised the implications and attendant dangers of such a viewpoint. The essence of the lecture was that the modern thinking Jew who does not live in an ivory castle and who considers the evidence adduced by modern scholarship impartially, must reject the traditional view of the Divine authorship of the Pentateuch as this is no longer tenable.

This point of view, admits Dr Jacobs, involves a re-adjustment – a new orientation, but which modern man must accommodate himself to if he wishes Judaism to have validity in the contemporary world.

I was sorry that Dr Jacobs did not in the lecture elaborate his views and indicate how this new readjustment would affect the practice of Judaism – the day-to-day life of this emancipated Jew. The logical extension of this new point of view is surely that the same approach be made when we consider the practical expression of our beliefs.

According to Dr Jacobs, should not our approach to mitzvot be moulded by what modern sociology has to teach us? In this view the value of the observances of the

Torah would not depend on their Divine origin, a most dubious scientific proposition, but because they represent man's attempts to formulate a way of life in accordance with some inner urge or aspiration which we might term, loosely, religious.

Of course, in addition, it would be admitted that in the performance of any particular mitzva the modern Jew is carrying out an act by which he is identifying himself with the corporate body of Jewry. Over the centuries these mitzvot have acquired a mystique and a value which cannot be rationally analysed.

But this brings us to the heart of the problem. The twentieth-century modern Jew who has had to readjust his whole concept of Revelation in the light of modern scholarship must also act similarly in the practice of Judaism. Contemporary thought has shown that many practices enjoined in the Torah can no longer have validity for us because research has shown they were the result of man's irrational fears and weaknesses, and often the consequence of man's lack of understanding of phenomena which science has now explained to us.

This, then, I believe is the logical outcome of the way of thinking as expounded by Dr Jacobs. It is fraught, as has been shown, with great danger, and, if widely disseminated, involves the virtual transformation of Judaism, so that Liberal Judaism, which is eschewed by Dr Jacobs, will appear as a bastion of conformity in comparison.

S. Reich,
Harrowside,
98 Northumberland St.,
Salford 7, Lancs.

I agree with Mr Reich, and those who follow his opinion, that a readjustment is required in Jewish practice as well as in the theory, if modern critical views are to be accepted. As I have tried to show in my book *A Tree of Life*, such a readjustment need involve no abandonment of the Halakhah, only that the Halakhah be seen in dynamic rather than static terms. There are risks, of course, but the alternative is to close the mind to the results of tried scholarship. Professor Louis Ginzberg, a pioneer in the kind of thinking I have been putting forward very tentatively over the years, speaks in this connection of the genetic fallacy. It is fallacious to conclude from the fact that institutions have a base origin, that they are valueless. I would argue that even if Freud's views on the origin of religion were correct (whether they are or not is a matter for investigation, not of faith) this would in no way discredit religion. For the religious mind God really does exist, and it is not for us to tell Him how He should have chosen to reveal Himself to mankind. Freud was tackling the question (a non-question for the believer): since religion is an 'illusion' or a 'collective neurosis', why has it retained its hold? For the believer, religion is decidedly not an illusion. My whole argument has been that faith cannot be invoked in matters that can be determined by investigation, otherwise one believes in a God who plants false clues to mislead His creatures.

What is Mr Reich's alternative? Does he, and those who think like him, feel obliged to hold that all modern thought is untrue, the work of Satan? I have never claimed (such a claim would be the height of absurdity) that Wellhausen has had the last word in Biblical scholarship. But to dismiss all historical scholarship in the name of faith is to prejudge the issue and lead to a schizophrenic attitude, in which every hypothesis is known and even admired as convincing and yet declared, on grounds of faith, to a be dangerous error.

The Society for the Study of Jewish Theology published a regular *Bulletin* in which lectures given to the Society by scholars and thinkers, Jewish and non-Jewish, were published. The *Bulletin* contained a 'Questions and Answers' section, consisting of the questions put to me in my talks to the Society and the answers I tried to give. Readers were invited to make their own observations on both questions and answers. Here are one or two questions and answers from the issue of the *Bulletin* dated December 1963.

Question: *How would you square the creation narrative in Genesis with the findings of modern science?*

Answer: This cannot be done. The sublime account of creation in Genesis has for its background the 'science' of the age in which it was composed, and it is a futile task to attempt to read our present knowledge of how the material universe came to be into it. We do not go to Genesis to obtain information about the structure of the universe but for the eternal truth it conveys that God is the Creator of all and that all things are subordinate to Him. The best way of reading the first chapter of Genesis is as a great hymn of praise to God as Creator, perhaps composed as a liturgical poem for recitation in the Temple. The thought patterns, the picture of the universe, the very vocabulary it uses all belong to the common ancient Near Eastern traditions, but in Genesis these are utterly transformed by the monotheistic idea. It is more than a little odd that Jewish apologists who are prepared to say that Genesis is not a scientific text-book sometimes go on to say in the next breath that Genesis can be defended scientifically by such highly dubious suggestions as that a 'day' means millions of years.

Question: *Is it your contention that God did reveal the whole of the Torah now in our possession but instead of revealing it all at once to Moses, as the fundamentalist says, He revealed it during successive epochs in the history of Israel?*

Answer: No, this is far too simple an alternative, and it fails to recognise the real changes which have come about as a result of historical conditions. Once you move away from the fundamentalist position you see the *Torah* as a dynamic process. You must acknowledge the principle of historical development, though this does not necessarily mean development in one direction. There are peaks and valleys, and not all the peaks come late in Judaism's development, not all the valleys early. What is needed today is a real sense of dedication to the *Torah* ideal but one that is not wedded to fundamentalism. The more dedicated non-fundamentalist Jews there are the better we shall be able to recapture the dynamism of the past.

Not everything that has come down to us from the past is of equal value. Some of it is of no value at all. But the question of establishing proper criteria is a very involved one, and many of us feel that it cannot be tackled merely by external tampering with Jewish institutions but by allowing Judaism to grow organically through the experiences of open-minded dedicated Jews.

Question: *Should the things you are saying be publicly discussed by laymen? Would it not be better to leave this to the Rabbis, who are well informed in Jewish matters?*

Answer: I agree that matters involving massive learning and scholarship should be left to the experts. There are certain technical problems which can only be tackled by those who have devoted their lives to learning. But the question of fundamentalism versus non-fundamentalism is not one of these. It is a problem which any intelligent Jew can see and deal with. Doctors do not normally discuss the advantages of treatment with laymen, but questions such as the value of a national health service are as much the layman's province as the professional's. I cannot accept the notion that Anglo-Jewry can be divided into two groups – the scholars, possessing esoteric knowledge, and the masses, for whom such knowledge is taboo. There are, of course, people incapable of appreciating our kind of discussion. I am no believer in the glorification of the common man. You know of the quotation *ad nauseam* of Abraham Lincoln's saying, 'God must love ordinary people, He made so many of them.' No doubt He had good reason for making so many of them, but this must not be taken to mean that Judaism is satisfied for us to be ordinary. Judaism surely wants us to cultivate the extraordinary in piety and comprehension. But I venture to suggest that men and women who are prepared to attend our meetings for two hours at a time can by no stretch of the imagination be classed as ordinary. They must not be dubbed the 'masses' and denied a voice in the interpretation of Judaism. They can teach the Rabbis as well as learn from them. Consequently, all the Rabbis can say is, let us work it out together. There is a problem here. We did not create it. We were born into this age and yet we love Judaism. Let us then 'reason together'. If

156

we are convinced that the search for *Torah* is itself *Torah* we should encourage all the best brains in Community to engage in the search, whether they belong in the ranks of the Rabbis or the laymen, a distinction which in any event is not too finely drawn in the Jewish tradition.

Soon after the inauguration of the Society for the Study of Jewish Theology, a rival organisation was formed called the Society for the Promotion of Jewish Learning, with Mr S.S. Levin as its Chairman, the Chief Rabbi as its President and Sir Isaac Wolfson as its Life-President. Sir Isaac and Lady Wolfson gave no less that £100,000, a very large sum in those days, to the newly formed Society, the gift to be spread over ten years. Though this was not stated explicitly, it was obvious that the new Society had been hastily formed as a counterblast to our Society. It was no accident that the address at the inaugural meeting of the Society for the Promotion of Jewish Learning was given by the Vice-Principal of Jews' College, Rabbi Dr J.J. Ross, and that the subject of the address was 'Torah Min-hashamayim – Divine Law'. It was a widespread misconception, Dr Ross stated, that when the traditionalists said the Torah came from Heaven they literally meant that some object landed from the sky on a particular day and at a particular time and place. This was, of course, a travesty of our critique of fundamentalism. Dr Ross carefully chose to ignore the real challenge to fundamentalism, that provided by Biblical Criticism.

Fully prepared to take us on, the Society declared its aim of undertaking publication of lectures and study courses so that the widest impetus could be given, as Mr Levin stated at the inaugural meeting, to 'spreading knowledge of authentic Orthodox Judaism and Hebrew literature'.

Our Society did not last very long because it was overtaken by events. But during its brief existence it did, I think, do some useful work, and it brought much satisfaction to its members, who believed they were fighting the good fight. The other Society (I hope I am not saying this in any spirit of gloating) made not the slightest impact and soon vanished entirely from the scene.

I might have continued in the position of Director of the Society had not events taken a new turn. As I shall relate in the next chapter, the position of Minister of the New West End Synagogue, my old congregation, had become vacant on the emigration of Dr Pearl for a pulpit in the USA. The members offered me the vacant position but this, too, was blocked by the Chief Rabbi. As the 'Jacobs Affair' entered into its second stage (my readers will, I hope, forgive me for dramatising it) the plot thickened.

11

THE JACOBS AFFAIR,
STAGE II

The Rev. Dr Chaim Pearl, successor to Dr Abraham Cohen in the pulpit of Singers Hill Synagogue in Birmingham, had accepted a call to the pulpit of the New West End Synagogue after I had left it to go to Jews' College. Dr Pearl, a distinguished scholar, eloquent preacher and caring pastor, was held in the highest esteem by the members of the New West End Synagogue. They were very sorry to let him go when he left them for the prestigious Conservative Synagogue in Riverdale, New York. (Dr Pearl served there for over twenty years, until his retirement to live in Israel.) Now that the pulpit was vacant again, my former congregants at the New West End wanted to extend a call to me, seeing in this a dignified way to resolve the controversy. It had died down by then, but the embers were still faintly glowing. The Honorary Officers of the New West End, Mr Bernard Spears, Mr Oscar Davis and Mr Frank Levine (a son of the Rev. Ephraim Levine, Emeritus Minister of the Synagogue) were eager to have the matter settled without fuss so that the community could put strife behind them. They anticipated no objection by the Chief Rabbi, who, they believed, would be only too eager to end the conflict, just as I for my part was willing to serve again in a synagogue under his jurisdiction. This was not to be, however, though I was told on good authority that even the members of the London Beth Din had urged the Chief Rabbi to accept the situation, arguing that, whatever my views, they would be capable of doing no harm in a pulpit long recognised as being somewhat outside the normal United Synagogue patterns in its 'reformist' tendencies.

To appreciate what happened next, it is necessary to know something of the peculiar bye-laws of the United Synagogue. An applicant for the position of minister in a congregation belonging to the United Synagogue was obliged first to obtain the Chief Rabbi's certificate, testifying that the applicant was a fit and proper person to hold such a position. It should be noted that there was no actual 'certificate' or written document to be signed by the Chief Rabbi. All the 'certification' meant was that the Chief Rabbi had to be consulted before the appointment could be made. The Honorary Officers, assumed that, since I had already been Minister of the New West End, at which time I had received the necessary 'certification' (the Chief Rabbi had in fact inducted me the first time round), there was no reason why they could not now seek the approval of the Board of Management of the Synagogue for the appointment to be made. The proposed appointment was voted on and accepted unanimously, not only by the Board of Management but also by the special selection committee which included five members of the United Synagogue panel for the appointment of ministers.

At this point, Mr Alfred Silverman, Secretary of the United Synagogue and a stickler for the strictest application of the bye-laws of that body, stepped in. He argued that since in this unprecedented case there was uncertainty as to whether or not a new certificate was required, it would be desirable to ask the opinion of the Chief Rabbi on the matter before going any further with the appointment. The Honorary Officers, despite their awareness that it was asking for trouble to put the Chief Rabbi on the spot in this manner, reluctantly agreed to Silverman's demand that he should be approached, and they did so in February 1964. To their consternation, the Chief Rabbi declared that his certificate *was* required and, furthermore, that he would withhold it in my case, so that the proposed appointment could not be made.

The Hon. Ewen Montagu had meanwhile retired from the Presidency of the United Synagogue, to be succeeded in that office by Sir Isaac Wolfson. The Honorary Officers of the New West End sent a letter to Sir Isaac strongly protesting against the Chief Rabbi's decision. It stated that, while anxious to maintain the Chief Rabbi's authority and the integrity of the United Synagogue, the Board of Management of the New West End was making known to the United Synagogue its intention to take all necessary steps to obtain the minister of the congregation's choice.

On Sunday, 1 March 1964, an Extraordinary General Meeting was held of the members of the New West End Synagogue, presided over by Mr Oscar Davis. According to the report in the *Jewish Chronicle* (6 March 1964) the meeting was attended by about 260 members of the Synagogue who, in the words of the *Chronicle* reporter, gave an 'overwhelming mandate' to the Honorary Officers and Board of Management of the New West End to contest the Chief Rabbi's objection to my appointment.

In the 'Incidentally' column of the *Chronicle* on the same date it was pointed out that the New West End had a tradition of independence. It had been responsible in 1892 for the convening of a conference by Chief Rabbi Adler which resulted in permission being given for some amendments to the order of service. The first Minister of the New West End, the Rev. Simeon Singer, was a Bible critic and a friend of the Liberal leader, Claude Montefiore. The Rev. Ephraim Levine was one of the sponsors of the Society for the Study of Jewish Theology. In addition to Mr Montagu, the Vice-President of the United Synagogue, Mr Frank Rossdale, was a member of the New West End and, the columnist saw fit to add, quite gratuitously I thought, that among the members of the Synagogue were 'Sir Barnett Janner, President of the Board of Deputies, Lord Marks, Lord Swaythling, Mr Harry Sacher, and many other distinguished names in the community'.

At the meeting, Alderman H.A. Leon, thrice Mayor of Richmond, reported on a deputation of members of the New West End (including himself), which had visited the Chief Rabbi. According to Alderman Leon, the Chief Rabbi had said that I would be better advised to seek a post at a university. When Alderman Leon begged the Chief Rabbi to reconsider his decision, the Chief Rabbi replied that only if I would agree to preach the rabbinic Judaism practised in the United Synagogue, both in and out of the pulpit, would he be prepared to accept me. To this end I was approached by the Chief Rabbi's Secretary, Rabbi A.M. Rose, who seemed acutely embarrassed by the mission the Chief Rabbi had imposed on him. So far as I could

161

gather from Alderman Leon and from Rabbi Rose, speaking on behalf of the Chief Rabbi, the message was that if I were to recant, the Chief Rabbi *might* agree to the appointment. I was particularly distressed at the suggestion that I was to toe the line in and out of the pulpit. Obviously, much as I wanted to go back to the New West End, I could not agree to do so on those terms.

Shortly afterwards, the Rev. Ephraim Levine, eager to support me in the earlier struggle but not so eager to see me back in 'his' old pulpit, asked me to call on him, saying that there might be a way out of the impasse. When I called at his home, he handed me a letter and said he had managed to obtain the Chief Rabbi's support for my candidature provided I signed it. Its contents amounted to a sheer declaration that I had been consistently mistaken in my views and had now come to see the error of my ways. I refused to sign. While passing the letter back to Rev. Levine, it accidentally slipped out of my hands and fell to the floor. Reporting on the incident to some of my followers, Ephraim Levine said that I had thrown the letter away in disdain. That is perhaps how such a letter should have been treated, but I was sincerely anxious to help achieve an amicable solution and tried to avoid intemperate words or actions.

Strange though it might seem, my relations with the Chief Rabbi, if not exactly cordial all of the time, were never really acrimonious. I think he genuinely believed he was upholding traditional Judaism against a man unwittingly contributing to its weakening. For my part, I saw the Chief Rabbi as a liberal-minded man, hurt to the quick that in the previous stage of the affair he had been accused of yielding to the pressure brought to bear on him by the London Beth Din and, recognising that there was much truth in the accusation, determined to show how firm he could be even when the London Beth Din counselled against the use of the heavy hand.

The whole matter was now being discussed in the Jewish and general press. No further steps were taken for the time being. Sir Isaac Wolfson had gone to Israel for Passover where, it was widely rumoured, he would meet with the Chief Rabbi, also in Israel for Passover, to persuade him to change his mind. Despite

Sir Isaac's denial, the rumour persisted. Dr Pearl had left for the USA a week or two before Passover and it was agreed that I would sit together with the other congregants during the festival, the pulpit and the minister's seat remaining unoccupied, in the hope that in Israel the Chief Rabbi would be persuaded by Sir Isaac.

Once the festival was over and in the absence of any further communication from the Chief Rabbi, the Honorary Officers requested me to put on my canonicals, sit in the minister's seat and occupy the pulpit. In a letter of protest the Secretary of the United Synagogue, Alfred Silverman, stated that I had also addressed a Bar Mitzvah. In fact I addressed the Bar Mitzvah not from the pulpit but at the *kiddush* in the synagogue hall, where I began by saying, 'Unaccustomed as I am to public speaking . . .'!

The Silverman letter, addressed to the Honorary Officers, began:

> The Honorary Officers of the United Synagogue have been informed that, on Saturday 11 April, despite the fact that he is not an accredited Officer of the United Synagogue and that the sanction of the Chief Rabbi had not been previously obtained for him so doing, Rabbi Dr L. Jacobs attended at your Synagogue dressed in canonicals, occupied the Minister's seat in the Synagogue and subsequently entered the pulpit and addressed a Bar Mitzvah.

'Dressed in canonicals' is rich – as if Jewish law recognises the wearing of canonicals as any indication that the wearer is a rabbi. Many Orthodox rabbis believed it to be a serious offence to wear canonicals on the grounds that this was following Christian modes of worship – *hukkot ha-goy*.

The Silverman letter went on to warn the Honorary Officers of the New West End that if they continued with 'such flagrant acts in breach of the Constitution', the Honorary Officers of the United Synagogue would have no choice but to bring the matter before a Special Meeting of the Council of the United Synagogue for action to be taken.

The Honorary Officers, with the exception of Mr Frank Levine, were undeterred and on 18 April I did preach in the synagogue on the theme of Judaism as a living faith (the text lending itself to this theme was from the *sidra* of the week, dealing with purification by means of *mayyim hayyim*, 'living waters') but I carefully avoided making any direct reference to the controversy, not wishing to be too provocative. The *Sunday Times* (19 April) carried a report on the incident on its front page under the heading 'The Rabbi Marches into Battle' together with a photograph of me, flanked by my sons, Ivor and David, walking to the synagogue through Holland Park. My opponents seized on this, accusing me of posing for the photograph on the Sabbath whereas, in fact, the photographer had lain in wait for us to leave my flat near the park, correctly guessing that this would be the route I would take to the synagogue.

These events took place at a time when the Christian community had become agitated over the Bishop of Woolwich's *Honest to God*. In a perceptive piece in *The Guardian* (18 April 1964) Christopher Driver wrote of the 'Jacobs Affair':

> The points of similarity with the 'Honest to God' row should not be overworked, for this is a debate about Biblical Criticism rather than about our image of God – that is, a debate which in the Church of England was fought a century ago. The true counterpart to Dr Jacobs is perhaps Bishop Colenso or Robertson Smith rather than the Bishop of Woolwich. If Dr Jacobs were a Liberal or Reform Jew, his views would have aroused no controversy, and some of his critics have suggested that he ought in logic and honesty to make the transition. But Dr Jacobs is Orthodox. He remains convinced that the traditional Jewish observances have a religious value in themselves – 'there are depths in the human soul which only ritual can reach' – but wants to maintain a critical attitude towards the Scriptures which lay down the observances.

This is a helpful summary of the argument by a non-Jewish writer, although, of course, Jewish observances do not stem solely, or even primarily, from 'the Scriptures' but from the interpretation of these found in the Rabbinic tradition, and in

Bar Mitzvah photograph of David (1965) with, left, Ivor and Naomi, and Shula, right

THE RABBI MARCHES INTO BATTLE

Rabbi Jacobs and his two sons marching through Holland Park to the synagogue, April 1964 (*Sunday Times*)

Cartoon by Len Gould drawn at the Protest Meeting against the Chief Rabbi's veto

Cartoon by Harry Blacker at time of the Jacobs Affair (by his kind permission)

Anglo-Jewry at least the term 'Orthodox' has had a meaning of its own, to denote observance of the traditions rather than the strict acceptance of dogma.

Notice was given that the Special Meeting of the United Synagogue Council, referred to by Mr Silverman, was to be held on Thursday, 23 April. The New West End leaders addressed a letter, dated 21 April, to all the members of the United Synagogue Council, setting out the history of the affair. I cannot think of a better way of describing the situation as our side saw it than by quoting this letter:

> In view of the resolution which will be placed before you at the Special Meeting of the Council on Thursday, we feel that we must give you the fullest information of what has recently passed in our efforts concerning the appointment of Rabbi Dr Jacobs.
>
> Although we have always maintained, for reasons which appear later, that no further authorisation by the Chief Rabbi was necessary, nevertheless many representations were made to the Chief Rabbi to state precisely what his objections were and the conditions which would satisfy him in approving the appointment. Rabbi Jacobs, too, called on the Chief Rabbi and assured him of his loyalty and acceptance of his authority.
>
> However, the Chief Rabbi has never stated his specific grounds of objection and has repeatedly suggested that Rabbi Jacobs should take up an academic post or go abroad. There is no evidence to support the statement publicly made that the Chief Rabbi has done everything to help Dr Jacobs. All the evidence points to the contrary, including the ban on Rabbi Jacobs conducting funerals when invited by bereaved families.

Here I might interrupt to observe that eventually the ban on my officiating at funerals held in grounds belonging to the United Synagogue was lifted, and to this day I am allowed to officiate on such sad occasions.

The letter continues with the history of the comings and goings, the letter I was given to sign by Ephraim Levine, the waiting over Passover while Sir Isaac met the Chief Rabbi in Israel and the final step the congregation took in inviting me to preach. After discussing whether the certificate was required and asserting that if so, it was hardly for the Chief Rabbi to decide the matter as a judge in his own case, the letter concludes:

We have done all we could to avoid conflict. It has arisen because the other parties to the dispute have not shown a similar attitude of conciliation. We have neither sought nor stimulated publicity. On the contrary, it was through our efforts that no word appeared publicly for the first two months of the controversy, to avoid embarrassment to the Chief Rabbi. The unfortunate consequences of this conflict are, we suggest, not the responsibility of those who are resisting injustice but of those who are seeking to perpetrate it.

All the Hon. Officers, members of the Board of Management and representatives on the U.S. Council, with the exceptions of Messrs F. Levine and F. Rossdale, are unanimous in our attitude and are the signatories of this letter.

We hope that, with the knowledge of these facts, you will, in the best interests of the U.S. and indeed of the whole community, oppose this resolution. Ruthless and repressive action to crush differing ideas is totally alien to a Jewish religious body and must fail in the end. Even at this late stage, we are convinced that the unity of the U.S. can be preserved by avoiding the precipitate action of this resolution and proceeding by further negotiation and conciliation.

Oscar B. Davis
Bernard Spears

Hon. Officers

Bernard Herson, LDS, RCS	Sidney Bright
William Frankel, LL B, JP	David Franklin

Isaac Gordon, MD, MRCP   Nathaniel Horne
Alan Jacobs   Lawrence Jacobs
Lewis Jacobs, MA, MSc.   Jack Kleeman
(Alderman) H.A. Leon,   Charles Marks
    MBE, JP
Donald Samuel
E. Stanning

Board of Management   *Representatives on Council.*

At the Special Meeting of the United Synagogue Council, described in the press as 'stormy', Sir Isaac, who presided, read out a lengthy statement in support of the Chief Rabbi and put forward a resolution that the Hon. Officers of the New West End be discharged. Sir Isaac refused to allow a secret ballot, insisting on a show of hands which, some felt, accounted for the large majority supporting the resolution, members being unwilling publicly to thwart the Chief Rabbi and Sir Isaac himself.

Sir Isaac's statement to the Special Meeting was printed and subsequently sent to all the members of the United Synagogue. It is not being over-suspicious to see the hand of Alfred Silverman, the Secretary of the United Synagogue, in all this. It was typical of the Silverman approach that there were constant references in Sir Isaac's statement and in the resolution to bye-law number this and bye-law number that. As a wag at the meeting remarked, whether or not the Torah was given to Moses at Sinai, the bye-laws of the United Synagogue certainly were, in Silverman's view. Sir Isaac himself, as I know from personal discussions with him at the time, felt that the whole matter was a little above his highly capable and businesslike but basically untheological head. The off-the-record discussions I had with him and his son Leonard (now Lord Wolfson) convinced me that he was really on my side in the struggle, and he did try behind the scenes to have the matter resolved so as to satisfy both parties. But Sir Isaac was, after all, President of the United Synagogue and, egged on by Silverman, believed in the final analysis that his loyalties were to that organisation and the Chief Rabbi right or wrong.

167

A new management for the New West End Synagogue was appointed at the Special Meeting of the United Synagogue and, on the following Sabbath, the members of this new management sat in the wardens' box in the place of the deposed Honorary Officers. It had been demonstrated that the Constitution of the United Synagogue reigned supreme.

The Secretary of the New West End Synagogue, Mr Isaac Kaska, a personal friend, was obliged in his official capacity to send me the following letter:

24 April 1964

Dear Rabbi Jacobs,

I am instructed to inform you that the Council of the United Synagogue at a Special Meeting held last night, for reasons which will be known to you, removed from office and deposed the Hon. Officers and the Board of Management of the New West End Synagogue and appointed in their stead to act as Managers of the affairs of the Synagogue Messrs Frank Rossdale, Samuel Boxer, Salmond Levin and Frank Levine.

I am instructed by the Managers to inform you that it is their wish that on no account should you appear in the Synagogue robed in canonicals or occupy the Minister's seat or enter the pulpit or address the congregation or preach to them or take part in the Service otherwise than in accordance with the Bye-laws and regulations of the United Synagogue. They further ask you not to address any meeting in the precincts of the Synagogue without their permission.

The Managers assure you that you will be welcomed in the customary manner as a member and a worshipper,

Yours sincerely,
Isaac Kaska
Secretary

As a postscript to this letter it might be mentioned that Isaac Kaska told me on his deathbed (as if I did not know it) that the whole matter could have been settled without fuss and in a manner acceptable to all the parties concerned had it not been for the intervention of Alfred Silverman.

The Observer (Sunday 26 April 1964), under the headline, 'Rift Empties Synagogue Seats', carried a front-page article telling of what happened on the previous day when the new Managers took over at the New West End. The article reads in part:

> Morning prayers were held almost as usual in the New West End Synagogue, London, yesterday. The synagogue was about a quarter full. It was the first Sabbath since the board of management had been dismissed by a delegates' meeting of the United Synagogue for supporting their new rabbi – Dr Louis Jacobs. The Chief Rabbi of the British Commonwealth, Dr Israel Brodie, had refused to confirm him in his pulpit.
>
> Not Dr Jacobs, but the Rev. Ephraim Levine, sat in the rabbi's chair. A previous holder of the office, he is Rabbi Emeritus of the Synagogue. Before the service began, a few members of the congregation arrived to remove their books in order to pray in a different synagogue. The former board of management were absent, though the new four-man board appointed by the United Synagogue were there, among them the son of the Rabbi Emeritus.
>
> Feeling among synagogue members at the treatment of Dr Jacobs is very strong. One prominent member of the congregation said yesterday, 'There has been much disappointment with the course adopted at the delegates' meeting on Thursday night. Sir Isaac Wolfson, in deference to the more extreme opinion, exercised his right to refuse a secret ballot' ...
>
> Curiously enough, too, some of the extreme right-wingers outside the United Synagogue tend to side with Dr Jacobs – because to them the whole institution of the Chief Rabbi is suspect. No one wearing an ordinary clerical collar could be the right representative of the traditional rabbi for them.

The remark by the *Observer* reporter that the extreme right-wingers kept themselves aloof from the whole controversy because the institution of the Chief Rabbinate was, for them, suspect in any event, is perceptive and contains a good deal of truth. But eventually the Chief Rabbi did manage to win a good deal of support among the right-wingers, largely because, as I see it, he was prepared to surrender the particular stance of the Chief Rabbinate in order to identify completely with the right wing in a way no previous Chief Rabbi had done.

Incensed at the press coverage of the affair and especially indignant at the role played by the *Jewish Chronicle*, the Chief Rabbi called a meeting of rabbis and ministers of the Anglo-Jewish community, on 5 May 1964, at which he stated his case. This statement, too, like that of Sir Isaac's, was printed and circulated to all the members of the United Synagogue. *Inter alia* the Chief Rabbi said:

> The travesty of our traditional Judaism has been featured in our monopolistic [*sic*] Jewish press for some time. There has been a consistent denigration of authentic Judaism and religious authority which has tended to create religious confusion and a spirit of divisiveness within our community and which in no small measure has contributed to the present situation. Whilst we believe in the freedom of the press, we should not allow this freedom to be abused and even turned into a tyranny as is attempted by the *Jewish Chronicle* which in recent years, no doubt for reasons of its own, has not presented an objective picture of the Anglo-Jewish scene, nor has it reflected the tradition and sentiment of Anglo-Jewry.

When asked how it was that he had allowed me to hold the position of minister to the New West End Synagogue from 1954 to 1959, and had also agreed to my appointment as Tutor and Lecturer at Jews' College, notwithstanding my views, the Chief Rabbi declared it was an 'act of faith' in a 'promising man passing through a phase of intellectual and spiritual struggle' whom it would be wrong to reject before he had reached a fixed position. In his view, my statement that 'In modern times the Jew no longer asks, "Why did God tell us to keep certain *Mitzvot?*" but "Did God tell us to keep certain *Mitzvot?*"', implied a rejection of the doctrine 'The Torah is from Heaven'. Here he ignored the fact that the pamphlet *The Sanction of the Mitzvot*, from which these words were taken, answers the question, 'Did God tell us to keep the *Mitzvot?*' in the affirmative, though I did not accept the fundamentalist understanding of the doctrine.

In the unkindest cut of all, the Chief Rabbi said that 'everything points to the fact' that I had been used as a central figure by a few resolute individuals who had openly declared their intention to bring about a new orientation in our community. I still have not discovered the identity of these 'few resolute individuals' and what they hoped to achieve in terms of a 'new orientation in our community', but I have to deny categorically that anyone tried to 'use' me for sinister or other purposes of their own. On the contrary, if there was any 'using' it was on my part, albeit for purposes I believed to be worthwhile. Practically every one of my supporters rallied round me not because of any theological issue but because they believed I had been treated unjustly. I wish it had been otherwise – that the personal aspect had been allowed to recede and that all my supporters had shared my theological views – but the central motivation, especially of the members of the New West End, was their sense of fair play.

By the time the Chief Rabbi's statement was made, the leading members of the New West End Synagogue, seeing that nothing further could be expected from the United Synagogue, had begun seriously to discuss the founding of a new independent synagogue with me as its rabbi. The Chief Rabbi alluded to this in his statement:

> I am saddened by the thought that a group of individuals are contemplating the promotion of a new synagogue outside the framework of the United Synagogue. I pray that under the impulsion of faithfulness to our sacred heritage and loyalty to our communal solidarity, no action will be

taken that may tend to create a schism in our old and all-embracing *kehillah*.

My supporters could only give the obvious retort: owing to the Chief Rabbi's attitude, the *kehillah* had ceased to be 'all-embracing'.

Despite the apparent finality of the statements by Sir Isaac Wolfson and the Chief Rabbi, some people were still determined to seek a resolution of the conflict, even at that late hour, with a degree of face-saving on both sides. I received a letter signed by Mr Michael Hunter, Chairman of the Inter-University Jewish Federation of Great Britain and Ireland, and Dr Jonathan Frankel on I.U.J.F. notepaper dated 30 April, informing me that a petition had been signed by members and a committee formed to have the case of the New West End Synagogue reopened. Oscar Davis, on behalf of his deposed colleagues, invited the members of the New West End Synagogue to a meeting at the Rembrandt Hotel, on Sunday 3 May, to receive a report on the situation and consider possible action. It was decided at the meeting to form a new congregation, but also to make a further attempt at conciliation, though this seemed doomed from the start. Accordingly, I had a meeting with Sir Isaac Wolfson and his son Leonard (only a few days after Sir Isaac's statement) where we worked on a letter, addressed to the Chief Rabbi, in which I begged him to have second thoughts. He could now do this without loss of face, I said, since it was clear that in any event most of the regular worshippers at the New West End would have me as their rabbi in the new congregation and it was surely better all round for me to be under his jurisdiction at the New West End. Sir Isaac took the letter to the Chief Rabbi the next day and importuned him to agree to my appointment but to no avail. The Chief Rabbi was in the position of a leader who had been accused of weakness and who therefore felt obliged to demonstrate his strength and courage even when wisdom dictated a more conciliatory attitude.

Resolutions were passed at the Marble Arch Synagogue (proposed by Mr Nathan Goldenberg, whom I did not know at the

172

time but who became a founder member of the new congregation and a very close friend) and at the Hammersmith Synagogue (both constituents of the United Synagogue) expressing solidarity with the desire of the New West End Synagogue to reappoint me as minister. But on submission to the United Synagogue they were ruled out of order.

On 1 May the *Jewish Chronicle*, in a hard-hitting leader, appealed for a reversal of the Chief Rabbi's decision. The leader concluded:

> Whatever may be the result in terms of institutions, the controversy is, and will be, a healthy one. Our community is taking a great interest in its religion, and it is a good sign that they are taking sides. From this Judaism as a whole will benefit. But if these important institutions, the Chief Rabbinate and the United Synagogue, are not to suffer, there is an urgent need, even at this late stage, to seek means to end the conflict. It is never too late to reverse an unjust and damaging decision.

But all these efforts at conciliation came to nothing. The Chief Rabbi had irrevocably committed himself and there was nothing further that could be said or done.

The Chief Rabbi and the United Synagogue had, of course, many defenders who published letters and articles, some of them to the point. The extreme right wing usually remained on the sidelines, and even included some who supported me in a kind of off-hand, indifferent way. However, my supporters were sent copies of *Newsletter*, published by the Neturei Karta representatives in London, containing a vitriolic personal attack on me. This proved less disconcerting to us when we became aware that this *Newsletter* was a scurrilous sheet (referring to Chief Rabbi Goren of Israel as 'the parachutist Green'), was illegally published without the publisher's address, and was printed, appropriately enough, on yellow paper. The *Newsletter* said:

> When he [Jacobs] professes to call himself a Jew – orthodox and all – and to stay within our fold with the sole aim

of seducing people to blaspheme our Holiness, defaming our religion, of uprooting the foundations, of corrupting the mind, of defiling the soul, and of being paid for it with fame and honour, then our only answer must be the Torah itself – 'Bring forth him that has cursed beyond the Camp and let all that have heard him lay their hands upon his head, and let all the congregation overwhelm him with stones' . . . Jacobs sold everything for a few words of flattery by Kessler and Frankel (of the *Jewish Chronicle*) who crowned him for his *epikors* with the so-oft repeated titles of Scholar, Academician etc. He does not stop, and has decided to become the main *Maysis* and *Maydiach* (one who stirs up people and leads them to worship idols) trampling underfoot the Holy Torah with the hypocrite's cry of 'honesty and broadmindedness' in his vanity and for his ignoble ambition . . .

Fortunately, I was never taken outside the camp to be stoned but I did receive anonymous letters and telephone calls urging me to 'repent'.

The Autumn issue of *Mosaic* (No.11, 1964) carried a leader and two articles on the affair. By this time the new congregation, the New London Synagogue, had been founded in St John's Wood. The articles were by founder-members of the board of the journal, Godfrey Silverman, a former student of mine at Jews' College, and Kenneth Zucker who became a founder-member of the New North London Synagogue. Silverman (no relation to the Secretary of the United Synagogue) sided with the Chief Rabbi, arguing that I had expressed the discredited theories of the German Bible critics in the last century and that I could hardly expect organised 'orthodoxy' (Silverman puts this word in quotes) to accommodate itself to my nonconformity. He went on to say, 'In an independent congregation, however, he will be free to preserve his cherished "norms" together with his dedicated supporters who will, I understand, now have a long Sabbath walk from Kensington and elsewhere to St John's Wood.' This snide remark about the long Sabbath walk was all too typical of the opposition and it was a remark often repeated, as if the members of the New West End or, for that matter, of other congregations in the United Synagogue, did not drive to the Synagogue on the Sabbath.

Kenneth Zucker's article argued the case better than I myself did at the time. After describing the theological issue, Zucker continued:

> In this situation there is a challenge to the resilience and vitality of Judaism, and to the depth of its faith. If the Chief Rabbi's attitude is typical, it possesses none of these qualities. He does not keep his mind open to the objections to the tradition. He does not refute them by logical argument. He simply takes refuge in dogma and calls the faithful to heel.
>
> Dr Brodie may be correct in his belief that the faith of some Jews can be upset if they were told that the old view of the Torah is untenable. That is a very important consideration but the danger will be far greater if orthodoxy is placed in the same predicament as the mediaeval Church which accepted as an article of faith the proposition that the earth was flat. To tie Judaism to a doctrine which is clearly false is to court disaster.
>
> It is said that any watering down of the belief that every word of the Five Books comes from Moses, will utterly undermine Judaism. If the truth led to that conclusion we would have no choice but to follow it. In fact there is nothing in the discoveries of modern research which, when viewed through the eyes of a religious Jew, need in any way erode his justifiable reverence for Torah, his belief in its divine impetus or his acceptance of the vast structure of law and commentary which has been built upon it. Of course the period of transition from a simple to a more sophisticated view, is a difficult one. But it need hold no greater terrors for us than those facing the generation which was compelled to accept that the picture of creation described in Genesis is not literally true.

Louis Jacobs deserves the highest credit for being the first English orthodox Rabbi to openly acknowledge the fact that these problems exist. He has gone further. He has attempted to show that acceptance of the conclusions already referred to is not incompatible with an outlook on Judaism that draws its faith and its strength from our traditions. It does not follow that his is the sole approach, that his conclusions are the only ones that can be held or that in the end they will prevail. The important point is that he has made the attempt. It is a mark of his opponents' sterility that their only reply was to cast him out as a heretic.

I can only add that the fear that my views would upset the faith of some Jews has proved to be unfounded. I do not know of a single person who has left traditional Judaism as a result of reading my books. As a matter of fact, it has been encouraging over the years to find rabbis and others, in this country and in the USA, assuring me that when they had become aware of the challenge presented by Biblical Criticism and been disturbed by it, they had found help through my writings in dealing with the problem and preserving their faith and their observances.

The non-Jewish religious press also commented on the affair, sides being taken according to the position of the particular paper with regard to the fundamentalist versus liberal debate in the Church. The *Modern Churchman* (July, 1964) devoted a leader to what it called 'a Jewish tragedy' under the heading 'Signs of the Times', in which it presented both sides as seen with Christian eyes:

> The element of tragedy is that the Chief Rabbi Dr Israel Brodie, and the United Synagogue which represents Anglo-Jewry [*sic*] and governs some eighty synagogues, fear that any further weakening of the *Torah* by liberal interpretation and any consequential slackening in the ritualistic laws must weaken the hold of the *Torah* on the minds of Jews. This would mean that what nowadays is primarily distinctive about a Jew, and what binds Jews together, would be first diffused and then lost. Incredible as it still is, Hitler slaughtered European Jewry. Almost as gravely, the acids of modern living, especially in the United States, eat away distinctive racial habits and opinions, so that there is a real fear that the Jews of New York are disappearing as

an ethnic group. The offence of Dr Jacobs with his rational and critical approach to the Book and tradition alike lies not in this or that view for itself, but in the threat of his whole teaching to the continuance of Judaism as a religion and the Jews as a people. On the other hand, Dr Jacobs and the members of the new [sic] West End Synagogue, and many Jews in all Synagogues, in understanding their religion and its writings cannot but stand by modern scholarship as they must stand by the truth.

The *Church of England Newspaper* on the other hand, also drawing the analogy with trends in the Church, was more sympathetic to the Chief Rabbi. In a leader (22 May, 1964), headed 'Split in Jewry', the editor wrote:

A crisis has blown up among British Jews and it is a mark of the position that they occupy in our society that it has received a large measure of publicity. It is also a sign of a cleavage that has always existed among Jews.

The Chief Rabbi Brodie refused to accept the nomination of Dr Jacobs for the New West End Synagogue and that synagogue, unable to accept Dr Brodie's ruling, has broken away from the United Synagogue. The charge against Dr Jacobs is that his attitude towards certain orthodox Jewish premises is unacceptable. In a long statement Rabbi Brodie declared that orthodox Judaism means acceptance of the 'absolute authority of the Bible' and the rejection of an 'individualism in religion . . .' full of vagaries and contradictions.

The leader went on to declare its sympathy with those on the Christian side who stood, like the Chief Rabbi, for this absolute authority and declared, too, that absolutes are not popular, so that 'the strong sympathy attaching to Dr Jacobs attaches also to attempts to overhaul our ideas'. It concluded:

The crisis among the Jews is an opportunity to re-examine what we mean by narrowness. We are unburdened by having to lean on the Law, so we must beware of driving

177

the analogy too far. But we must not be afraid of asserting again and again that far from fitting our faith to the times, we must do the opposite.

It cannot have been gratifying for the Chief Rabbi to find supporting his stand a paper that still believed that the Law is a burden.

The *Church Times* (8 May 1964) used the occasion to take a swipe at the fundamentalist *English Churchman*:

The Chief Rabbi has indeed been the target of much criticism over the affair; but he may be consoled to know that the *English Churchman* is on his side. This paper said last Friday, 'It is a battle which has been raging for many years now, and we are glad that, so far, the Chief Rabbi has remained firm in his determination to hold back those who would undermine the "old view" of the Scriptures.'

12

THE NEW LONDON SYNAGOGUE

Over 300 members of the New West End Synagogue assembled on Sunday, 3 May 1964 at the Rembrandt Hotel in Kensington, for a Special Meeting with Mr Oscar Davis in the Chair. The walls of the Rembrandt Hotel are covered with reproductions of the great master's paintings. Observing these, some of us recalled the remarks of Rabbi A.I. Kook, that in Rembrandt's paintings one could see an expression of the idea, found in the writings of the Jewish mystics, that there is a 'hidden light' proceeding from the darkness, a remark that we thought might augur well for our future.

The resolution before the Meeting read:

> That this meeting of members of the New West End Synagogue approves the actions of their Honorary Officers and Board of Management taken in pursuance of the mandate given to them at the Extraordinary General Meeting on 1 March 1964, and protests strongly at the treatment accorded to the Synagogue and its elected representatives at the hands of the Honorary Officers and Council of the United Synagogue.
>
> That the members of the New West End Synagogue here assembled reaffirm their desire and determination to follow the spiritual guidance and leadership of Rabbi Dr Louis Jacobs.
>
> That in consequence of the foregoing, it is hereby RESOLVED to constitute an independent Orthodox Congregation under the name of the New London Synagogue, in the tradition of the New West End and under the spiritual leadership of Rabbi Jacobs. All members of the community are invited to join in this endeavour to serve Judaism.
>
> At the same time, this meeting affirms the intention as

individuals and members of the New West End Synagogue, to work for the return of the United Synagogue to its own traditions of tolerance and the 'Progressive Conservatism' referred to in the preamble to its Bye-laws.

After a very fair summary of the situation by the Chairman, his co-warden at the New West End, Mr Bernard Spears, put the resolution to the assembly. I was then called on to speak, the Chairman promising the meeting that my speech would not be long – only six to seven minutes. I do not think that I kept to the time-limit (which speaker does?) but it did think it right and proper to define what the term 'Orthodox' in the resolution could mean. We had been accused so often of misleading people on this score that I felt I had to try to spell it out. Refreshing my memory from the tape-recording of the meeting I see that I said in this connection:

> The question, friends, is not what the term Orthodox means in other parts of the world – it has many different meanings – but what has Orthodoxy meant in the United Synagogue and in Anglo-Jewry. If by Orthodox you mean an attitude of mind which shows no hospitality to modern scholarship and modern thought and the inquiring mind, then I would say that we shall certainly not be Orthodox and we shall be proud not to be Orthodox. It was never the fashion of the New West End Synagogue to have the kind of Judaism taught and preached suitable only for know-alls leading a congregation composed of docile sheep. However, if by Orthodoxy you mean – and the words are not ours but are taken from the preamble to the Constitution of the United Synagogue – 'Progressive Conservatism', then we are as Orthodox as the next man. I hope that one of the things we will do in the new congregation will be to work out the implications of the term 'Progressive Conservatism'.

I continued in this vein, stressing that if we were successful in setting up the new congregation we would look upon it as a quest, a searching for the truth of the Torah.

180

Many points were raised in the discussion and people sought clarification on some of the issues. Among the speakers was the Hon. Ewen Montagu, Sir Isaac Wolfson's predecessor in the office of President of the United Synagogue. Loyal as ever to the office of Chief Rabbi and its holder, irrespective of who held that office, Ewen blamed it all on the London Beth Din for exerting pressure on Chief Rabbi Brodie. Others at the meeting took strong issue with Ewen, pointing out that even if the Beth Din did exercise pressure it was, after all, the Chief Rabbi who had yielded to the pressure. In fact, as we have noted previously, far from having any objection to my appointment to the New West End, the Beth Din had urged the Chief Rabbi to yield. Be that as it may, it was heartening to everyone present to hear a former leader of the United Synagogue speak in favour of the resolution. Ewen remained a member of the new congregation till he passed away.

At the end of the meeting, the resolution was passed by a vote of 300 for, 11 against. We thus had a congregation with hundreds of members and some funds donated by well-wishers, but no building in which to worship. The search began for a temporary hall in which services could be held. One of those approached for the hire of a hall was the vicar of a prominent Anglican church whose hall was not in use on Saturdays. 'Certainly not,' he irately exclaimed, 'I'm a proud fundamentalist and you won't catch me helping anti-fundamentalists, not even of the Jewish variety!'

On the first Sabbath after the meeting, we held services at the hall adjacent to the Sephardi synagogue in Lauderdale Road, where we were disturbed by loud music from a record-player put on by a Mr Parnes who thought it a mitzvah to interrupt the devotions of the heretics, even if this involved profaning the Sabbath. The *sidra* of the week gave me a ready-made text for our new venture: 'And ye shall proclaim freedom in the land for all the inhabitants thereof' (Lev. 25:10). I also quoted the Hasidic saying, 'He who has no place anywhere has a place everywhere.' That was all right in theory. In practice we were moved on by Rabbi S.D. Sassoon, acting Haham of the Sephardic community during Dr Gaon's absence abroad. Eventually we hired a large room at the Princes Hotel in Kensington where, in euphoric mood, we worshipped during the summer months. We had no Chazan. The services were conducted by members of the congregation who were familiar with the melodies used at the New West End. It was a kind of Anglo-Jewish *stiebel*: that is, it was a blend of Anglo-Jewish decorum but with more than a dash of *stiebel* warmth. Not everyone's cup of tea, but it worked.

Throughout the summer the search went on for a permanent home. Salvation came from a totally unexpected quarter.

The St John's Wood Synagogue in Abbey Road was a constituent synagogue of the United Synagogue. Its Rabbi, Dr Solomon Goldman, was a close friend of mine and had refused to take any part in the agitation against me. In fact, he, the Rev. Dr I.H. Levy (loyal as always) and the Rev. Isaac Livingstone of the Golders Green Synagogue addressed a private letter to the Chief Rabbi begging him to reconsider his decision to bar me from the pulpit of the New West End Synagogue. During my time at the New West End, Dr Goldman, Dr Levy, Rabbi Bernard Casper of the Western Synagogue and I used to meet weekly at each other's homes to discuss theological topics. Dr Goldman was eager to do all he could to help in the matter of acquiring premises for the new congregation. The old building in Abbey Road had become too small to accommodate the large congregation and a splendid new building had been put up around the corner in Grove End Road. The congregation, or rather the United Synagogue, had sold the old building to a property developer, Mr E. Alec Colman, a devout Jew whose heart would not allow him to demolish a building in which his fellow-Jews had prayed for almost a hundred years. Mr Colman had finally had to steel himself to appoint a firm of architects, Messrs Alexander Flinder & Associates, to build a block of flats on the site of the synagogue and this firm had been given a tender by a firm of demolition contractors to pull down the house of worship.

At this stage Mr Colman, when informed that we were looking for a site on which we could build our synagogue, offered us the building and the two adjacent houses at considerable loss to himself and his plans for the development of the site, requesting no more than the price he had paid. Some of our enthusiastic members were sufficiently carried away by all this to see the direct hand of God at work. Be that as it may, we had the opportunity of acquiring a lovely synagogue (built by Collins who built the famous Collins Music Hall) in which Dr Hertz and his successor, Rabbi Brodie, both of whom lived around the corner in Hamilton Terrace, had been regular worshippers, occupying the special Chief Rabbi's seat. It really did look as if this was an instance of direct divine providence, though I encouraged my supporters to be sceptical of any too close a theological interpretation.

Despite efforts by the United Synagogue to prevent the sale (believe it or not, they were prepared to see the building demolished rather than permit us to use it as a synagogue!) we did manage to purchase the building, thanks to the generosity of our members including Sir Jack Lyons, the Jacobs family, the Kleeman family, the Stone family, the Franklin family, Sir Emmanuel and Lady Kaye, Mr and Mrs Basil Samuel and Mr Louis Mintz, who was a tower of strength throughout. Soon after we had acquired the building, John Betjeman came along to congratulate the congregation on saving for posterity a superb example of late Victorian architecture. Alex Flinder, the architect given the job of building the block of flats that was to have been erected on the site, came along to one of our services to see the people who had been indirectly responsible for his losing his commission. Alex may have come to scoff, but he remained to pray, becoming a leading member of our congregation and serving for years on the Executive.

Mention must also be made of Mr H.I. Simons. 'Toddy' Simons, who belonged to an old Anglo-Jewish family and was a life-member of the Council of the United Synagogue, was a staunch upholder of the old Anglo-Jewish traditions. He was of enormous help in the establishment of the congregation, not least in seeing to it that we did not deviate too far from these customs.

A zealot from the St John's Wood Synagogue, aghast at the thought that I would be sitting on the very seat that had been graced by the august posteriors of two Chief Rabbis, got into the building at the dead of night with a hatchet in his hand and proceeded to demolish the seat. The result is that I now sit on a very comfortable, newly-furbished seat – 'fundamentalism' at its best, so to speak.

We called our new Synagogue the New London Synagogue (*bayit hadash*, 'new house', in Hebrew). Services were held in the new building we had acquired towards the end of the summer of 1964. We had the good fortune to engage Mr George Rothschild as our Chazan and eventually had an excellent choir under the direction of Mr Martin Lawrence. We still had to work out a Constitution, but an *ad hoc* Executive and Council was formed with the two former wardens at the New West End, Mr Oscar Davis and Mr Bernard Spears, both of whom had done so much in bringing our plans to fruition, serving as wardens. Mr David Franklin was appointed Treasurer, not only looking after the financial affairs of the new congregation but playing a very active role in raising the funds required for the success of the enterprise.

The building had been neglected by its former owners, whose efforts had been put into the building of their new home. Fortunately, Professor Misha Black, a world famous authority on design, advised us on how to make the most of the building, showing us how to preserve its Victorian character while getting rid of some of the clutter such as the plastic cornucopia above the Ark. We acquired a number of Scrolls, donated by generous members, and Mr Gerald Benney, the distinguished silversmith, was hired to provide the beautiful ornaments for the Scrolls and a very unusual but highly effective *Ner Tamid*.

We had to face the problem of marriage registration and that of providing for burials. In English law, the Jewish religious marriage ceremony counts, at the same time, as the civil ceremony. But this privilege is only granted to a 'congregation of Jews', and the Act of Parliament states that, for a congregation to be recognised for this purpose, the President of the Board of Deputies has to testify that it is a *bona fide* congregation of people professing the Jewish faith. Since the President is bound by the Constitution of the Board to consult the Chief Rabbi on all religious questions, successive Presidents have only been willing to make the required statement if the Chief Rabbi first approves.

Thus, indirectly, and with no support in English, law, the Chief Rabbi can prevent the President of the Board from making the statement that will enable a congregation to enjoy registration of marriage. In practice the Chief Rabbis have used their office in this way to prevent any congregation refusing to accept the authority of the Chief Rabbi from having a Marriage Secretary. In the last century, the Reform Synagogue was obliged to take the drastic step of having a special Act of Parliament enacted to give them the same privilege. It is ironic in this connection that the Gateshead community, which looked askance at the whole institution of the Chief Rabbinate, refused to satisfy the condition that it accepts the Chief Rabbi's authority, so that, for a long time, marriages in Gateshead had to be conducted under the aegis of a Newcastle synagogue which had accepted that authority. We had to struggle at first to obtain a Marriage Secretary, though when Chief Rabbi Jakobovits was elected the problem was solved and we had a Marriage Secretary without being compelled to recognise his authority. But for the first two or three years, the local Registrar of Marriages had to be present at every one of our marriage ceremonies. This gentleman used to sit in the body of the synagogue, his registers open before him, while I, as officiating rabbi, had to ask bride and groom, 'Will you, X, take Y . . .?', in order to satisfy the requirements of English law.

As for burials, since these are conducted in this country through the synagogue, we had to have either a cemetery of our own or access to one, in order that an adequate burial scheme could be organised. We had been on the best of terms with the independent Western Synagogue and we were able to come under their burial scheme, with a cemetery in Tottenham and later at Cheshunt. A number of our members, who belonged to the United Synagogue and had contributed for many years to its burials scheme, continued to do so. This occasionally led to difficulties when I was asked to officiate at a funeral in a United Synagogue cemetery of one of my congregants who had remained a member of the United Synagogue burial scheme. At first the authorities of the United Synagogue refused to allow me to officiate on such sad occasions because, they maintained, that would amount to a recognition of my status as an Orthodox rabbi. Eventually, however, as recorded earlier, wiser counsels prevailed and I am now allowed to officiate at funerals in United Synagogue cemeteries.

In May 1965 Chief Rabbi Brodie retired at the age of 70 and was knighted by the Queen. The search for a successor was energetically pursued by Sir Isaac Wolfson. By the time Dr Jakobovits (now Lord Jakobovits) had been elected Chief Rabbi, the New London had become completely 'disestablished', which was our eventual aim. Nevertheless, when Rabbi Jakobovits arrived in London to spy out the land and consider the offer, Sir Isaac Wolfson's Secretary, Captain Myers, telephoned me to arrange for Rabbi Jakobovits to visit me at my home. I assumed that Dr Jakobovits would wish to explore the possibility of a *rapprochement* between the Chief Rabbinate and the New London Synagogue as desired by Sir Isaac. If this meant the New London again becoming part of the United Synagogue it was an outcome none of us contemplated for one moment. But out of courtesy to Sir Isaac and to Rabbi Jakobovits I told Captain Myers that I would be glad to welcome the Rabbi to my home. However, no sooner had Rabbi Jakobovits arrived in London than Captain Myers telephoned again to say that Rabbi Jakobovits felt that it would compromise him if he called on me so would I mind calling on him instead at his hotel. I replied that I certainly would not agree to this because it could be construed as if I was eager to defend myself and was courting an invitation to join the United Synagogue, which I personally did not want and, even if I did, owed it to my supporters to resist. In yet another telephone call, Captain Myers suggested that Rabbi Jakobovits and I should meet on neutral ground, or, as it seemed to me, in no-man's-land.

I suggested Holland Park as a suitable venue. It was near enough for both of us and secluded enough for no one to be likely to see us. Like other events in this saga, it was cloak-and-dagger stuff. I said that there was no need for either of us to wear a red carnation as identification since we already knew one another. False beards were also out – we both had real ones.

So it was that on a bright sunny morning the future Chief Rabbi and I strolled around the flower-beds in Holland Park, discussing the future of the Anglo-Jewish community. Neither of us had any clear idea about the expected outcome of the meeting. In what amounted to an apology for his intervention in the Jews' College affair, Rabbi Jakobovits said that he had no idea at the time that I depended on Jews' College for my livelihood, implying that had he known he would not have written what he did. He did make it clear, however, as I recall, that he distanced himself from my views if not from my person. When he became Chief Rabbi he did his best to be friendly and I think I reciprocated, but the suggestion that the New London Synagogue should come under his jurisdiction was never raised again. We certainly could not countenance this and I had the impression that he, too, was unenamoured of a prospect that would prove thoroughly embarrassing all round. Years later, when the New London Synagogue was attacked by our old foes, the members of the London Beth Din, the Chief Rabbi kept his peace and made no comment. On the other hand, some of us had qualms about our community becoming affiliated to the Board of Deputies for the very reason that the Chief Rabbi and the Sephardi Hakham were that body's sole religious authorities. Yet, since Reform and Liberal synagogues were also affiliated to the Board, the problem of authority apparently causing them no sleepless nights, we believed that the cause of communal unity was too important to be jeopardised by such misgivings. Since then, our representatives have occupied, and continue to do so, positions of importance at the Board. In 1988 our members June Jacobs and Eleanor Lind were elected Chairmen of two of its Committees.

Our Hebrew classes met at first in the two old houses on the site. These were later demolished and the site sold, for a very small amount, considerably less than its real value, to the Jewish Welfare Board for the erection of the Ellis Franklin House. Mr Ellis Franklin, as related earlier, had been a prime mover in the formation of the Society for the Study of Jewish Theology. His widow, Muriel, an energetic, sprightly, cultured lady, became Chairperson of our Ladies Committee, and his son, David, our first Treasurer, so it was appropriate that the site should be given over to this purpose.

Shortly afterwards, another great benefactor, Mr Jack Posnansky, told me that he intended to pay for the erection of a synagogue hall and classes at the side of the synagogue. When I said, 'My Honorary Officers will be pleased', Jack said that he had made the offer because he knew that his 'Honorary Officer', his wife, would be pleased.

At our first Rosh Hashanah service in our new home, I felt obliged in my sermon to return to the question of the 'Orthodoxy' of our congregation. We had described ourselves as an 'independent, Orthodox congregation' and I tried once again to define these terms so that there would be no misrepresentation. I argued again that in an Anglo-Jewish context we were fully entitled to call ourselves Orthodox. In our congregational life, I said, we were fully observant and in their personal lives our members were as observant as members of other congregations who laid claim to Orthodoxy. Where we differed from some congregations was in our refusal to equate Orthodoxy with a refusal to inquire. The word 'Orthodoxy' was, in any event, a relative term, used originally by the reformers as a term of reproach. As for 'independent', I said:

> We are an independent congregation. We have decided to take our destiny into our own hands, to work it out for ourselves. The system we have come up against of rigid control from above is peculiar to Anglo-Jewry and is otherwise unknown either in Jewish history or in the Jewish world of today. If there is any meaning to the Jewish boast that there is no priesthood in Judaism and that the Jewish ideal is that of a kingdom of priests, a priestly people, then we cannot afford to maintain the notion of ecclesiastical domination.

It was not all solemn, determined work. Shula and I were able to relax in a whirl of dinner and cocktail parties, just as in our days at the New West End when we were first introduced to a very active social life. I recall a party given by our members Ellis and Alma (later Baroness) Birk where I had a long conversation with the Editor of the *Daily Mirror*, who, to my embarrassment, went on and on about how much he sided with me in the controversy. It was a rapid come-down when, afterwards, he introduced me to his wife and said, 'Darling, meet the Chief Rabbi. I have just been telling him how much I agree with him!'

Among our younger stalwarts at the New London were the brothers Victor and Jonathan Stone. Their father, Hyman, had been a warden of the New West End Synagogue where Shula and I were befriended by him and his wife Dorothy. Victor Stone became and remains the Hon. Solicitor of the New London. Jonathan Stone spent, I would estimate, around 1,000 hours editing the first issue of the ambitious journal *Quest*, published in September 1965. The journal, very attractively produced by Paul Hamlyn, had a cover designed by Felix Topolsky and the list of contributors included Dan Jacobson, Gerda Charles, Alfred Rubens, Isaiah Berlin, Alexander Baron, Nathaniel Tarn, Charles Spencer, Edward Jamilly, Lionel Davidson, Chaim Bermant, Ruth Fainlight, Arnold Wesker, Michael Hamburger, Josef Herman, Alan Montefiore, Dannie Abse, L.A. Moritz, Ignaz Maybaum and Louis Weiwow, – almost everyone who was writing on Jewish themes in this country. Jonathan Stone contributed an article on English silver on which subject he was a widely acknowledged expert. I contributed an article, 'Reflections on a Controversy', which I thought provided an adequate summary of the affair from my side. I included this article in my book on the development of Jewish law, *A Tree of Life*, in the chapter 'Towards a Non-Fundamentalist *Halakhah*.' In 1967 this was followed by *Quest 2* on the theme 'The Jew', edited by Alma Birk and Clive Labovitch, and containing articles by a similar galaxy of literary talent. Among the articles was one by the famous non-Jewish religious writer, Monica Furlong, in which she described a visit to the New London Synagogue. An anonymous writer described 'The Making of a Chief Rabbi' in which he showed how little say rabbis have in determining the choice of the man to whom they will owe allegiance. Rabbi Dr Solomon Goldman, Minister of the St John's Wood Synagogue, wrote the article 'Love Your Competitor'. This was not an attempt to deal with the relationship between his community and ours but an analysis of the moral problems faced by businessmen. Dr Goldman never failed to be courteous and friendly without the slightest trace of the rancour a lesser man might have felt towards invaders of his territory.

The two volumes of *Quest* have now become collector's items. They were part of the determined effort to have our synagogue promote literature and the arts. Under the direction of the Stone brothers, Amia Raphael and Anna Horowitz, beautiful objects were made for ritual use in the service. Anna, together with her husband, the composer Joseph Horowitz, and Mr Sam Goldman, later Chairman of the synagogue, organised a series of concerts in the synagogue at which some of the most famous artists in the musical world performed, among them, Daniel Barenboim, at whose Bar Mitzvah I had officiated at the New West End. This had coincided with the 85th birthday of Viscount Samuel, who was also called up to the Torah on that day. In my address from the pulpit I was able to say that we were celebrating the birthdays of two Jews, one who had long been world-famous and one who would undoubtedly be world-famous in the future. Daniel remembered my prophecy. When he did indeed acquire his international reputation he used to send me a greeting card each Rosh Hashanah and when I asked him if he would perform at one of our concerts he accepted without hesitation. The first of these concerts was given by the London Philharmonic, conducted by Joseph Horowitz, in 1965 and repeated, with the works of different composers, in 1966 and again in 1967. Louis Kentner gave a piano recital in 1966; the Melos Ensemble played Handel and Beethoven in 1967; there was a family concert at which our children's choir sang together with the Kings Singers; the Amadeus Quartet performed in 1973, and in 1974 there was a piano and violin recital by Yehudi and Hephzibah Menuhin.

At these concerts, the Ark had a screen placed in front of it, though, strictly speaking, this was not necessary. I could see no Halakhic objection to having a concert of good music in a synagogue. On the contrary, we at the New London saw our concerts as a means of bringing the sacred in closer touch with the secular. However, soon after the first concert, the Chief Rabbi attacked the venture as 'sacrilegious'. Letters to the *Jewish Chronicle* also questioned the propriety of concerts in the synagogue. To our surprise and delight, Rabbi Dr Alexander

Carlebach, Rabbi of the Belfast Hebrew Congregation, wrote an article in the *Belfast Jewish Recorder* in support of concerts in synagogues, quoting Rabbinic sources that such concerts do not contravene the Din, and pointing out that only two things are forbidden in synagogues: levity and secular activities. On the question of levity, Rabbi Carlebach wrote:

> How can concerts of serious music be termed as 'levity' in this context? Merely to put the question shows its absurdity. Anyone who has ever attended a concert of such music and has witnessed the reverent attention and concentration with which the audience listens to the performance will readily reject the insinuation of levity.

As for the question of 'secular activity', Rabbi Carlebach wrote:

> Jewish theologians are rightly fond of stressing that for Judaism there is no absolute dividing line between the two domains, that religion ought to permeate and sanctify all aspects of life.

As it may be recalled, Rabbi Carlebach's daughter, Tirza, married my son, Ivor, but this article was written before he became my *mechutan* and, in any event, Alex Carlebach was too honest a man to let such considerations stand in the way of the expression of what he believed to be the truth. Rabbi Carlebach concludes:

> I cannot help thinking, therefore, that by extending the use of the synagogue to such functions as concerts, lectures, symposia and the like, one extends the realm of the sacred to the wider fields of human sensibility and experience from which religion in the narrow sense of the word can but profit.

Exactly our sentiments, which we were pleased to have confirmed from a distinguished Orthodox authority.

On the matter of concerts in synagogues, 'Toddy' Simon, zealous as usual for the Anglo-Jewish tradition and the honour of the New London Synagogue and ready as always with facts and figures, wrote a letter to the *Jewish Chronicle* (2 April 1965) in which he pointed out that both Chief Rabbi Solomon Heschel and Chief Rabbi N.M. Adler had been installed to the accompaniment of string orchestras; that the band of the Royal Horse Guards played during the dedication service of the New Synagogue in 1837; that musical accompaniment at the installation of Chief Rabbi Hertz in 1913 was only cancelled because he had suffered the loss of his father a few days before the service; and that in 1938, as part of the 75th anniversary at the Bayswater Synagogue, a full orchestra performed within the synagogue, two Dayanim of the London Beth Din, Dayan Lazarus and Dayan Gollop, being present, Chief Rabbi Hertz only being prevented from attending through illness.

The first Annual General Meeting of the New London Synagogue took place on Sunday, 23 May, 1965, with Mr Oscar Davis in the chair. The chairman declared that the synagogue had made progress in the first year of its existence 'beyond anyone's wildest dreams'. A constitution had been drawn up and, when presented to the meeting, was passed unanimously. The constitution provided for women members not only to vote at meetings but to be eligible to serve on the Council and Executive. We have had, in the person of Miss Ethel Wix, a woman Treasurer of the synagogue, and indeed there is no obstacle to a woman becoming Chairman of the synagogue. The notion that it is contrary to Jewish law for a woman to occupy any position of trust and authority in the community is still held by the Chief Rabbi and the United Synagogue, but is based on a ruling by Maimonides, writing against an Islamic background, which, if consistently acted upon, would have disbarred Golda Meir from becoming Prime Minister of Israel – a position the Orthodox accepted, however reluctantly.

Our children in the Hebrew classes were taught Hebrew with the Israeli/Sephardi pronunciation rather than the European/Ashkenazi version, and we thought it right and proper to adopt this style in our services to avoid confusing the children with two different systems. On the first Passover we used, as a trial run, the Israeli pronunciation. I read the Torah and Dr Jack Joels the

Dedication of Ellis Franklin Hall. Mrs Muriel Franklin; Chief Rabbi Jakobovitz; author (*Jewish Chronicle*)

Mr Harold Wilson at J.I.A. Dinner of the New London Synagogue. Mr David Gestetner, right; author, left (*Jewish Chronicle*)

Author and Shula receiving guests at a dinner to celebrate the First Anniversary of the New London Synagogue, May 1965. Shaking hands Lord Cohen of Walmer; left, the Hon. Ewen Montagu and Mrs Montagu

Broadcasting on the BBC Overseas (Hebrew) Service, May 1964

Haftarah, whereupon I jokingly remarked in my sermon that it was not a real trial since I read the Torah with a Manchester accent and Dr Joels the Haftarah with a Scottish accent. The resolution that the Israeli pronunciation be adopted was passed unanimously at the meeting.

Mr David Franklin, the Treasurer, reported at the Annual General Meeting that the building fund had received in cash and promises £100,000 towards the £175,000 needed. Thanks to generous well-wishers the New London has always managed to be financially viable.

The first Anniversary Dinner of the New London Synagogue was held at the Drapers Hall on Thursday 20 May 1965, presided over by the Hon. Ewen Montagu, former President of the United Synagogue. Sir Alan Mocatta proposed the toast to the New London Synagogue in what I thought was a less than whole-hearted manner by implying that, as a Sephardi, he was aloof from petty Ashkenazi squabbles. He evidently felt it his duty to be present at the dinner and to propose the toast because of his struggle for my acceptance at Jews' College. But Sir Alan did say that there could be no doubt about the future success of the New London because it had men and women of sincerity in its formation. In replying to the toast I said that the ideals of the New London Synagogue could be summarised in one word, 'quest', the title of our journal shortly to appear. I quoted, 'When inquiry was denied at the door, doubt came in at the window.' (I do not recall the source of this apt quote. Subsequently, I searched the dictionaries of quotations but could not find it. I remember reading it somewhere but where I still cannot say.)

Name-dropping again, I fear, I recall Mr Bernard Spears welcoming the guests among whom were Eva, Marchioness of Reading, Lord Swaythling, Lord Cohen of Walmer, Lord Segal, Sir Louis Gluckstein, Mr Maurice Edelman, MP, Mr David Weitzman, QC, MP, Mr Victor (later Lord) Mishcon, and Mr F.M. Landau, a Treasurer of the United Synagogue. Some of the VIPs present were members of the Reform and Liberal Synagogue, and Jonathan Stone was highly critical of having as honoured guests at the dinner people who did not subscribe at all to our philosophy of Judaism but who had been invited solely because of their name. He was probably right. This anniversary dinner was, in fact, our first and last. We did not repeat the experiment. Referring to Mr Landau's presence, Bernard Spears remarked, 'I am told definitely that he does not represent here tonight either the United Synagogue or the Chief Rabbinate. Most of us wish that his colleagues were all as tolerant and understanding as he is.' The connection with the United Synagogue was also evident in that the response to the toast to the guests was given by Sir Bernard Waley-Cohen, a former Lord Mayor of London, son of Sir Robert Waley-Cohen, former President of the United Synagogue, who was constantly at loggerheads with the London Beth Din and, for that matter with Chief Rabbi Hertz. The Rev. Dr I.H. Levy recited grace at the dinner. Thus, after a year's steady progress, the New London Synagogue indulged in a degree of self-congratulation; prematurely, some said.

During my time with the Society for the Study of Jewish Theology, I had begun to work on a study of Maimonides' thirteen principles of the Jewish faith. This was completed just before the storm broke over my re-appointment to the New West End and, fortuitously, was published by Vallentine, Mitchell in 1964, just as the storm was receding. In this book, *Principles of the Jewish Faith*, I examined each of Maimonides' principles in turn, seeking to trace its history in subsequent Jewish thought and its sources in the earlier tradition. I let myself go on Maimonides' eighth principle – that the whole of the Torah was conveyed by God to Moses – and I tried to spell out the obvious: that, before the rise of critical, historical scholarship, Maimonides' 'fundamentalist' view was intellectually respectable, although it is, in our present state of knowledge, untenable. My aim was not destructive but was to explore how the Halakhah could still be maintained as the word of God, though seen in dynamic rather than static terms. Lou Mintz, anxious that my views should receive a wide circulation, had 150 copies of the book specially bound and sent one of these copies to each of his friends. Basic Books in the USA published an American edition of the book, which was received with acclaim by Reform and Conservative reviewers, with horror by most (but not all) of the Orthodox. Years later, *Commentary* magazine reprinted the work in one of its special editions and, later still, B'nai B'rith in the USA reprinted the book in its Adult Education Series.

Not very long after this, I was appointed to teach Talmud at the Leo Baeck College. This College, on paper, was modelled on the Hochschule in Berlin as non-denominational, in that it concentrated on Jewish studies without any direct reference to the leanings of its students to either Reform or Orthodoxy. The theory seems to have been that the students would first equip themselves with the knowledge required of every rabbi, whether Reform or Orthodox, and could then pursue the special studies that would enable them to follow whichever denomination, Reform or Orthodox, they preferred. Whatever the theory, in practice the Leo Baeck College trained only Reform and Liberal rabbis. Open though the College was (in theory) to students for the Orthodox rabbinate, no such students ever applied for admission to the College. Even if they had and had eventually received ordination at the College, that fact alone would have been sufficient to disqualify them for the Orthodox rabbinate.

I accepted the position at Leo Baeck, after discussing it with the Honorary Officers of the New London Synagogue, undeterred by the risk that my opponents would seize the opportunity to say, 'We told you so.' I did not see it as in any way compromising my theological position. I was not, and never have been, a Reform or Liberal rabbi. In fairness to my congregation and to the College itself, I made it clear that my role at the College would be purely academic. Unless it were held that the very teaching of Talmud to students for the Reform or Liberal rabbinate was itself Reformist, a view to which I could not subscribe, there was basically no difference between teaching at Leo Baeck and teaching Jewish studies at a university. On the whole the arrangement worked well. For a time I even served as Chairman of the Board of Studies at Leo Baeck.

In this way I managed to keep a foothold in the academic world without neglecting my duties at the New London Synagogue. I lectured from time to time at various universities;

supervised and examined students for higher degrees; read papers at academic conferences such as those of the Society for Old Testament Studies and the British Association for Jewish Studies, of which body I was President for a year. I also managed to find the time to contribute articles to learned journals, especially the *Journal of Jewish Studies*. But I suppose a full-time working rabbi can never be more than an amateur in serious Jewish studies. I had to wait until the year 1985 before I became a professional academic. In that year I went to the Harvard Divinity School as List Visiting Professor.

I am convinced that too much introspection and self-analysis is out of place in an autobiography. With rare exceptions, when these are attempted they are not done well. My experience of severe self-scrutiny in the Musar half-hour at Gateshead has, in any event, put me off for good from the semi-morbid preoccupation with what makes one tick. Nevertheless, I have to say at this stage in my story that throughout my career I have been torn between the assumption of different character roles. Viewed with suspicion by the Orthodox and, to a lesser degree, by Reform, unable to come down definitely on either side of the academic versus practical rabbinic demands, and having supporters, some of whom thought I was too radical, others that I was too timid, I have known something of what the Germans call *Zerrissenheit*. I have tried to preserve a calm exterior but this has, I am afraid, often cloaked an inner turmoil. This was to the detriment of my family who, I might add, never complained and bore with me despite what it must have cost them. Having said this, I shall leave further exploration into my character out of this narrative.

The general Press had not forgotten the Jacobs Affair entirely. The Colour Supplement, for example, of the *Sunday Telegraph* for 1 April 1966, devoted to an examination of the Jews of Britain, carried on its cover (to my consternation) a photograph of my face against the background of the New London Synagogue building. There I appear, my hands and body out of sight, gazing suspiciously at the camera and wearing a broad black hat over my eyes, looking for all the world like a character out of the old

196

gangster films. For all that anyone knew to the contrary, I could have been holding in my hands a sawn-off shotgun concealed in a violin case.

In this *Supplement* Chaim Bermant wrote a witty piece on six Jews, of whom I was one. This is how he put it:

> Doubt is the prerogative of the laymen. Rabbis, at least in the Orthodox community, are appointed not to ask questions, but to dispense revealed truth. This was at the heart of the Jacobs Affair and when it blew up it seemed as if the Jewish community might be torn asunder. But Anglo-Jewry is very English and the controversy died down long before everyone was quite sure what it was about. Today Rabbi Jacobs ministers to the New London Synagogue, an independent congregation formed as a result of his exclusion. Its practices conform in every important respect to that of any Orthodox synagogue in London. The members may be a little less devout but where they are deficient in their belief in God, they make up for by a belief in Jacobs.

This last remark was no doubt intended as a joke (I noticed at the time that the date was, after all, 1 April) but I have had to meet criticism that the New London Synagogue was the 'Jacobs Synagogue', formed by friends who were warm in my support but with no ideas of its own. All of us at the New London tried hard to give the lie to this by placing the emphasis on the theory by which we stood, not on the personalities who tried to give expression to it.

The New London Synagogue became affiliated to the Conservative body, the World Council of Synagogues. In July 1968, we were hosts to the Seventh Annual Convention of the World Council at which the key address was given by Professor Louis Finkelstein, whose invitation to me to come to the Jewish Theological Seminary, of which he was Chancellor, had started the whole affair. Louis Finkelstein, author of *The Pharisees* and other books, was a world-renowned scholar and thinker and a leader of the Conservative Movement in the USA. He was a strictly observant Jew, like Professors Abraham Joshua Heschel and Saul Liebermann and other teachers at the Seminary. Leaders of the Conservative Movement from the days of Schechter and Louis Ginzberg saw no incompatibility between the acceptance of the findings of critical scholarship and complete loyalty to the Halakhic process.

Our hosting the Convention was the occasion for a typical outburst by the right-wing Agudat Israel paper, *The Jewish Tribune*. This paper had regularly commented on the Jacobs Affair, alternately dismissing me and my supporters as of no significance and seeing us as a great threat to Judaism. The paper seems to have been obsessed with the notion that I was an innocent who was being manipulated by the *Jewish Chronicle*, particularly by its editor, William Frankel, for the purpose of allowing Conservative Judaism to take over Anglo-Jewry. That the New London Synagogue should host the Conservative Convention enabled the *Tribune* to say, 'We told you so.'

The issue of the paper which appeared just after the Convention (10 July 1968) had an editorial with the heading (with double exclamation marks), 'Conservatives, Out!!' The editorial read:

The New London Synagogue and its minister, Dr Louis Jacobs have at last come out of their shell. If there was ever any doubt – and there was extremely little – as to Dr Jacobs' ultimate intentions within the Anglo-Jewish community, he has now declared his colours by acting as host to the World Council of Synagogues, a 'Conservative' organisation which held its Conference in London this week. Indeed, if there was ever any doubt – and here again there was extremely little – as to the wisdom of Dr Brodie, during his tenure of office as Chief Rabbi, to veto Dr Jacobs' appointment as Principal of a College which trains Orthodox ministers, his action is now fully vindicated.

By giving the so-called Conservatives a foothold in Britain, Dr Jacobs has ensured that his name will for ever rank in the annals of Anglo-Jewry among those who have helped to destroy Torah Judaism.

198

THE NEW LONDON SYNAGOGUE

Conservative Judaism is as alien and repugnant to orthodox Judaism as is that expounded by the Liberal and
Reform Movements. It is an American export commodity
which is aimed at bluffing the public into believing that its
contents are genuine. At best it is a religion of convenience
and at worst it is a cult calculated to impress the weak, the
timid and those who seek to run away from themselves and
their past.

Despite the persuasive efforts of the *Jewish Chronicle*
which has championed the cause of the Conservatives for
some years, Anglo-Jewry will not be tempted by this *Ersatz
Religion*. It will uphold and strengthen traditional Judaism
and will treat with contempt the efforts of those who are
out to destroy the community's traditional spiritual make-
up and organisational structure.

Like many an attack on the New London Synagogue for sup-
posedly introducing a new and alien philosophy of Judaism onto
the Anglo-Jewish scene, this Editorial conveniently overlooks
the facts: that 'progressive conservatism' *is* the religious position
of the United Synagogue, as outlined in its Constitution; that
historical scholarship of the highest order had been practised
at Jews' College; and that Chief Rabbi Brodie's predecessor,
Dr Hertz, was the first graduate of the Jewish Theological
Seminary, the College for the training of Conservative rabbis.
Time and again we found ourselves having to defend ourselves against this charge, that we had simply adopted American
ways, essentially foreign to the Anglo-Jewish community. It
made it more difficult that most of us were, indeed, wary of
throwing in our lot entirely with a Movement, no matter how
close we were to it in our thinking, that might compromise our
ability to develop in our own way. We had not struggled for
independence only to surrender it to toe even a more congenial
party line. So we did host more than one Convention of the
World Council and were affiliated to that body; I did become a
member of the Conservative rabbinic organisation in the USA,
the Rabbinical Assembly; but we avoided using the actual name
'Conservative' for our synagogue because of its American con-
notations. When the Conservative Movement in Israel used the

Hebrew term 'Masorti' we were easier with this, but the subject remained a problematic one.

The New London Synagogue continued to prosper, its membership growing week by week. It would be futile to speculate on the motives of all who joined the new congregation but I do not delude myself that many became members solely because they agreed with my theological views. There were, however, a few members, of whom Lou Mintz was the most vociferous, as he was the most encouraging, who urged the formation of a Movement, preferably a branch of the Conservative Movement in the USA. Many of us were more interested in tending our own garden rather than in empire-building and for good reasons. We had not tasted the sweet fruits of independence to surrender it, as we would have had to do to some extent had we pursued the wider aim. Also, the United Synagogue owned the very buildings of its synagogues in London and very few sympathisers could be found ready to build again right from the beginning as the members of the New West End Synagogue had done. In the provinces, too, the constitution of the Orthodox Synagogues generally included a clause to the effect that the Chief Rabbi was the sole religious authority. Even to those who thought it important, theology was not sufficiently powerful a force to bring about a change in a synagogue's constitution.

Furthermore, Anglo-Jewry already had too many religious divisions – Orthodox, Ultra-Orthodox, Reform and Liberal – to warrant yet another grouping appearing on the scene. As for a Conservative Movement in Anglo-Jewry, while we did not wish to hide our very close connection with the theory of that Movement in the USA, as I have said earlier in this book, and while I had become a member of the Rabbinical Assembly and the New London Synagogue a member of the World Council of Synagogues, we felt that to import the patterns of what was after all an American phenomenon into the very different climate of Anglo-Jewry would have been less than authentic, particularly since we had claimed that traditional Anglo-Jewish Orthodoxy had been 'Conservative' all along and we wished to fight from within. I cannot pretend, however, that our attitude did not disappoint those in the community who were looking for a lead.

Looking back, I am prepared to say that *perhaps* Lou Mintz was right and we were wrong.

For all that, efforts were made to enlist the support of the provincial congregations, but without success. I recall particularly the efforts of the Garnethill Synagogue in Glasgow to join with us. The Executive, Council and Minister (The Rev. Dr I.K. Cosgrove) of Garnethill were determined to become independent of the Chief Rabbinate so that they could be organised together with the New London in a loose body with the same aims. David Franklin and I flew to Glasgow one Sunday to discuss the project with the Executive and Council of Garnethill, all of whom were very enthusiastic. We were met at the airport by Sheriff Lionel Daiches and Dr Cosgrove. After tea at Sheriff Daiches' home, off we went in his car to the home of the President of the synagogue where the meeting was to be held. Unfortunately Dr Cosgrove, used to visiting the home of the former President of the synagogue, directed us there without thinking. It so happened that the new President had not thought fit to invite the former President to the meeting. When, shamefacedly, Dr Cosgrove had to explain what he was doing visiting the home of the former President with me and David Franklin in tow, the secret was out, and the former President, piqued at not being in on the project, became a determined foe to it, canvassing strong opposition. At the special Annual General Meeting of the Garnethill Synagogue called for the purpose, the discussion went on into the morning hours, and when a vote was taken, although a majority of members voted in favour of disaffiliation from the Chief Rabbinate and affiliation with us, the proposal did not quite manage to obtain the two-thirds majority required for a change in the constitution. A best-laid plan had thus come to naught.

Another failure was at the Singer's Hill Synagogue in Birmingham. The Executive and Council were solidly with us in theory; however, they had heard that Rabbi Dr Louis Rabinowitz, a candidate for the position of Chief Rabbi, then vacant, would be appointed, and they wished to support this tolerant Rabbi in what would be a severe struggle with the right wing. By this time we were so thoroughly disillusioned by our abortive attempts at creating a Movement that we decided to let the matter rest, at least for the time being, arguing that it was evident that our most promising role was to help create a mood in Anglo-Jewry cutting across the usual divisions.

Though the New London Synagogue decided to go its own way it was never parochial or sectarian. Our members were active in the Jewish Welfare Board and in all the usual phil-anthropical organisations; we had our representatives on the Board of Deputies; we founded the New London Housing Trust to help provide accommodation for the homeless in the Borough of Hackney, and, like other synagogues, we did our share for the cause of Soviet Jewry. Under the able leadership of Mr David Gestetner, our JIA Committee raised huge sums for Israel. On Tisha Be-Av our special service to commemorate the Holocaust is now attended by scores of people from all over London, as is our service on Purim when Mr George Rothschild, our Cantor, intones the Megillah in his own inimitable way. Our Adult Education programme attracts audiences from every section of Metropolitan Jewry. Dr M. Friedlander, an extremely able edu-cationalist, conducted a class on Tuesdays in modern Hebrew, and on Thursdays a course in the dynamic periods of Jewish history. My Talmud class on Monday evenings is attended by many who are interested in this branch of Jewish learning. At this class we generally read a page of the Talmud each week. David Gestetner, through his firm, supplies us with photocopies of the pages for all participants, in the margin of which they can make notes to keep for further study. I have noticed that generally at the opening Talmud class of the season, a visitor, new to the class but coming in response to the advertisement in the *Jewish Chronicle*, will ask how all these complicated, purely academic discussions are relevant to Jewish life. What such a visitor expects is to be told how to be a good Jew, how to lead a good Jewish life. I have never been particularly good at telling people how to be good and have to point out that, in any event, the point of the exercise is the study of the Torah for its own sake, not only as a pointer to the leading of the good life but itself the living of the good life as understood by Judaism.

Soon after the New London Synagogue had been established it was decided to have a Chairman, elected by the Executive, to preside over its affairs. We have been fortunate in our Chairmen

THE NEW LONDON SYNAGOGUE

who managed to guide the synagogue in its quest and, when it was attacked, to defend it with skill and confidence but without aggressiveness. The first chairman was Mr Bernard Spears. He was followed in office by Mr Sam Goldman, who was followed by Mr Alec Jacob. Mr Jacob was followed by Mr David Cohen, and he by Judge Alan Lipfriend. The present chairman is Mr Hans Bud.

13

THE NEW NORTH LONDON SYNAGOGUE

An offshoot of the New London Synagogue, the New North London Synagogue, was founded in 1974 by my son Ivor and Mr Michael Rose, a sympathiser with our aims from the beginning, together with a number of other young or youngish people, most of them married with small children.

Shortly after the inaugural meeting, the following statement of objectives and first priorities was issued, under the heading 'New Highgate and North London Synagogue' (this was the original name because the first site was intended to be in Highgate):

> Our Synagogue was founded at a meeting in Highgate on Sunday 3 November 1974, when a group of young families resolved 'to constitute an independent congregation for the advancement and promotion of the practice and teaching of traditional Judaism under the name THE NEW HIGHGATE & NORTH LONDON SYNAGOGUE, in the tradition of the New London Synagogue'. A Deed of Trust was approved and the first Management Committee was appointed, consisting of Ivor Jacobs and Michael Rose (Joint Chairmen), Ralph Selig (Treasurer), Alan Orelle (Secretary) and Simon Kester.
>
> Our objectives are to create a synagogue which will be a real community, where traditional Judaism is taught and practised in a way which is intellectually honest and satisfying to its members; which is independent of outside control; and which will in due course provide all communal necessities including education, study groups, communal welfare, marriages and a burial scheme. The ideal eventual size of the congregation is regarded as being

between 300 and 400 members so that it is financially viable but not so large as to run the risk of becoming impersonal.

Our theology is based on the teachings of Rabbi Dr Louis Jacobs. Essentially this means that we regard Judaism as dynamic rather than static and the Mitzvot are valid to us, not because we believe that they were dictated at a certain point of time, but because they are founded in Israel's response to God in history. The effect of this is to make the discovery of the whole range of Jewish thought and practice an exciting quest, rather than a burdensome routine.

Although we regard ourselves as a child of the New London Synagogue this venture began with a group of individuals and is not being promoted by the New London. We have been independently constituted and our aim is, eventually, to be completely viable and self-sufficient, to grow up into a flourishing and worthy partner of our parent Synagogue. Our members will be able to subscribe to the New London's burial scheme and all the facilities of the New London Synagogue will be open to our members so long as we are not able to provide them ourselves.

Within the Anglo-Jewish Community our function is to offer a third choice, traditional Judaism which does not involve acceptance of untenable ideas. We will do our best to avoid controversy and, if we are criticised, we will reply with logic and vigour but without rancour. Our long term aim is to build a bridge within the community, and not to create another division.

Our first priority is to purchase a house which can be used as a small community centre, combining a Synagogue with accommodation for a Minister. We will meanwhile make enquiries with a view to finding a suitable Minister and in the interim period services will be conducted by our members, and will be held in temporary premises – either a hall, if a suitable one can be found, or in our own homes.

We attach the greatest importance to education and an education committee has been formed with a view to starting classes for children in the 4 to 8 range as soon as possible.

A study group has been arranged, and will meet regularly. We also have an active Ladies' Committee, and the first steps have been taken to set up a group for young people in the 13 to 16 age range.

An initial entrance fee of £5 per family is charged for membership. Husbands and wives will count as separate members and will have one vote each at General Meetings. A decision regarding the rate of half-yearly subscriptions will be taken within the next few months, and a constitution will be drafted and presented for discussion before the first Annual General Meeting, to be held in the summer of 1975.

IVOR JACOBS   MICHAEL ROSE
88 Willifield Way,   Heath Winds,
London NW11   Merton Lane,
                               London N6.

This carefully worded document, amounting to a manifesto, sets out the full programme for the new congregation, a programme that was realised in practically all its details.

The first target of our 'daughter congregation' was to have a nucleus of 50 families by the end of the year, a target they reached with ease. At first the members of the new congregation met in a variety of church and school halls, but they eventually found a suitable site with a degree of permanence in Finchley. This, the Manor House, had been a convent school with magnificent grounds. The purchase of the whole site would have been quite beyond the financial capacity of the budding congregation, which in any case had no need for the huge house and grounds. Consequently, a Consortium was formed consisting of the New North London Synagogue, the Leo Baeck College and the Reform Synagogues of Great Britain (RSGB). Leo Baeck college has been housed ever since at Manor House (now called the Sternberg Centre, in gratitude for the munificence of Sir Sigmund Sternberg in helping to finance the project). The RSGB administration is now also carried out from this centre. The New North London owns the previous convent chapel, which it has transformed into a beautiful small synagogue, with an adjacent large room and kitchen. The facilities of the Sternberg Centre are also available to the congregation.

The New North London had neither Rabbi nor Chazan, but Mr Leslie Lyndon, a founder-member, gifted with a pleasant voice, had studied Chazanut, and he served as Chazan to the congregation in a voluntary capacity. He was later joined by Mr Ronnie Cohen and Mr Henry Newman and a number of other congregants able to lead the services. For the time being I served as rabbi of the congregation with regard to ritual questions and the like. Later, Mr Jonathan Wittenberg, a student for the Rabbinate at Leo Baeck College, served as Student Rabbi to the new congregation. (Jonathan's father had been a warden of the New London Synagogue and Jonathan had had his Bar Mitzvah there.) Sermons were delivered by the members of the synagogue. Although affiliated to the New London Synagogue, the New North London congregation felt itself free to be innovative. The services were completely traditional but while there was no actual mixed seating there was no *mehitzah* (partition) between the men's section and the women's. Women as well as men gave sermons, served on the Board of Management (Susy Stone later became co-chairman of the congregation) and were counted in the *minyan*. Although the synagogue functioned well, the reading of the Torah at first left much to be desired. Michael Rose, Ivor and some others did their best but it soon became evident that a skilful reader had to be hired. A learned young man from outside the congregation was prevailed upon to take on the job but it was not long before some local rabbis brought pressure on him to desist. Eventually the problem was solved when members became more proficient at reading the Torah and when Jonathan Wittenberg helped out.

Thus in ten years, the New North London managed to achieve its target of 300 families, possess a permanent home, engage in the various educational activities referred to and become a fully established, independent congregation. It was particularly gratifying to me that the document drawn up by Michael Rose and Ivor with the full approval of the other founder-members placed the emphasis on the theological issues. From time to time, both at the New London and at the New North London, it became evident that some people were joining not so much because of the affinity they felt with these congregations but because of their dissatisfaction with the United Synagogue or with Reform or Liberal congregations. Such negative reasons for joining are, perhaps, also good reasons but are basically inadequate. According to the saying attributed to the Kotzker Rebbe, 'If I am I because you are you and you are you because I am I, then I am not I and you are not you. But if I am I because I am I and you are you because you are you, then I am I and you are you.' All the more welcoming was this original statement of aims. Neither the New London nor the New North London has been quite so idealistic and tolerant all the time, but both congregations have tried to see themselves as furthering worthy ideas and fighting for their principles. In 1987 Jonathan Wittenberg was appointed full-time Rabbi of the new North London Synagogue.

The example of the New North London certainly encouraged many thinking members of the Anglo-Jewish Community to explore the possibility of having a closer association with the New London Synagogue or, at least, with the ideas for which it stood. The difficulty still remained of establishing synagogues of our stamp, like the New North London, but in 1980 the Masorti Movement was founded with the aim of attracting interested individuals who would work for the non-fundamentalist approach to tradition while remaining with their own synagogue, be it Orthodox or Reform. The name Masorti (meaning 'traditional') is the name for Conservative Judaism in the State of Israel, where the pattern of life obviously differs from that in the USA and requires Conservative Judaism to have a different slant. It was thought preferable to use the Israeli term rather than the American since the pattern of Jewish life in this country also differs from that of the USA. It differs from the pattern of life in Israel as well, but we did not want to press this too much in the direction of further fragmentation. I was elected President of the Masorti Association and Mr Ashe Lincoln, QC, served as Chairman. Mrs Jacqueline Chernett, indefatigable in pursuit of its aims, became the Director of the Association.

A further development took place in 1984 when the Edgware Conservative Synagogue was founded (with Jackie Chernett as Chairperson) and soon after all three synagogues joined to form the body we called the Masorti Assembly of Synagogues. It is a loose organisation in that each constituent synagogue preserves resolutely its own independence and autonomy. For instance, on the question of women's participation in the service, the New London Synagogue is the most traditional, with separate seating; the New North London, as noted above, also has separate seating but without a *mehitzah*, and women deliver sermons; while the Edgware Conservative Synagogue has mixed seating and women are called up to the reading of the Torah. There is a tacit understanding that the patterns adopted by any one synagogue belonging to the Assembly do not commit the other members to that pattern. At the time of writing, two further Masorti congregations have been established and now belong to the Assembly – one in Ilford and one in South London.

One of the differences between the New London Synagogue and its 'daughter congregation', the New North London, was that the former began as an offshoot of the New West End Synagogue, the members of which had decided to make their own choice of minister. The essential principle at stake was, for them, the question of independence and freedom from outside control. The theological issues were no doubt of interest to some but they were not in the forefront of the struggle. The average member of the New London Synagogue had as little need to ask himself what he stood for theologically as he had while still belonging to the United Synagogue. It was quite otherwise with the newcomer on the scene, the New North London, the members of which had, in the main, to make a conscious decision to join a new congregation, a decision which was bound to be based on attitudes towards theological questions. We saw above how the first co-chairmen tried to provide a programme for the new congregation and proper directives for its future. The attempt to draw up such directives was made more than once at the New North London. Here, for instance, is a statement of Michael Rose and Leslie Lyndon, co-chairmen of

the New North London in 1975. (The statement was published
in the Newsletter of the congregation, No.4, dated 21 April
1975). I quote parts of this equally challenging and perceptive
statement:

> Jews today tend to identify their religious standpoint by
> reference to 'right' and 'left', the yardstick being how much
> one does or does not do, how far one is officially permitted
> to ignore Jewish observance.
>
> Our congregation does not fit these categories. We are
> not trying to get away from the Jewish tradition, on the
> contrary it is the force which draws us together. For us,
> the conflict between Orthodoxy and Reform belongs to
> the past; our approach, as Franz Rosenzweig once said, is
> 'from the periphery to the centre'.
>
> Our point of departure is an attachment to traditional
> Judaism, based on an appreciation of the values it embodies
> and the determination to live by it and hand it on to our
> children. But we do not begin with an 'a priori' set of
> demands as to the degree of observance we expect from
> our members. We wish to create an atmosphere in which,
> against the background of a fully observant congregational
> life, people will feel free to discover for themselves which
> aspects of Judaism give relevance to their own lives. There
> is the famous quote – again from Rosenzweig – who when
> asked whether he laid Tefillin, replied, 'Not yet.'

It was stimulating and encouraging to the members of the
New London Synagogue to see how the 'offspring' of their
congregation was mapping out its own way yet was inspired by
the ideals and ideas of the parent synagogue.

14

THE JACOBS AFFAIR,
STAGE III

The only firework in the third stage of my quarrel with the
London Beth Din turned out to be something of a damp squib.

Once the New London Synagogue had been established it
became necessary to consider what we were to do about those
matters which, in Jewish Law, require a Beth Din. I was on my
own, whereas a Beth Din had to be composed of three rabbis
at least. We had no desire, in fact, to set up a rival Beth Din,
even if we could have done so. There was enough 'divisiveness'
(a favourite expression of Chief Rabbi Brodie) already in the
Anglo-Jewish community and we did not wish to add to it. In
matters of *kashrut* supervision and the drawing up and delivery
of a *get* (this latter has only been required on two occasions)
we could leave things in the capable hands of the London
Beth Din. But the adjective 'capable' could by no stretch of
the imagination be applied to the way in which the London
Beth Din handled conversions. The Beth Din was so strict in
accepting applicants for conversion that very few indeed could
meet the excessive demands made on them. When, for instance,
a Jewish couple adopted a baby whose mother was not Jewish,
although according to the *din* the infant can be converted by a
Beth Din, the adopted parents, Jewish though they were, had to
satisfy the London Beth Din that they were prepared to lead a
fully observant life, to the extent of never switching lights on and
off on the Sabbath and obeying other standards of observance
not required of members of the United Synagogue. In the case
of a young man or woman willing to be converted the person
concerned had to undergo a very rigorous course of training,
including a stay for half a year, at least, in a strictly observant
home in Stamford Hill or Golders Green. No Beth Din elsewhere
in the world imposed so many obstacles to conversion. The

result was that in this country, no conversions, over which the London Beth Din had sole authority, could take place in the Orthodox community without a trial period extending, usually, for five to seven years, if they took place at all.

It was impossible for me to subject the families of our congregants to these ridiculous procedures, unknown, as I have said, elsewhere in the Jewish world and unknown in Anglo-Jewry until the fairly recent ascendancy of the right wing. Although ideally a Beth Din of three rabbis should be convened to supervise a conversion, the *din* allows the procedures to be carried out by three persons, only one of whom need be a rabbi (this because only a qualified rabbi would know the procedures to be followed). On the comparatively rare occasions when conversions were required to take place at the New London Synagogue (either for purposes of marriage or because a couple wished to adopt a child) I, consequently, set up a Beth Din for the purpose, composed of two laymen in the congregation and myself, and all the procedures were followed required by the *din*. The main procedures were circumcision for a male and immersion in a *mikveh* (ritual bath) for both males and females. The trouble was, at first, that we had no access to a *mikveh* – no *mikveh* in London was available to us for conversions. By a sheer stroke of good fortune we did manage to obtain access to a *mikveh* outside London and, although this meant a day spent out of town for every conversion, all went well without fuss and to everyone's satisfaction.

Complications set in when an increasing number of prospective converts, thoroughly browned off at the rebuffs they had suffered at the hands of the London Beth Din, and unwilling to be converted by Reform or Liberal rabbis, began to approach me to arrange for a conversion to be done 'according to the *din*'. My attitude was that while I did have an obligation to the families of my own congregants, I had no such obligation to the members of the United Synagogue. This was the responsibility of the Chief Rabbi and the London Beth Din. Nevertheless, on occasion, where the circumstances were too heart-rending to be ignored, I did arrange conversions on behalf of people who were not members of my synagogue. Whenever I did this I felt obliged to point out that while everything was done according to the *din* I could give no guarantee that the conversion would be recognised by the London Beth Din.

Among the instances where I felt obliged to help, after an incredible rejection by the London Beth Din, two in particular stand out in my memory. A girl whose natural mother was not Jewish was adopted as an infant by a Jewish couple, who brought her up as their own daughter without informing her that she was adopted and technically not Jewish (since she had not been taken to the *mikveh*). When the girl grew up and discovered that she was not their natural daughter and would have a problem were she to marry a Jewish boy, she went to live in Israel where she was formally converted by none other than Rabbi Ovadiah Yosef, later the Sephardi Chief Rabbi of Israel and a renowned authority on Jewish law. The young woman returned to this country, fell in love with a Jewish young man and, armed with the famous Rabbi's conversion certificate, anticipated no problems. She was mistaken. The Beth Din did not actually say that they did not recognise Rabbi Yosef's conversion. How could they? What they did say was that they only allowed those converts who had been converted by them to be married in the United Synagogue. The parents and the young couple came to me in desperation, begging me to marry them at the New London Synagogue. I could not see any reason for refusing to do so.

The other case was even more bizarre. Again this concerned a Jewish couple who had adopted a little boy. There was some uncertainty whether the boy's natural mother was Jewish. The boy attended the Jewish Youth Study Group, eventually becoming so *frum* that he kept his head covered with a *yarmulka* all the time and did not carry a handkerchief when going out on the Sabbath. When he was about to marry an equally observant Jewish girl, the Beth Din declared that not only did the young man require conversion (here they were in the right since the Jewishness of the boy's natural mother had not been definitely established) but insisted on treating him as if he were an original applicant for conversion, informing him that he had to prove his sincerity by leaving his home to live in one of their 'safe houses'. They were unable to inform him when his conversion would take place, to say nothing of when the couple could be married. Any reasonable Beth Din would have regularised the position without further ado by having the young man immerse himself in the *mikveh*; it could all have been done to everyone's satisfaction in half-an-hour. At this stage, I was approached by Mr Moshe Davis, Chief Rabbi Jakobovits's Secretary, putting the case to me and requesting my help. I replied that I would do so provided he came in with me to form the ad hoc Beth Din required for the conversion. Mr Davis said that this was impossible since he could not be seen as openly defying the London Beth Din. I went along with the conversion, on purely humanitarian grounds, and Moshe Davis did attend the marriage ceremony at the New London Synagogue and also recited the *sheva berakhot* at the festive meal. Soon after, Dayan Swift, in his capacity of official zealot, attacked me from the pulpit of the Golders Green Synagogue for performing unauthorised conversions, as if the Chief Rabbi had to 'authorise' conversions done under the aegis of the New London and as if the Chief Rabbi, through his Secretary Moshe Davis, had not taken any part in the affair. I could not believe that Moshe Davis had acted entirely off his own bat without consulting the Chief Rabbi, off the record, at least.

After this attack, the Chairman of the Synagogue, Mr Sam Goldman, and I met with the Chief Rabbi at his home. I protested that it was not my responsibility but his to deal with conversions in the general community, and that I was tired of undertaking conversions that should have been undertaken by his Beth Din if they had any human feeling. The Chief Rabbi was sympathetic but implied that his hands were tied and he could do nothing about it.

Worse was to follow. The London Beth Din began what I can only describe as a smear campaign, hinting that if people were married at the New London Synagogue questions would be raised when their children wished to be married. What this really meant was that questions would be raised as to whether or not there was any legal impediment to the marriage, e.g. whether the bride was Jewish or whether she had been married before and had not received a *get* from her former husband. Of course, if such an investigation were carried out it would be established that all was above board. But the Beth Din allowed the word to get around that it meant there was a question mark against every marriage performed under the aegis of the New London Synagogue. Dayan Swift, I learned, had approached the mother of a young man married at the New London Synagogue asking her to encourage her son to be married again at the headquarters of the United Synagogue at Woburn House.

My congregants at the New London were themselves beginning to ask questions and I had no recourse but to write an article in *Forum*, the journal of the New London Synagogue, explaining the position. I wrote in this article:

The following statement on the question of personal status in Jewish law will, I hope, clear up some of the difficulties expressed by our congregants and others in the Anglo-Jewish community . . .

In Jewish law a marriage between two persons both of whom profess the Jewish faith is valid provided there is no legal impediment. A legal impediment in this context means where the union is proscribed by the list of forbidden unions in Leviticus; where, for instance, a previous marriage had not been dissolved by a *get* or where there is close affinity or consanguinity between the man and the woman. The marriage is effected by the delivery of the ring, in the presence of two witnesses, attended by the declaration, 'Be thou betrothed unto me by this ring according to the law of Moses and of Israel.' The special order of service is, of course, demanded by the tradition – the chuppah and kiddushin benedictions – but their absence has no effect on the validity of the marriage . . .

It follows that, provided there is no legal impediment, it is impossible to invalidate a marriage solely on the ground that it took place in a Liberal or Reform synagogue. This has been acknowledged more than once by the Chief Rabbi, yet one hears all too frequently snide remarks to the effect that marriages performed outside the aegis of the United Synagogue or similar Orthodox bodies are questionable . . .

The further point must be made that normally when people ask whether this or that marriage is valid they mean:

215

will the children of the marriage be kosher in Jewish law, will they be allowed to marry in an Orthodox synagogue? But here, again, there is considerable confusion. The status of the child is only affected where the mother is not Jewish or where there is a legal impediment of the kind mentioned above.

Where no such impediment is present the children are kosher in any event since, in Jewish law, a child born out of wedlock (i.e. where no marriage at all took place) is perfectly kosher and may marry in an Orthodox synagogue.

Where there is a legal impediment, the child is not kosher to marry in an Orthodox synagogue but that is because of the impediment, not because there was no marriage. The only meaning that can be given to the question of whether or not a marriage is valid is not in connection with the children, but whether, according to Jewish law, the couple may now live together as man and wife and, as we have seen, provided there has been the delivery of the ring in the presence of two witnesses with formal declaration of marriage, there is no question the marriage is valid for this purpose. Their children will be kosher in any event, even if they were not married at all, and they may live together as husband and wife because they *are* husband and wife.

To apply all this to marriages at the New London Synagogue: since we do not perform any marriages where there is a legal impediment, the status of the children is unaffected in any event. The children of all our marriages are perfectly kosher. They can be married in the most Orthodox of synagogues. If any of our congregants, having been reassured about the question of the kashrut of the children, are still worried about whether, having been married in our synagogue, their marriage is valid for the purpose of them living together as husband and wife, they need not have the slightest fear; all is perfectly kosher. Whether, to introduce the personal note, which, unfortunately I have to, I am *persona non grata* to some Orthodox Rabbis, is irrelevant. Couples married in the New London Synagogue are not married by me (the concept of a Rabbi 'marrying' a couple has no meaning in Jewish law; the Rabbi is not a Christian priest; indeed, he is not a priest at all). They are married by the fact that the marriage ceremonies (i.e. the delivery of the ring in the presence of witnesses with the formal declaration) have been carried out in the proper manner.

I continued, in this vein, with the question of conversion and adoption and concluded:

> To sum up. The procedures of the New London Synagogue in matters of personal status are in full accordance with traditional Jewish law. We cannot claim that we have an especially humane attitude because that would imply that the law is not itself humane. Nor can we claim that we are 'modern' in our interpretation since the situation we have described is that which is inherent in the law itself. This defence of our procedures would not be required at all were it not that Orthodox officialdom is now determined to act in these matters in a manner far in excess of other Orthodox Rabbis and with an attitude beside which the Neturei Karta are a model of tolerance and sobriety.

The *Jewish Chronicle* (16 September 1983) carried a report of my statement under the lurid headline 'Worse than Neturei Karta' and the Beth Din had to reply.

There thus began another controversy, this time in matters not of theory but of practice. I like to think that even if I had adopted a fundamentalist approach I would still have opposed what I considered to be the inhuman attitude of the Beth Din in the matter of conversion.

A word should be said about the history of the London Beth Din's attitude, totally different from the tolerant attitude typical of the Anglo-Jewish rabbinate in the early decades of this century. In the book *Conversions to Judaism*, published in the USA, the editor notes that the London Beth Din was far stricter and far more reluctant to accept converts than any other Beth Din in the world. His explanation is that when Oliver Cromwell was approached by Manasseh ben Israel to allow the Jews to be re-admitted to England, Cromwell, according to this reading, was willing to re-admit the Jews but had qualms that if the Jews did come here they would try to convert English Christians to Judaism. Cromwell, therefore, so this story goes, extracted a solemn promise from Manasseh that when the Jews were re-admitted they would not engage in conversionist activities. The writer concludes that the members of the London Beth Din, staunch English gentlemen that they are, keep the promise made to Cromwell and refuse to accept converts unless there are quite exceptional circumstances.

This is nonsense. The fact is that until Dayan Abramsky was appointed Head of the London Beth Din, that body was as tolerant as any other. Dayan Abramsky, often at loggerheads with Chief Rabbi Hertz, brought all the influence of his strong personality to bear on his colleagues at the Beth Din, who stood in awe of him and were overawed by his erudition. It was Dayan Abramsky, not Oliver Cromwell, who was responsible for the attitude of the Beth Din in this and in other matters. For instance, hindquarter meat had been sold by butchers under the jurisdiction of the Beth Din, but Dayan Abramsky caused it to be banned on the grounds that there were too few meat 'porgers' and that those who did exist could not be relied on to do the job properly.

The London Beth Din, at the time I wrote my piece in the New London *Forum*, was composed of Dayanim Kaplan, Lerner and Berger. Dayanim Kaplan and Lerner were mild scholars who might have taken no action were it not for Dayan Berger, a young zealot upon whom the mantle of Dayan Swift seems to have fallen. Dayan Lerner was, in fact, an old friend from Manchester Yeshivah days. He and I took Semichah at the same time. He was rabbi of the New Synagogue in Manchester during the time I was rabbi of the Central Synagogue and at this time we lived next door to one another. When Rabbi Lerner moved to Leeds and later to Newcastle we kept up a correspondence until the first stage of the Jacobs Affair, when he dropped me like a hot potato.

The Beth Din chose to reply indirectly through the Clerk to the Court, Mr Marcus Carr. In a typically high-handed statement to the *Jewish Chronicle* (30 September 1983) Mr Carr said:

The London Beth Din does not normally feel obliged to comment on unfounded generalisations such as those appearing in the *Jewish Chronicle* of 16 September from Dr Louis Jacobs. However, in view of the confusion that the statement may cause, I am instructed to inform the public that marriages performed by Dr Jacobs, even in cases where both parties are eligible for marriage according to Jewish law, have no more halachic validity than marriages contracted in a Register Office in civil law. Conversions under the auspices of Dr Jacobs have no validity whatsoever in Jewish law.

This statement is a masterpiece of imprecision if ever there was one. What is meant by the apparent distinction between the marriages I performed which have 'no more halachic validity than marriages contracted in a Register Office' and my conversions which have 'no validity whatsoever'? Evidently, the Beth Din did hold that our marriages have some validity (the Beth Din requires a *get* to dissolve a marriage that took place in a Register Office) while our conversions have none. It is a novel idea in law that there can be 'some validity' but not total validity. Validity in Jewish, as in civil, law is an either/or concept. A marriage can hardly be termed partially valid, just as a man cannot be partially dead.

In the same issue of the *Jewish Chronicle* it was reported that Dayan Berger had been asked by the paper to clarify Mr Carr's statement. The Dayan gave as the reason for the lack of validity of our marriages that the halachic requirement of the status of the witnesses was not being complied with in all cases, but he declined to explain what he meant by this. Just as vague was the Dayan's reply to the question whether a *get* would be needed if such a marriage were dissolved. The Dayan said, 'As for the need for a *get* on the dissolution of such a marriage, as with civil marriages, each case must be submitted to the Beth Din to be decided in the light of its particular circumstances.' What can these 'particular circumstances' be? The halakhic authorities are divided on whether a *get* is required to dissolve a civil marriage. Those who rule that a *get* is required apply the rule to every civil marriage. Those who rule that no *get* is required do not require it for any civil marriage. There are no 'particular circumstances' according to both sets of authorities. If the Dayan meant that a *get* would be required because of doubt as to which set of authorities are to be followed, he should have said that the marriages *might* be valid.

In any event, all the talk about the invalidity of our marriages was no more than an attempt to mislead the public. The man in the street, when told that a marriage is invalid, imagines this to mean that the children of the union are illegitimate since the parents had not contracted a valid marriage. But, in Jewish law, there is no such concept as the illegitimacy of children (a *mamzer* is the issue of an adulterous or incestuous union and is disbarred from marrying, although he is 'legitimate') so that wherever a couple is married (or, for that matter, even if they have not been married at all) the status of the children is in no way affected. Dayan Berger had to admit this when he replied to a question put to him by the paper on the status of the children: 'In cases where the parties were eligible to marry in Jewish law, an invalid ceremony itself does not affect the status of the children.' We now had substituted an 'invalid ceremony' for an 'invalid marriage'. What an 'invalid ceremony' can mean was again left undisclosed. If witnesses do not meet the requirements of the law it is the marriage that is invalid. What possible meaning can there be to an 'invalid ceremony'?

The *Jewish Chronicle* (now edited by Mr Geoffrey D. Paul) in the same issue carried a leader headed 'Jacobs Affair II', which observed:

> On the face of it, the problem between the Beth Din and Rabbi Jacobs is insoluble. Dr Jacobs is insistent that all marriages which take place under his auspices – and all conversions – were totally in accord with the halacha, Jewish religious law. The Beth Din is adamant that neither marriages nor conversions supervised by Dr Jacobs (the reference to 'Dr Jacobs' in the Beth Din statement is unquestionably intentional) are Jewishly valid. However the Beth Din does make the important declaration that the children of marriages between people 'eligible to marry in

Jewish law' are fully Jewish, that is, they are able to marry Orthodox Jews. The question for the layman is, then, if the children are totally acceptable to the Orthodox community, how are their parents' marriages invalid? The Beth Din will not explain. It can reasonably be asked whether it has done its duty by bringing in a verdict without publicly presenting the evidence on which this judgement was based or, alternatively, supporting the verdict with a stated case.

The leader went on to suggest that by the reference to the 'witnesses' the Beth Din was implying that I was not a valid witness because of my theological views. As to conversions, it pointed out that Israeli religious courts have permitted the conversions of many settlers on secular kibbutzim where there is not the smallest probability of any basic Jewish observances.

Dayan Swift passed away (in September 1983) while all this was going on. In a memorial address for him on 9 October, Dayan Berger took the opportunity of replying to a letter challenging his attitude – a letter written by the co-chairmen of the New North London Synagogue and published in the *Jewish Chronicle* of 7 October. The Dayan said that no amount of compassion was going to move a Dayan to condone a conversion that was patently invalid. Dayan Berger also referred to me as a 'compassion-monger', the nicest compliment I have ever been paid. A friend and congregant, writing in the *Jewish Chronicle* (4 November 1983), pointed to the marked silence of the Chief Rabbi on the matter. 'The fact that he has been so silent can only mean that he does *not* agree with the statement of the Beth Din.' In fact the Chief Rabbi preserved his silence throughout the whole row.

In the same issue of the *Jewish Chronicle*, Mr M. Milston replied to Dayan Herman (of the Federation of Synagogues' Beth Din), who had written to say that I *was* invalid as a witness:

> With reference to Dayan Herman's casting doubt on the validity of Rabbi Jacobs as a witness (incredible as it may seem), may I refer him to a source which, I am sure, he knows only too well – that of tractate Sanhedrin

24b, which states that only dice-players, usurers, pigeon-flyers or seventh-year produce traffickers are ineligible as witnesses. Admittedly, Rabbi Jacobs traffics produce, but it is on a daily basis and is not a seventh-year produce. It is Judaism.

Looking back, especially, on the conversions I arranged to be carried out, I think I can say that in almost every case I succeeded in saving people for Judaism when the attitude of the Beth Din would have driven them away. I conclude this chapter with a letter I received from a young woman whose father was Jewish but not her mother. All her relations were Jewish, she became totally dedicated to Jewish life and was a diligent worker for the cause of Israel. I did no more than the majority of rabbis (excepting the London Beth Din) would have done. We convened an ad hoc Beth Din, asked her the questions we were supposed to ask about her sincere wish to be formally converted, and then arranged for her to go to the *mikveh*. After the ceremony the young lady cried tears of joy at the privilege of being formally admitted into the ranks of the Covenant people. The next day I received the following note from her:

Dear Rabbi Jacobs,
I am writing to thank you for making it possible for me to become Jewish, and for being so supportive, and motivating throughout my conversion.
Despite the fact that I have always felt a strong commitment to my Jewish roots, I knew that I could not be considered as such, according to Jewish law. However, I now have a complete sense of identity, and can look forward to leading a proper Jewish life.
Once again, please accept my gratitude which I feel I cannot express in writing.
With my deepest sincere thanks,

X Y.

15

FILMS, RADIO AND TELEVISION

Largely because of the controversy in which I had become involved, I began to receive invitations to appear on television. The new channel, BBC 2, began broadcasting in 1964 during the very week when Dr Brodie made his statement to the assembled rabbis and ministers. On the next day, a television crew came to my home, cameras and all, and recorded an interview with me which was shown the next evening as a feature of the new channel. I tried to be as circumspect as possible, but it was difficult. If I remember correctly, the interviewer was Cliff Michelmore and he let me down lightly. On the evening when the interview was to be broadcast I had been addressing a meeting in Hampstead Garden Suburb on my views. We left the meeting and, with a sense of euphoria, went to a nearby house to watch the interview, thinking it fortuitous that the new channel should have come on the air just at this time and looking forward to a huge rating. We learned afterwards that a freak blackout had coincided with the programme, so that while a few of us did see it, many people in London could only look at blank screens. Evidently, the Chief Rabbi still had some pull 'up there'.

This was followed not long afterwards by an interview on ITV with Bernard Levin. Levin was doing a well-advertised series of half-hour interviews with mavericks from various walks of life, to which class he evidently thought I belonged. Another inter-viewee – I fancy that Levin, in his concern for proper English usage, would be appalled at the term – was Enoch Powell, discussing politics. I had already been bracketed by the press with the Bishop of Woolwich, and here I was teamed, however loosely, with another man whose views I did not share at all. But such is the price to be paid for being anti-establishment.

Levin was very fair and tolerant. Among other things, he asked me how my acceptance of Biblical Criticism could be squared with my observance of the dietary laws. Although Levin is Jewish, he did not allow this fact to intrude, but I did sense that he was not entirely objective and uninvolved in asking a question that he had perhaps thought about himself at some stage. I gave my usual reply, that whatever the origin of the dietary laws – that was a matter to be decided by scholarly investigation – they had provided the Jew for over two millenia with a vocabulary of worship and were instruments for the attainment of holiness in daily living. Levin, in turn, rather gently responded, 'It all depends on what you mean by holiness.'

Later on I took part in a series of programmes on prayer in the 'Religions of Mankind' series run by ITV. By this time I had become used to complete strangers stopping me in the street to say, 'I saw you on television last night.' They do so no more. *Sic transit gloria mundi.*

In 1984 I appeared in another programme on ITV, part of the series on spirituality in world religions. The interviewer was Karen Armstrong who had just completed a hugely successful TV series on the life of St Paul. So far as my television appearances were concerned I seemed to be keeping up with the *goyim.* At the time of the controversy, an Osbert Lancaster cartoon depicted the Archbishop of Canterbury saying to the Chief Rabbi, 'You must be glad that the Bishop of Woolwich is a *goy!*'

Among the radio programmes in which I participated was one of my 'spiritual quest' for the Open University. They paid very well and I still receive royalties each time the talk is broadcast. Like many other rabbis, I have been interviewed not infrequently on Michael Freedland's programme 'You don't have to be Jewish'. I was also one of the advisers for the TV programme 'The Long Search'. I advised the producers, among whom was Michael Feuerstein, to get away from the stereotyped images of a service in the synagogue, *kiddush* in the home and a Bar Mitzvah in order to concentrate more on Jewish intellectual life. They took my advice and had some excellent footage on life in an Israeli Yeshivah, with students hammering away at one another in fierce Talmudic debate. My exposure in my youth to Hasidism, with its doctrine of self-annihilation, and to Musar, in the Gateshead Kolel, with its denigration of any attempt to seek the limelight, did not prevent me from participating in these events but did diminish my enthusiasm and enjoyment of them. I always saw Rabbi Dessler or the Hasidim in the background protesting, 'Shame on you!' When the programmes were shown at home I could hardly bear to watch them.

When the highly gifted artist, Jacques Kupferman, did a full-length portrait of me in my canonicals and it was presented by Dr Abraham Marcus, who commissioned it for the New London Synagogue, it was put up on a wall in the room where Board meetings were held. At these meetings I always took pains to sit with my back to the painting, pointing out to the Board that it was expecting too much of a rabbi always to view with equanimity the appearance of another rabbi at a meeting!

My first experience of filming was when the New London Synagogue allowed Mr John Schlesinger to film the two Bar Mitzvah scenes for his *Sunday Bloody Sunday* in the synagogue. The hero of the film is a Jewish homosexual doctor. When we read the script some of the members of the Council thought it unfitting to use a synagogue for the making of a film with such a theme. Mr Schlesinger explained that by no stretch of the imagination could it be construed that we were in any way condoning homosexual practices. The film in fact showed the misery and tragedy of what is so inappropriately called 'gay' life. Moreover, and it was this argument that won the day, if a Bar Mitzvah scene was to be shot it was surely better that it should be done where an eye could be kept on the proprieties so that the scene would present Judaism with dignity instead of the vulgarity which often attends the dramatising of such scenes.

. . We were all amazed at the care with which Schlesinger and his associates went to work. For example, he thought that a real synagogue should have stained glass windows, which the New London did not have. So Schlesinger had dummy stained glass

225

windows made for the purpose. He pressed a number of our congregants into service as 'extras', each receiving £6 a day, which they donated to charity. There were in fact two separate Bar Mitzvah scenes – one where the doctor was present at his nephew's Bar Mitzvah, the other when the doctor's memory carries him back twenty-five years to his own Bar Mitzvah at the same synagogue. Schlesinger had all the extras fitted out in two sets of clothing, one for the contemporary scene, the other for the scene of twenty-five years earlier. When the film was shown to the public, I received an irate letter from a staid matron in the community protesting that the New London Synagogue should never have agreed to help Schlesinger make the film. This was not because of the homosexual theme, which she did not refer to at all, but because of the vulgarity of the dinner scene which took place the day after the Bar Mitzvah. I replied that we had no say and nothing to do with anything that happened in that part of the film, only in the part which took place in the synagogue. Nor could I agree that the dinner scene was all that vulgar. I wrote, 'Beside the similar scene in *Goodbye Columbus* it was a model of decorum.'

My real film *début*, however, came when Barbra Streisand invited me to be a technical adviser for her film *Yentl*. I had been introduced to Streisand by Jeanne Kupferman, the writer, wife of Jacques, who had painted my portrait, and whose son had been Bar Mitzvah at the New London Synagogue. *Yentl* was based on a story by Isaac Bashevis Singer with the film script by Jack Rosenthal. My task was to go over the script with Jack Rosenthal to weed out any inaccuracies and later, when the film was being shot at the studio in Wembley, to do the same. To be frank, I told Streisand, I found the original story quite daft. Even in a *stetl* at the beginning of the century it was not such a heinous offence for a girl to study the Torah that her father would have to put up the shutters before teaching her in case someone observed the terrible sin. I also thought that it was pretty drastic for the heroine to have to disguise herself as a boy in order to study at a Yeshivah when her desire to become proficient in Jewish learning could have been satisfied by the teaching of her father. Women were undoubtedly put in their place in that time and milieu, but not to that extent.

FILMS, RADIO AND TELEVISION

Barbra retorted that the film was a work of fiction, not a documentary.

So there I sat in the studio in one of those canvas director's chairs – though it did not have my name at the back and I had no eyepiece to shade my eyes from the glare of the arc lamps in true Hollywood fashion – ready to pounce on errors. I did not find many. One, I recall, was a photograph of the Hafetz Hayim and another one of the Lubavitcher Rebbe on the wall of the rich man's house in the film. I pointed out that the Hafetz Hayim would have been a young man, not a venerable sage, at the period of the film and the Lubavitcher Rebbe an infant. Barbra had these photographs removed and two others put up in their place.

During the filming of Yentl I had an uncanny experience; pure coincidence, no doubt, but alarming at the time. The Wembley studio had been fitted out as an old-time Yeshivah, with several hundred holy books lying along the shelves. These books, though I did not know it at the time, had been lent for the filming by my friend Rabbi Dr H. Rabinovitz. A good deal of time a film is being shot is spent simply sitting around by those not actually engaged in the shooting of a particular scene. One morning, sitting in boredom in my chair, I realised that there was no cause for boredom, surrounded as I was by hundreds of Hebrew books. I took out a book at random and began to read when I noticed a letter placed within its pages addressed to Rabbi Rabinovitz beginning, 'Dear Harry', and in a handwriting that seemed oddly familiar. To my astonishment, I looked closer to find that it was a letter I myself had written fifteen years before!

Another coincidence (I refuse to believe that either of these two incidents was anything but coincidental) concerned an article in Commentary magazine on the wedding of the Belzer Rebbe in B'nei B'rak, written by Rabbi Herbert Weiner. An editorial note to the article stated that Rabbi Weiner intended to publish a book with the intriguing title 9½ Mystics. A year or two after I had read the article, I was writing about Hasidism and, remembering that there was an article on Belz in Commentary, of which magazine I had a complete run, I took down the issue containing the Weiner article and my eye fell on the editorial note. I said to Shula, 'I wonder if this book 9½

Mystics is out yet. If it is I would like to buy a copy.' Just then
the telephone rang and when I answered it a voice said, 'This
is Herb Weiner.' I had never met Herb Weiner and had never
corresponded with him and yet there he was in London on a
visit and telephoning me at almost the exact moment when I
was reading an account of his forthcoming book, a book on
mysticism at that. Many a Hasidic miracle-tale is based solely
on such sheer coincidences – at least, my Litvak background
compelled me to see them that way.

During the filming of *Yentl* I noticed with curiosity how
the light of the arc lamps was bounced off a white back-cloth
rather than pointed directly at the scene that was being shot.
This, I was informed, is a technique used by British cameramen
and produces far better effects. Next Yom Kippur I took as my
text for the Kol Nidre service the verse, 'Light is sown for the
righteous', with which the service begins. Drawing on my film
experience, I was able to suggest that the spiritual light of the
Torah has a better illuminative effect if it is introduced gradually
and indirectly rather than in an attempt to achieve too much at
once which could result in an off-putting glare. The light has
first to be *sown*, then the rich fruit will grow.

I saw that Barbra Streisand had a strong desire to get the
message across that the Jew loves the Torah. She also wished
to promote the women's liberation movement, for which the
story of a girl's success in the man's world of Torah learning
was a highly attractive theme. On one occasion she asked Jack
Rosenthal to substitute, in the script, a reference to Rashi for
one to Maimonides. 'Why?' I asked. 'Well,' she said, 'I have
discovered that Maimonides did not have too high an opinion
of women, whereas Rashi had three daughters who were learned
in the Torah'!

Ever since my Yeshivah days I had wanted to own a *stender*,
the wooden stand, rather like a lectern, on which the large copy
of the Talmud is placed during study. In the mock-Yeshivah at
the studio there were a number of these stands. After the filming
was over I was allowed to take one of them home. I found it to
be very much a Hollywoodish affair, only *looking* like a real
stender. Yet it served its purpose and I still use it as a reminder
of an interesting interruption of my normal activities.

The New London Synagogue bought a block of seats at the early showing of *Yentl* in London, the amount raised by the sale of these to members contributing towards our building fund. The members of the congregation and of my family waited eagerly to see my name in the credits. It did duly appear, towards the end of a long list, as *Dr* Louis Jacobs.

The London Beth Din would have been pleased.

16

VISITS ABROAD

Few of us are uninfluenced in later life by the experiences of our youth. Having been in contact both with members of the Musar school and with Hasidic Jews, my attitude to travel has been an ambivalent one. Hasidism, generally speaking, encourages travel to distant lands and far-off places, not only to visit the Rebbe but as a good in itself, because of its doctrine that each person has some place containing holy sparks corresponding to the holy sparks in his own soul. He is bound to journey to that place in order to rescue the holy sparks which have an affinity with his own particular soul's root; only he, and no one else, can reclaim *his* sparks. Musar, on the other hand, urges its adherents to stay put (except for the purpose of Torah study in a famous Yeshivah or at the feet of a great master) and not waste time on travel that could be spent so much more profitably in study. Possibly my experiences of Musar have given me a jaundiced view of the movement, but it has always seemed to me that the teachers of Musar frown on almost everything that makes life enjoyable, travel being no exception.

I did not come from a family of great travellers. The farthest we ever got from home when I was a child was on the annual holiday to Blackpool. I was twenty years of age when I first visited London, for the wedding of a fellow-student at the Manchester Yeshivah who had married a London girl. After I became a rabbi, however, I did make frequent journeys abroad, not only when on holiday but also and chiefly in order to undertake lecture tours and engage in similar educational activities.

Not long after I came to the New West End Synagogue, I was invited by the Paris branch of the American Jewish Committee to meet Zechariah Schuster and Georges Levitt to consider a project they wished me to do for them. This was to prepare a popular booklet on Jewish ethical values. Although I was taken to see the Eiffel Tower, the Louvre and some of the other sights, most of my time in Paris was spent in meetings and discussions around the nature of the proposed booklet. I felt rather like the Yeshivah student who said he was perplexed by the poor reputation Paris had; wherever he went in Paris, they were busy studying the Torah!

After I had been at the New London Synagogue for several years I made a ten-day speaking and teaching visit to Denmark, Norway and Sweden, arranged by the Chief Rabbi of Denmark, Rabbi Bent Melchior. Rabbi Melchior, like his father whom he succeeded as Chief Rabbi, had been a prominent member of the Association of European Rabbis. This was a body of Orthodox Rabbis and included the British Chief Rabbi and the members of the London Beth Din. At the same time, Rabbi Melchior senior was a Vice-President of the World Council of Synagogues, the Conservative organisation. None of his colleagues had dared to challenge the older Rabbi Melchior and accuse him of entertaining dual loyalties, but when the younger Rabbi Melchior succeeded his father, he was gradually elbowed out of the Association of European Rabbis because of his membership of the Conservative World Council. It was courageous of Rabbi Bent Melchior, then under fire, to have invited me, especially since a small group in his community (aided, unfortunately, by some members of the Association) had it in for him.

During this Scandinavian trip, Shula and I were given full VIP treatment. It was evident that *persona non grata* though I was to the British Orthodox establishment, the communal leaders of Copenhagen, Stockholm and Oslo were not only tolerant of my views but shared them to a large extent. I conducted a seminar at the University of Copenhagen; led a week-end study group for young people in the Danish countryside; spoke in English and Yiddish in Oslo (there had recently been an influx of Yiddish-speaking Polish Jews into the Norwegian capital), and spoke at meetings in Stockholm, the Rabbi of which city, Rabbi Morton Narrowe, was a prominent Conservative rabbi. It appeared that Scandinavian Jewry had the attitude towards the Jewish tradition previously typical of Anglo-Jewry, before the determined swing to the right had taken effect.

Another European visit I shall never forget was to Moscow in 1980. A number of congregants at the New London Synagogue, active in work for Soviet Jewry, organised a visit to Moscow by Shula and me, together with two others who sympathised with the plight of the refuseniks. Ostensibly we were in Moscow as tourists but our real purpose was to visit the refuseniks and conduct a number of study sessions with these brave folk. In the event, our visit coincided with the clampdown by the Soviet authorities on refusenik activities so the study groups had to be cancelled. I was able, however, to meet some of the refuseniks and bring them various books of Jewish interest. In the arbitrary way of the Soviet customs people, I was searched at the airport for drugs(!) but was allowed to bring in Hebrew books. My copies of *The Times* and the *Guardian* were confiscated. Someone suggested that this was because the customs officer wished to read these newspapers himself.

We were housed in one of the official hotels near Red Square. At each of the floors of the hotel sat a large Russian lady patiently recording the times of all our comings and goings. On one occasion, the four of us were followed by a member of the KGB. When we got out at the wrong underground station, this man followed us whilst pretending to be reading the posters outside the station. Had we known Russian we would have given him the address of the refusenik we were visiting in order to save him the bother!

On another occasion, all four of us were being shown round the Kremlin by a woman guide who spoke excellent English. We noticed that a Russian man and woman had attached themselves to our party. At first we imagined that these two were there to spy on us but soon realised that they were really there to spy on the guide. It was all very comical as well as tragic. The guide, adopting the official line, showed us proudly the treasures amassed over the centuries by the various Czars. This pride seemed more than a little odd at first, until we came to appreciate that in the Marxist philosophy historical change was inevitable but this was no reason for refusing to admire the aristocratic and capitalist past which has also followed inexorable laws. I was reminded of the remark by the Reform leader,

Samuel Holdheim, who defended his radical departures from Talmudic law by saying, 'The Talmud was right in its day and I am right in mine.' The same guide expressed her astonishment that we believed in God. Science, she protested, had exploded the idea that there is a God. 'What do you believe in?' we asked. She replied, 'We believe that the world is controlled by a huge space-machine up there which no one has ever seen.' Chesterton was right when he said it is not true that if you do not believe in God you believe in nothing. If you do not believe in God, you believe in anything.

During our Moscow visit, I had a long session with a young refusenik, Mr Ilya Essas, now in Israel. Essas had been educated in Vilna, had painfully taught himself Hebrew, and had studied Talmud with an old man who was a graduate of the famed Yeshivah of Volhozhyn. Over the years Essas had read widely books on Judaism in English, including my book *A Jewish Theology*. Essas was thoroughly familiar with my argument in the book but, as a proud fundamentalist, took vigorous exception to all I had said. So there we sat, he vehemently denouncing my heresies, and I glowing with delight that in spite of all his troubles, this brilliant young man could be concerned with theological niceties. Attack away, I felt like saying, it does my heart good.

On the Sabbath, Shula and I went to the Moscow Synagogue, housed in a splendid building, for the morning service. The young rabbi recited the prayer for the Government which included the words, 'Bless the Soviet Union, the shield of peace (*magen ha-shalom*) for the whole world.' The President of the Synagogue sat with the rabbi on the Bimah (platform) and, when I was called up to the Torah, I realised that I was expected to shake hands with the man. I was later told that he was in semi-government employ, his job being to keep an eye on the congregants to see that they did not step out of line. In the afternoon we met the refuseniks, who would not enter the synagogue, but congregated outside to discuss their fate. The police, evidently accustomed to the sight, rarely tried to disperse them. I was warned against spies disguised as refuseniks and, sure enough, a suspicious-looking character sidled up to me, asking me to deliver a letter to a London address. Forewarned, I quickly moved away, noticing appreciative glances from the real refuseniks. On our return to London, Shula and I both addressed a large meeting in the New London Synagogue in which we told of our experiences and gave due praise to the heroes and heroines we had met.

I first visited Israel in my New West End days, when Shula and I were members of an Anglo-Jewish Association delegation to the newly established State. The AJA had been strongly anti-Zionist in the past but it all changed once the State of Israel had come into being. We were taken on the usual sight-seeing trips including a boat-ride on Lake Kinneret, the Sea of Galilee. On the way there, the bus passed the tomb of Maimonides in Tiberias. I demanded that the driver stop the bus so that we could visit the last resting-place of the great sage. A member of our party, a refined and cultured, but Jewishly ignorant, English gentleman said, 'Why should we stop to see the grave of a notorious heretic?'! Stop we did, however, when I observed that there were, in fact, two tombs. When I asked why, the custodian replied with a twinkle in his eye, 'One for the Sephardim and another for the Ashkenazim.' A young Hasid, pointing to one of the graves, said, 'This is of the Rambam himself, the other is of his father.'

Among the dignitaries our delegation visited was Rabbi Yitzhak Nissim, at the time Sephardi Chief Rabbi of Israel. Rabbi Nissim declared, as a Sephardi rabbi would do, that all the really great Halakhic authorities were Sephardim. He proudly pointed to the shelves in his study reaching from floor to ceiling and remarked that all the important books on the shelves were compiled by Sephardim. He had, he said, a few books by Ashenkenzi rabbis but kept them in a corner at the bottom of the shelves. What he did not say was that the books in the corner were by illustrious Ashkenazi rabbis such as Ezekiel Landau and Moses Sofer, whereas the majority of the Sephardi authors whose books graced the upper shelves were virtually unknown in Halakhic circles.

After our daughter, Naomi, had married a sabra, Sasson Bar-Yosef, and had settled in Jerusalem now undivided after the Six

Wedding of son Ivor to Tirza
Carlebach, 14 November 1967

Wedding of daughter Naomi to
Sasson Bar-Joseph, 12 August
1969

1. Grandson Daniel –
son of Ivor and Tirza

2. Granddaughter Paula –
daughter of Ivor and Tirza

3. Granddaughter Ziva – daughter of
Naomi and Sasson

4. Granddaughter Noa –
daughter of Naomi and Sasson

5. Grandson Michael –
son of Naomi and Sasson

Day War, our visits to Israel became frequent. Sasson's parents, Moshe and Hadje, hailed originally from Iraq. They had eight children, Sasson being the youngest. The oldest was a girl, Ziva, who was a nurse at Hadassah Hospital. Ziva was killed in 1948 when a convoy proceeding to the hospital under the supposed protection of the British forces was attacked by the Arabs. All seven sons later married and when they had daughters, called them Ziva after their murdered sister. Naomi and Sasson also have a daughter named Ziva after the aunt she has never seen. Perhaps not surprisingly, then, the whole Bar-Yosef family was very much to the right in Israeli politics. The older boys had been members of the Irgun Zvai Leumi in their teens and Jabotinsky was the family hero.

Fascinated as I have always been by Hasidism, I tried whenever possible to *daven* in a Hasidic *stiebel* when in Jerusalem. Sasson, politely and with amused tolerance, often accompanied me on my visits to this for him, strange world of Eastern European piety. For my part, it was a revelation to see my writings on Hasidism come alive in vibrant, Yiddish-speaking conventicles.

My other *mechutanim*, Alexander and Marga Carlebach, had also settled in Jerusalem. Shula and I were, of course, always made welcome at the Carlebach home, where we met many prominent Israelis and visitors to the country from England and the USA. After our visits to the Carlebach home, a witness to the good quality of life in Jerusalem, Shula and I were tempted to follow their example and go to reside in Israel. We did not yield to the temptation. Our ties with England were too strong and by this time I had the most powerful moral obligation to remain rabbi of the synagogue which, after all, had been established to provide me with a pulpit from which I could express my views. For the same reasons, I declined offers I have had from time to time to occupy a pulpit or receive a university appointment in the USA.

During a visit to Israel when the controversy was at its height, Shula and I were invited to a reception at the home of Dr Israel Goldstein, the famous Zionist and Conservative rabbi, where we met Mr Zalman Shazar, President of the State of Israel. Shazar, under his previous name of S. Rubascheff, had published a book in Berlin in 1925, with M. Soloweitchick, on Biblical Criticism in Jewish sources (*Toledot Bikoret ha-Mikra*) and seemed particularly interested in the way I had argued for the acceptance of the discipline by observant Jews. 'Next time you are in Israel', he remarked, 'please speak on the subject to the group that meets regularly at my home.'

That did not come about, but I did speak years later on the theme of 'Attitudes to Zionism in Anglo-Jewry' to the group of scholars and thinkers which met monthly at the residence of the then President of Israel, Mr Yitzhak Navon. It was heart-warming to observe that, for all his anxieties about the future of the State, the President could find time to have a study and discussion group over which he himself presided and to which he contributed. The parallel in Britain would be monthly meetings to discuss English history and British philosophy, held by Her Majesty at Buckingham Palace.

During another visit to Israel I spoke at a celebration at the Hebrew University on Mount Scopus. The occasion was the planting of a rose garden in memory of Mr Shalom Gordon given by his wife Tanya, the artist, and daughter, Amia Raphael, a friend and founder-member of the New London. I spoke on the theme of a rose as a symbol for the divine Presence, as this appears in the opening passage of the Zohar in a comment on the verse, 'As a rose among thorns' (Song of Songs 2:2). Rabbi Louis Rabinowitz, who had written extensively on the flora and fauna of the Bible and the Talmud, was present and I remember discussing with him the meaning of a 'garden' in the Bible. This would seem to have been something like a vegetable garden, since all the evidence goes to show that the cultivation of a flower garden was not introduced until the Middle Ages in Europe. A rose in the Song of Songs would be a wild flower growing among the wheat sheaves.

On a number of occasions I did a lecture tour of Jewish communities in the USA, among them New York, Chicago, Boston, Los Angeles, San Francisco, Dallas, Houston, New Orleans, Albuquerque, Minneapolis, Indianapolis, Syracuse and Albany. It is the usual practice in the USA for the chairperson to introduce the guest speaker with a formal 'presentation'. The introduction was usually tactful but there was the inevitable reference to the Jacobs Affair. My ploy, when beginning my talk, was to tell the famous 'howler' of the little boy whose teacher had requested the class to write something on King Alfred. Please, said the teacher, avoid the hackneyed story of Alfred burning the widow's cakes. There is so much you can write about King Alfred without dishing up that old tale. The boy produced a piece in which the sentence occurred, 'After this, Alfred came to the house of a woman. But the less said about this the better'! Nevertheless, I was usually asked to explain my position and where I differed from the Chief Rabbi. And, whatever the subject of my lecture, at question time I was asked to say something about the set-up in the Anglo-Jewish community, about which most American Jews have only the haziest of notions. They admired the Board of Deputies in achieving a communal unity beyond their own capacity but were astonished at the hierarchical structure of the United Synagogue and its complete pooling of all resources, to which with their stern notions of local independence, they could not for a moment subscribe.

My first lecture tour to the USA was in 1963 while the controversy surrounding my appointment to the New West End was at its height. Under the auspices of the B'nai B'rith Adult Education Department, directed by the indefatigable Lilly Elderman, alas no longer in the land of the living, I was one of a team of three guest lecturers at summer schools in North Carolina, Dallas and San Antonio. My colleagues in the mountain retreat some 70 miles from North Carolina (built by an American millionaire and with nauseatingly pious signs everywhere declaring that one is never nearer to God than on a mountain) were Professor Ellis Rivkin and Professor Eugene B. Borowitz. This was my first taste of the American fondness for Jewish learning. Some of the students, all of them of mature age, had travelled hundreds of miles in order to participate.

The Dallas school took place at a converted ranch near the city. One evening, we were treated to a lecture and display by a one-time cowboy. He performed the trick of shooting out a candle while looking at it backwards through a mirror, but told us that the Hollywood notion of the cowboy being quick on the draw was nonsense, since if one tried to draw at such a speed he would probably shoot himself in the leg. Another illusion dispelled.

My colleagues at Dallas and San Antonio were Zalman Schachter and Marshall Sklare, the distinguished sociologist. Zalman Schachter was an extraordinary character – a Lubavitcher Hasid, a friend of Thomas Merton and Gerald Heard, and a rabbi who was fast becoming a guru to young Jews anxious for spiritual experience. I used to take issue with Zalman when I sat in on his lectures, particularly when he tried to sell the idea of reincarnation to his audience. I also thought it inappropriate for a lecturer at this kind of summer school to try to put across his own version of Judaism rather than approach the subject more or less objectively. But generally the three of us got along well, trying not to appear to be competing with one another.

Zalman certainly had a way with him. Within one or two days he had his audience eating out of his hand. He observed, during the daily *minyan*, that the men were wearing very small *tefillin*. At the following prayer-meeting he said, 'In Texas everything is bigger. Even the *Ribbono Shel Olam* is bigger in Texas. So please go and buy for yourselves real big Texan *tefillin*.'

Zalman was not always so successful in promulgating his ideas on spirituality; some of them seemed extreme to his audience. One day a married woman in Zalman's class complained about his lecture on sex: 'He tells my husband to have God in mind during the marital act. But I want my husband to have me in mind!'

During the Sabbath Zalman wore the traditional garb of a Hasidic Rebbe; *streimel*, long black coat and a silken *gartel*. But as soon as the Havdalah had been recited, he whipped off his *streimel* and coat to be seen wearing shorts and sleeveless shirt underneath – one of the boys again. On Saturday night, after a long day of study and prayer, various recreational activities took place in the large hall of the ranch. Some of us played poker, though not for money. Others shot pool, the hall being bathed in the ghastly light of the ranch reminiscent of the gambling saloon of the cowboy films. Zalman had invited a young rabbi to pay him a visit at the ranch; the young man evidently required spiritual counsel. When he entered the room, the young man saw me dealing cards, Zalman holding a billiard cue and a general air of dissipation (though not for real – but the young man could not have known this). The look of dismay on the rabbi's face had to be seen to be believed. His thoughts were clear enough, 'Here I have come for spiritual guidance and appear to have stumbled into a den of iniquity.'

The participants at the school had made arrangements for me to be made an Honorary Citizen of Texas and I have a large, golden certificate to prove it. At the presentation ceremony I was fitted out with a broad-brimmed cowboy hat and the assembly sang in unison, 'The Eyes of Texas Are Upon You.' I now proudly display the certificate on the wall of my study together with one I received when, on another visit, I was made an Honorary Citizen of New Orleans. I am unaware, however, of the special privileges, if any, of which an Honorary Citizen of Texas and New Orleans can avail himself.

From Dallas, the next stop for the three of us was at a similar ranch in San Antonio. It was a Sunday and the journey by the infrequent bus service would have taken five hours. One of the participants at both summer schools undertook to take us there by private plane, by which means he had arrived at Dallas. Marshall Sklare cried off, because, so he said, such a method of transportation would not be covered by his insurance policy. However, Zalman Schachter accepted the lift and I, not wishing to be outdone by a Hasid, also accepted. I nearly changed my mind when I saw the plane – like one of those with struts in the old films, with only four seats. But it was too late for me to back out. 'Not to worry,' said the pilot in his Texan drawl, 'I've been flying for eighteen years and have never had an accident.' 'There's always a first time,' I thought to myself as worry I did. Zalman sat next to the pilot in front while I sat on my own in the back seat. To my horror, once we were airborne, the pilot and Zalman became engaged in a vigorous discussion about Hasidism. 'Keep your eyes on the road,' I shouted above the noise of the engine.' 'Oh that's all right,' was the reply, 'This plane virtually flies itself. I often read a novel while flying it'! Once my nerves had stilled it was, in fact, an exhilarating experience to fly like a bird in a glorious, cloudless vast expanse of Texan sky.

After the San Antonio summer school, I was taken to the airport to catch the flight to Washington where I was due to speak the next day. At that time there had been a number of hijackings of American planes by the Cubans. When I went to the men's room at the airport, I noticed that a policeman, his hand on his revolver, was eyeing me with suspicion. He sauntered over, his hand still on his gun and requested me to follow him. I was extremely puzzled until the 'cop' mumbled something about Cuban hijacks and I realised that, with my beard, I had something of a Cuban look. I insisted on being taken to the manager at the airport where with the help of Marshall Sklare and the sight of my British passport my innocence was established. I could now express my indignation that one of Her Majesty's subjects should be treated in such a manner. Profuse apologies all round.

My troubles were not over. The flight to Washington was one of the most frightening I have ever experienced. There was a violent storm over Washington and from the window of the plane we could all see the White House, while the plane circled again and again, unable to land. Up in the air I was very much down in the dumps, wondering what I was doing in an American plane so far from home after having come close to being arrested as a dangerous criminal. Once the plane had landed, however, all was well. The welcoming party from the B'nai B'rith office told me that the account of my 'arrest' had been on the radio. The newspapers the next morning carried a photograph of me, prominence being given to my beard, and with what can only be described as a cynical smile, over which was the heading, 'British Rabbi Arrested'.

My most memorable invitation to speak in the USA came about quite by accident. In 1965, the United Nations was organising a series of celebrations to commemorate its 20th anniversary in San Francisco, where the original charter had been signed. The celebrations were to be preceded by a service in which representatives of all the great religions of the world would participate. It was even rumoured that the Pope himself would attend, but in the event he sent a personal message read out at the gathering by the Cardinal Archbishop of San Francisco.

Dr Jacobs 'a perfect suspect' at Houston airport

Celebration of 20th anniversary of Vatican II Declaration on the Jews, Chicago, October 1985. Author, Cardinal Archbishop of Chicago, Chairman of Chicago Board of Rabbis

Convocation, Harvard Divinity School, September 1985

U Thant, the Secretary-General of the United Nations Organisation, represented Buddhism and there were representatives of Islam and Hinduism, as well as all the major Protestant Christian denominations.   The question, much agonised over by the organisers, as I later learned was who would represent Judaism. If a prominent rabbi belonging to one of the three denominations – Orthodoxy, Reform and Conservative – were to be chosen, the other two would protest and, even if the denominational problem could have been solved, there would still have been the difficulty of choosing one rabbi rather than another. The organisers finally decided that the best course would be to invite the philosopher Martin Buber, to whom none would object, to represent Judaism. Unfortunately, Buber was too ill to attend, and he suggested that I should be invited as a neutral figure. An English rabbi, unknown to the majority of American Jews, would be acceptable to them for that very reason. And so it happened. Shula and I were provided with first-class seats on the plane and off we went. We had never before travelled in such style. Sitting across the aisle from us was Groucho Marx smoking his cigar, from whom we obtained his autograph for our children. Arriving at San Francisco we were whisked off by motorcade and police escort to the Hilton Hotel where we had been given a suite for the duration of our stay. Talk about the corridors of power!

The celebratory dinner, attended by all the UN representatives and the religious leaders, was a gala occasion. It was held on Friday evening so we had to walk the short distance to the hotel in which the dinner was held. Arriving there we found that a special vegetarian meal had been provided for us. The Cardinal Archbishop, sitting next to Shula, leaned over and said to me, 'Although today is Friday I have received a special dispensation from the Pope to eat meat. Couldn't you have obtained a dispensation from the Chief Rabbi [sic] to enjoy, for this occasion, a non-kosher meal?' At the reception which preceded the dinner I met the Episcopalian Bishop Pyke, then in trouble with his church for his theological unconventional views. 'Brother,' he said, with his arm around my shoulder, 'we are in the same boat.' Bishop Pyke later created another stir when he wrote a book in which he claimed that the dead can communicate with the living and that he had himself received such communications from his dead son. The Bishop's life ended tragically. He was travelling by car in the Judean desert and the car ran out of petrol. The poor Bishop expired in the desert.

The special service was held at the San Francisco Cow Palace, with an audience of 40,000. I had never addressed anything like such a gathering and, looking down, I began to appreciate what speakers mean when they talk of a 'sea of faces'. I was probably deluding myself, but I imagined that I could see Shula's face as a speck in the distance wishing me to speak well on behalf of Judaism. There was a choir of 2,000 formed from the choirs of the churches in the surrounding area. It was, in a way, a *kiddush ha-shem* ('sanctification of the divine name') that the representative of Judaism was invited to be the first speaker because, as the organisers explained, Judaism was the oldest of the world's major religions and the Hebrew prophets the first to dream of a world in which war was no more. I took for my text the priestly blessing, exploring its implications for the establishment of peace on earth.

Members of an extremist Protestant, fundamentalist sect carried banners of protest and, as the speakers arrived at the Cow Palace, hurled abuse at the Bishops who were to participate for 'worshipping the gods of Judaism, Islam, Buddhism and Hinduism'. I could not help thinking that our fundamentalists are better-behaved than Christian fundamentalists. It appeared that even in the USA at the United Nations I could not escape the issue of fundamentalism. Small wonder that I have been accused of being obsessed by the subject.

After the service, the speakers and their spouses were taken to Trader Vic's, where Shula and I were again provided with a vegetarian meal, as were the Muslim speaker and his wife. We could not enjoy the food served to the other guests but consoled ourselves that we were able, at least, to enjoy the drinks offered, unlike our Muslim friends.

My longest stay in the USA was when I spent the academic year 1985–86 as Visiting List Professor in Jewish Studies at the Harvard University Divinity School. Albert List, a wealthy Jewish philanthropist, offered to endow a chair at the Divinity

School so that post-graduate students at the School might be introduced to Jewish learning and scholarship at University level. The University Officers decided not to make this important appointment permanent until the Faculty of the Divinity School had had time to fully consider the suitability of candidates in an unprecedented situation. Harvard already boasted the excellent Centre for Jewish Studies, under the direction of Professor Isadore Twersky, the distinguished Jewish mediaevalist. But this was the first time that a Chair in Jewish Studies was being established at the Divinity School, to cater largely, though not exclusively, for Christians pursuing post-graduate studies in the Old and New Testaments, in comparative religion and in the philosophy of religion. For the interregnum it was decided to invite four older men each to serve as Visiting List Professor for a year. The appointees were professors Judah Goldin, Eugene B. Borowitz, Jacob Petuchowski and myself. My invitation came out of the blue to my complete surprise – and, naturally, gratification.

I received ample notice of the appointment and proceeded to discuss with Judge Alan Lipfriend, the Chairman of the New London Synagogue, and the other Honorary Officers, what was to be done during my absence. My contract with the New London (for several years there was, in fact, no contract at all) made no provision for leave of absence but, since I had taken no sabbatical during the 22 years I had served, the Honorary Officers and Council were willing to grant me leave for the academic year at Harvard. Fortunately, my colleague, Mr George Rothschild, Cantor of the Synagogue, agreed to shoulder many of the extra responsibilities. During my absence he addressed Bar Mitzvahs, preached a number of sermons and was generally helpful in all sorts of ways, ably assisted by Jonathan Wittenberg, the student for the rabbinate at Leo Baeck College mentioned earlier, who had been Bar Mitzvah at the New London and who was officiating as student Rabbi at the New North London. In addition, a rota was drawn up of congregants willing to deliver an address during the Sabbath morning service. For weddings and funerals we were able to draw on the services of my friend Dr I.H. Levy. Everything went smoothly in the event, so much so that when I returned for about six weeks during the vacation

I said I had better hurry back as soon as the spring semester at Harvard was over!

The Divinity School provided us with accommodation at the Center for the Study of World Religions, attached to the School, where Dr John Carman, Head of the Center and Acting Dean of the Divinity School, his charming wife Inika and the Center staff were as lavish in their welcome and hospitality as only Americans can be. Nothing was spared to make us feel thoroughly at home. The Center itself is a place where visiting scholars belonging to various religions can stay while pursuing research in their chosen field. Professor Marc Saperstein and his wife, Roberta, also did much to smooth the transition from pulpit rabbi to university professor. In the common room at the Center the symbols of the various religions were on display on tables or stands and it all amounted to comparative religious studies in action, so to speak. Every week there was a get-together of the members of the Center family and, from time to time, a Divinity School dinner. On these occasions, arrangements were made for us to be provided with kosher food.

During the autumn semester I taught two courses – one on the Principles of the Jewish Faith and one on Jewish Law. The first was obviously of interest and relevance to the Christians in the course but the other course was also well-attended. I should not have been surprised. The Harvard Divinity School was not the place for glib and trite generalisations about the spirit of the law versus its letter. Although only a few of the participants knew Hebrew, they all had trained minds, and we were able to discuss freely and objectively the nature of Judaism in its theological and legal aspects. The students did their homework, reading the texts I had chosen and other relevant material. When they turned in the papers they had written for me at the end of the semester, most of them were good enough to deserve an A grading. I understand that there had been something of a grading inflation at American universities, partly as a result of the backlash against student unrest in the 1960s. But even at inflationary rates an A grading was not to be sneezed at.

During the spring semester I also taught two courses – one on Jewish Mysticism, the other on Talmudic Reasoning. Once again, the popularity of the course on Mysticism was not surprising – Mysticism is now very much the in thing – but that there should have been a keen interest in Talmudic methodology was rather astonishing. We studied texts in the English translation of the Soncino Press. When I announced this course I realised I was taking a big risk, but as it turned out the lack of Hebrew and Aramaic was no hindrance to understanding the texts. In a strange sort of way, the fact that there could be no concern with philological questions made for greater concentration on the ideas. By the end of the course, some members of the class were able to employ Talmudic dialectics as to the manner born.

There is, of course, a strong women's liberation movement in the USA, with Harvard very much in the forefront. Equality of the sexes was taken for granted; the slightest hint at inequality was hotly resented. For instance, a woman (for females to be called 'girls' was unacceptable and considered patronising) in my class, when we were reading a text from Maimonides, suddenly said, 'I don't like this guy Maimonides. He always says "he" when he should be saying "he or she".' I could not help replying that in most instances Maimonides did mean 'he or she' but that, in any event, he happened to live long before Columbus discovered America. The course in Jewish Mysticism came as a godsend to the feminists, what with the Kabbalistic doctrine of the *Shekhinah* as a female element in the Deity and the appearance of women Rebbes in Hasidism. This did not prevent some members of the class writing good papers in which they observed that, after all, the Kabbalists were male and theirs was a man's view of womanhood. The line, 'I don't need your compliments, thank you very much', was sometimes implied even when not actually expressed. On one occasion, when I opened a door for a young lady, she said, 'After you, Professor,' in a tone which implied I had commited a social gaffe. I could not help saying, 'Evidently, one must be careful *not* to be an English gentleman at Harvard.'

The Weidener Library at Harvard with its eleven million books is a book-lover's paradise. The Judaica and Hebrew sections, under the supervision of Dr Charles Berlin, have all the learned journals and practically every book published during the past

245

two hundred years available on open shelves in the stacks. As a faculty member I could take out as many books each day as I could carry and keep them for six months. Almost every day I took the ten-minute walk to the Weidener, returning loaded with borrowed books. I was able to borrow books I had seen referred to but had never before read or even seen.

At Harvard there is an intellectual atmosphere second to none. In Harvard Yard in the mornings one could see students hurrying from lecture to lecture, standing eagerly discussing the latest views of the professors on philosophy, politics, economics and religion, or simply sitting quietly on the grass reading. There were lectures galore on every conceivable subject, given by Harvard professors or by visiting scholars. At the Divinity School and at the Center for the Study for World Religions, I came into contact with a plethora of fresh ideas on religion and there was much debate 'about it and about', albeit conducted with the politeness and understatement I had thought peculiar to Britain. There was no rowdiness at Harvard. The students, who had to pay heavy fees for their tuition, were too determined to get their money's worth to fritter away their time. Yet on a warm evening the coffee-shops, ice-cream parlours and bookshops were crowded by well-behaved but cheerful students who, while they wished to achieve good results, did not want to be, in the Harvard jargon, over-achievers.

At the Faculty Club, at seminars and lectures, I heard brilliant men and women expound their views, sensible, reasonable or outrageous, and I became so infatuated with it all that I almost forgot I was a rabbi in a London pulpit. Almost but not quite. I appreciated that in my congregation there was not only an abundance of intellectual stimulation but also a breadth of view not found even at Harvard, the broadmindedness present in a congregation drawn from many different walks of life. I was glad to be a Harvard professor for a time. I was even more glad that I could return to my pulpit when it was all over.

During my Harvard year, I lectured also at other universities – York in Toronto, McGill in Montreal, Brandeis, Yale – and in Jewish communities. Every lecturer on Jewish topics in this country knows how rare it is for a fee to be offered. Even travelling expenses are not always provided. It is quite different in the USA. There the question is always asked, 'What is your fee?' Before I delivered the Simon Ravidowitch lecture at Brandeis, Professor Marvin Fox, Head of the Department of Jewish Studies, telephoned me to say that while by American standards my honorarium might not be too magnificent, it would be by English standards. I replied that by normal English standards any fee at all would be magnificent. Professor Fox then observed that years ago he had been told the same thing by the famous historian, Cecil Roth.

One of my out-of-town excursions during the autumn semester was to Chicago, where I had been invited to deliver the Solomon Goldman lecture at Spertus College. Byron Sherwin, Vice-President for Academic Affairs at the College, was a trusted friend from the time I first met him when I had delivered the Goldman lecture on an earlier occasion. Shula and I were made welcome at the Chicago home of Rabbi Seymour and Naomi Cohen, our dear friends. Seymour was Rabbi Goldman's successor at the Anshe Emet Synagogue, where I delivered a lecture on Hasidism on Friday night at a sumptuous dinner. My Spertus College lecture was given on 27 October 1985 (the 850th anniversary of Maimonides' birth), my subject being attitudes towards Maimonides on the part of the Kabbalists and Hasidim.

On the evening of 27 October a celebration took place at Mundelein College on the 20th anniversary of *Nostra Aetate*, the Vatican II declaration on Catholic–Jewish relations. It was organised jointly by the Chicago Board of Rabbis and the Catholic Archdiocese of Chicago, with Cardinal Bernadine as the Catholic speaker; I was invited as a representative of Judaism. The whole affair was organised with American aplomb – a choir, actors declaiming from a stage, a procession, soft music and spotlights; all a little Hollywood but quite moving. In my address, I quoted the tradition according to which the Hebrew word for 'and he kissed him' (*va-yishkahehu*) in Genesis 33:4, describing the reunion of the brothers Jacob and Esau, has to be written in the Scroll with dots over it. One Rabbi in the Midrash holds that these dots denote strong reservation, an ancient version of the American 'Tell it to the marines'. But another Rabbi declared that, on the contrary, the reunion was real and the animosities of the past forgotten. The dots are for emphasis, as if to say, see, it can really happen. Jews believe that Vatican II was completely sincere and our Catholic friends believe that we are completely sincere in our desire to forge strong bonds of friendship. The heroes of the evening were Pope John and Professor Heschel, pioneers in Christian–Jewish dialogue. A drawing of these two was projected large on to the backcloth, Pope John looking, as one of the actors declaimed, like everybody's uncle and Professor Heschel like everybody's grandfather. The order of proceedings stated that the Cardinal, the President of the Chicago Board of Rabbis and I were to embrace and receive a gift of the framed drawing, of which there are only three copies in existence. It was the first time I have ever embraced a Cardinal in public. The first time I had ever embraced *anyone* in public. But, I thought, being in America, that's the way the cookie crumbles.

Although most of my lectures at Harvard and elsewhere on this visit were purely academic, I did not entirely escape from the old controversy. One evening, for instance, I addressed a large public meeting under the auspices of the Holy Blossom Temple in Toronto and the Department of Jewish Studies at York University on 'Tradition and Authority' in which I defended the non-fundamentalist understanding of the doctrine 'The Torah is from Heaven'. The Rabbi of the Holy Blossom Temple is Rabbi Dov Marmur, a friend from the days when he was Rabbi of the Reform Synagogue in Alyth Gardens in London. There was quite a heated discussion after the lecture, but Dov told me that many Orthodox Jews who had hitherto refused even to enter the precincts of a Reform Temple came to the meeting, not all of them to challenge my views. On another occasion, I was invited by the newly-formed Orthodox Synagogue at Newton Center, near Boston, to speak on 'Towards a Non-Fundamentalist Halakhah', the title of a chapter in my book *A Tree of Life*. Here, too, Orthodox Jews, some of them ordained rabbis, seemed profoundly concerned with the need for observant Jews to face up to the challenge of modern critical scholarship. There are Orthodox Jews who do not share the frightening certainties of the fundamentalists and are not afraid to see Judaism as a quest.

For several years Harvard University had an arrangement with the Central Synagogue in New York for an annual lecture to be delivered at the Synagogue by a Harvard Professor. I was asked to deliver this lecture and I accepted. After the lecture I was sent the following letter which speaks for itself and also shows how coincidences occur in lives.

Dear Rabbi Jacobs,

In a sense, this letter is long overdue. I should have written long ago. However, since late is better than never, this belated note will have to do.

A few weeks ago, I had the privilege and pleasure of listening to you at Shabbat services at Central Synagogue. Since I had to leave a bit earlier than the conclusion of the service and the Oneg Shabbat I was unable to chat with you, and know in any case that there would be others and what I had to say to you would be better written . . .

How did I come to you? You might be interested. I was a young kid of 15 years old and was at the summer camp Ramah. During the winter months I was in attendance at the Ramaz School, a good modern Orthodox day school. While at Ramah, I was introduced by an overzealous Bible instructor to Biblical Criticism. This instructor must have had a spark of Wellhausen in him, because he took a particular and rather sadistic delight in destroying a young boy's faith in the Bible. I was rather bereft and felt as though the ground had been pulled out from under me. When I think back on it, I recall that I felt as though I were all alone, and who could help me?

I wandered back to my bunk, and along the way met the counselor who was assigned to the bunk next door. Sensing that I was disturbed, he asked me what was wrong. I told him. A little smile came over him, and he said, 'I know what you're feeling. Come with me. I have just the thing for you.' I went with him and he handed me a slim red volume. 'Here, read this,' he said. 'You'll be fine in the morning.' With that theological medicine, I discovered in my hands the book, *We Have Reason to Believe* by someone named

Louis Jacobs. The counselor was right; I began to feel better in the morning. (The counselor happened to be English and was studying at the Seminary. I believe he was the son of the Cantor at the New West End Synagogue. His name was Elkan Levy). . .

A final thought: When Elkan gave me your book in Camp Ramah, I read it that night. The next day, a burden had lifted from my being. As I walked along the Camp road, I met another camper with whom I was friendly. She saw me smiling; she knew that the day before I was quite sullen. 'Why are you so happy today?' she asked. 'Because I have discovered a wonderful writer who's helped me tremendously.' 'Oh?' she replied. 'Yes,' I said. 'He's wonderful. And you should remember his name. Yes, remember it. His name is Rabbi Louis Jacobs. Will you remember it?' She looked quizzically at me but then shook her head in agreement. 'Oh, I'll remember his name. If you say so.'

She must have remembered it. Her name was – is – Vicki List. Daughter of Mr and Mrs Albert List.

A coincidence? Not for believers.

Very sincerely yours,
Perry Berkowitz

17

BOOKS

Although I am the author of thirty books, I still share the sentiments of Gilbert Murray who, when he saw someone reading a book he had written, was tempted to go over and say, 'That's not a book. *I* wrote it.' I have never been a professional writer; at least, not in the sense of one who earns his living by the pen. Some of my books were written from an urge to explain my position, some for the purpose of expounding some aspect of Jewish religious thought I happened to be interested in at the time, and some were written because I had been commissioned to write them. I now realise that I would have profited, financially and in other ways, if I had had a literary agent but, mistakenly, I adopted a do-it-yourself policy, even to the extent of doing my own typing. Until a few months ago I did all my typing with one finger on a small portable machine, but my sons, Ivor and David, who work in the printing business, have at last prevailed upon me to invest in a decent electric typewriter full of amazing gadgetry, the intricacies of which are more difficult, for me at least, to master than a page of Talmud.

I have been fortunate in my publishers: the Jewish Chronicle Press, Vallentine, Mitchell, Darton, Longman & Todd, Oxford University Press (for the Littman Library books), Cambridge University Press, Routledge & Kegan Paul – all based in Britain; Keter Publications in Israel; and Behrman House, Basic Books, Hermon Press and Rossel Books in the USA. The fact that I have had a variety of publishers is accidental; the books were varied in theme. It was not because of my falling out with any of my publishers, with all of whom I have maintained, I think I can say, cordial relations. Royalties on my books are a welcome addition to my income but, except for famous authors, no large sums are obtained from writing. I have never actually been out

251

of pocket from my writing (particularly since I do not employ a typist) but neither have I made anything remotely approaching even a small fortune.

Leaving aside those of a popular nature, my books and articles have covered three fields: Talmudic, theological and mystical.

Whatever expertise I have in Talmud was acquired through my studies at the Manchester Yeshivah and the Gateshead Kolel, supplemented by the Talmud classes I have conducted in the congregations I have had the privilege of serving, as well as at Leo Baeck College. As it is said in the Talmud itself, one learns more from pupils than from teachers. I have also read as widely as I could works of modern Talmudic scholarship, in which so much important work has been done in applying critical and historical method to the ancient texts. It is a moot point whether traditional methods of Talmudic analysis, as employed in Yeshivot, can be combined with modern methodology, but I have tried in my work to explore this possibility; in the process, my critics would no doubt say, falling between two stools or, to quote the Yiddish saying, dancing at every wedding.

The attempt to combine both methods is evident in the three books I have written on the Talmud: *Studies in Talmudic Logic and Methodology; TEYKU: The Unsolved Problem in the Babylonian Talmud*; and *The Talmudic Argument*. I also published a number of articles on Talmudic themes, among them 'Are There Fictitious *Baraitot* in the Babylonian Talmud?' in the Hebrew Union College Annual; 'Evidence of Literary Device in the Babylonian Talmud' and 'Further Evidence of Literary Device in the Babylonian Talmud'; 'An Analysis of three *Sugyot* in the Babylonian Talmud'; 'How Much of the Babylonian Talmud is Pseudepigraphic?' and review articles on the works of Professor Abraham Weiss, the pioneer of literary analysis of the Talmud. All of these were published in the *Journal of Jewish Studies*. They are largely expository but there is perhaps something of an original thrust in my attempts at detecting such literary devices in the Talmud as contrivance and arrangement of the material by the editors in a dramatic sequence leading to a surprising conclusion, almost as in a work of pure fiction.

The Talmud is certainly more than a mere record of the Amoraic debates. It is a literary work by anonymous editors, who worked on material they had from earlier times. I have also tried to show, particularly in *The Talmudic Argument*, that modern scholarship can gain from a knowledge of Yeshivah-type analysis of concepts, provided this is not used in a manner that runs counter to the results of historical investigation into the texts.

We Have Reason to Believe, the book that started all the trouble, was my first essay into Jewish theology, not counting my little book *Jewish Prayer* (a popular work which has gone into four editions). In this book I put forward my view that the findings of the Bible critics cannot simply be waved away and that the only conclusion to be reached is to acknowledge that there is a human as well as a divine element in the Bible, including the Pentateuch. Until the controversy broke, two years after the publication of *We Have Reason to Believe*, the book was largely ignored. No one pounced on me for entertaining heretical views and even one or two Orthodox journals reviewed the book not unsympathetically. As I have said, the charge of heresy was made public when Dayan Grunfeld showed the book to the Chief Rabbi, warning him that it would be a disaster to appoint the author of the chapter on the Torah as Principal of Jews' College. Shortly afterwards, I took up the theme again in my book *Jewish Values*, in the chapter on 'The Study of the Torah', where I tried to explore the idea of Torah study as involving critical as well as analytical method and suggested that the quest for Torah is itself part of the Torah. *We Have Reason to Believe* went into a second edition and, later, a third, in which I added an epilogue replying to my critics.

My lengthy book, *The Principles of the Jewish Faith*, takes each of the principles laid down by Maimonides to examine how each found its expression in Jewish thought. My thesis in the book was that while a modern Jew could in all honesty still subscribe to Maimonides' basic principles (laid down, it must not be forgotten, eight hundred years ago) this did not mean that the great teacher's formulation was the last word Jewish theology had to utter, a fairly obvious position I thought at the time and still do. The essential question with regard to each of the principles is not what Maimonides said *then*, but what he would say if he were alive *today*. The book also discusses the general question of dogma in Judaism, about which so much has been written since Moses Mendelssohn. I showed that theological ideas, while certainly present and to be accepted in Judaism, were fluid to a degree so that much depended on who was doing the formulation. Naturally, in my discussion of Maimonides' eighth principle – that the Torah is from Heaven – I let myself go in an attack on fundamentalism. The book was supplied with extensive bibliographical notes and it became a kind of textbook on Jewish theology, used as such in theological colleges, Jewish and non-Jewish. An American edition of the book was published by Basic Books; much later, the book was re-issued in a book club edition by the magazine *Commentary*, and now a new American edition has been issued, published by Jason Aronson Inc.

In *Faith*, published in 1968, I tried to examine the nature of religious belief, showing how the term *emunah* ('faith') had changed from the Biblical and Rabbinic sense of trust in God to the mediaeval belief that God exists, through to the existentialist and other modern concepts. The book defends the idea of God as Person. On the strength of this book and *Principles of the Jewish Faith*, I was invited by the American Jewish Committee to do a lecture tour in the USA. Basic Books launched their edition of *Faith* during this tour, which was attended by Professor Mordecai Kaplan, whose 'naturalistic', non-personalistic philosophy I had attacked but whom I, like so many others, admired for his complete honesty and intellectual integrity. When I remarked, 'Dr Kaplan, how very nice of you to come to the launching of my book,' Kaplan graciously replied, 'Why not? Although our views differ, we are both asking the same question: what Judaism means for the modern Jew.'

For several years I did a regular column on current theological literature, both Jewish and non-Jewish, for the American journal *Judaism*, providing surveys of recents works on such topics as 'Prayer', 'Mysticism', 'Science and Religion', 'Hasidism', 'Philosophical Theology', and 'Theology in the Responsa'. As a result of the latter, I began to collect material on theology in the writings of the great Halakhists, which appeared in my book *Theology in the Responsa* in 1975. Here I tried to show that the Halakhic authorities treated theological questions in their Responsa with the same rigour and seriousness they employed in their purely legal discussions.

Darton, Longman & Todd, a non-Jewish publishing house with an interest in religious books, published my main work *A Jewish Theology* in 1973. (Behrman House published the book in paperback form and corrected the numerous printing errors which had, unfortunately, crept into the hardcover edition.) Not surprisingly, in view of the suspicion with which theology is treated in some Jewish circles, there had been only two such full-scale treatments of the subject before mine. These were *Jewish Theology* by Kaufmann Kohler and *Jewish Theology* by Samuel S. Cohon, both written from the Reform perspective. Unlike my predecessors, I put an 'A' in the title because on such a topic as Jewish theology it seemed absurd to me for a writer to claim that he is presenting the definitive work. 'A Jewish Theology' implies the idea of a quest, which I had become convinced was an essential idea. When I have been accused (quite often) of theological vagueness and tentativeness, I have replied that theology – the science of the transcendent – is bound to be vague by its very nature, so that it is better to be vaguely right than definitely wrong. This book, too has been widely distributed and with its copious notes has also become a kind of textbook – not so much on theology itself (can one have a textbook on theology?) as on the history of theological thought in Judaism.

There must have been an interest in Jewish theology in some parts of the Jewish world, since both *We Have Reason to Believe* and *A Jewish Theology* won book prizes; the former, the Abramowitz–Zeitlin Prize in 1963, the latter the *Jewish Chronicle* Book Award in 1974. The aims of the Abramowitz–Zeitlin Fund were 'to encourage men of ideas and writers to compose literary works which will clarify for people brought up "on the knees of science" the faith of Israel, its Torah and its mitzvot'. This was an Israeli award and I was unable to be present for the special meeting in which it was formally given: a friend, Judge Nahmani, receiving it in Jerusalem on my behalf. The panel of judges included the great exponent of mediaeval Jewish philosophy, Professor Hugo Bergmann, Judge Silberg of the Israeli Supreme Court, Professor Churgin of the Orthodox Bar-Ilan

University and the famous Talmudic scholar, Professor E.E. Urbach. The judges for the *Jewish Chronicle* award were Chaim Raphael, T.R. Fyvel and the Editor of the *Jewish Chronicle*.

A curious footnote to the Jacobs Affair should be mentioned here in connection with *We Have Reason to Believe*.

Mr Henry Shaw, while Director of Hillel House, compiled a guide to Jewish books entitled *Your Jewish Bookshelf* and this was published by and on behalf of the United Synagogue in 1970. The guide recommended *We Have Reason to Believe* as 'a popular work on Jewish religious thought'. The *Jewish Chronicle* (17 April 1970) noted that it was largely because of the theological views expressed in the book that I had been rejected as a candidate for the principalship of Jews' College and refused permission to reoccupy the New West End pulpit. Did this betoken a change of heart on the part of the authorities of the United Synagogue? When questioned on this, Mr Raymond Goldwater, chairman of the United Synagogue publications committee, said: 'We did not feel that we should exclude the book merely because its views do not coincide with that of the Chief Rabbi or the Beth Din.' He added that the Shaw booklet had been sent to the Chief Rabbi for his approval and went on to say, 'The recommendation of Dr Jacobs's book represented no change in the official United Synagogue view, in so far as it was possible for an institution to hold a view.' Reading between the lines, it was obvious that the United Synagogue leaders had no wish to pursue the Affair further at that time and, truth be told, that seems to have been the attitude of the Honorary Officers to this day.

Laughable though it is to claim expertise on the idea of God (what can be more ridiculous?) I yielded to the request by the editors that I contribute an article on 'God' for the Macmillan *Encyclopaedia of Religion* (edited by Mircea Eliade) and for the *Dictionary of Jewish Theology*, edited by Arthur Cohen and Paul Mendes-Flohr. The Macmillan article was largely historical and, as I wrote to Arthur Cohen when he invited me to do the article for his volume, 'Since you are asking me to do the impossible, then, provided it is clear that it is impossible – as it is to anyone who has ever given thought to religion – I might as well do it and, in the process, say why it is impossible.' Theology should be concerned to leave the way open for its own demise by showing, as Maimonides and other Jewish thinkers have tried to do, that the greater the success one has in apprehending God, the more one appreciates how small a degree of apprehension there is or can be. Solomon Schechter, in his *Rabbinic Theology*, remarks that the best theology is not consistent. I have my doubts about the correctness of this observation, but it is surely right to say, if one may put it in this way, the best theology has suicidal tendencies.

My book *A Tree of Life: Diversity, Flexibility and Creativity in Jewish Law*, published in 1984, falls somewhere in between my Talmudic and theological interests. The major part of the book is concerned with the development of Jewish law from Talmudic times and can qualify as 'Talmudic' but the final chapter, 'Towards a non-fundamentalist Halakhah', is theological.

On the theme of Jewish mysticism, I translated Cordovero's *Tomer Devorah*, with the English title 'The Palm Tree of Deborah'. This work by the sixteenth-century Kabbalist of Safed discusses the doctrine of *Imitatio Dei* as understood by the Kabbalists. Another translation was of a Hasidic classic, *Kunteros ha-Hitpa'alut*, which I translated as 'Tract on Ecstasy', an acute analysis of mystical states of mind by the early nineteenth-century Habad teacher, Dov Baer of Lubavitch, who succeeded his father, Shneur Zalman of Liady, as leader of the Habad group in Hasidism. Dov Baer's rival for the succession was another profound religious thinker and Kabbalist, with an acosmic philosophy of Judaism. My study of this thinker, Aaron of Starosselje, was called *Seeker of Unity*.

I had acquired an interest in the mystical philosophy of this Hasidic school from my teacher in Manchester, Rabbi Dubow, and from Rabbi Rivkin, the rabbi who gave me Semichah, both of them Habad/Lubavitch Hasidim. I also wrote *Hasidic Prayer* for the Littman Library. The Editor of the Israeli publishing house, Keter, Dr Geoffrey Wigoder, approached me to compile a series of texts in translation in which the Jewish mystics bared their souls in describing, unusually for them, the nature of their mystical experiences. This had never been done before.

The book was called *Jewish Mystical Testimonies* and was later also published by Schocken in hard cover and paperback.

These works led to my being summoned during my stay at Harvard in 1985 to serve as an expert witness in a case that came before the American courts. Rabbi Yosef Yitzhak, the father-in-law of the present Lubavitcher Rebbe and his predecessor, had died intestate. He had two daughters, the wife of the present Rebbe and an older daughter. The son of the latter laid claim to the magnificent library of rare books the Rebbe had amassed, claiming that these actually belonged to the Rebbe, even though most of them had been purchased by him with money he had received from the Hasidim, who counter-claimed that this only gave the Rebbe custodial rights and that the books belonged to the movement. I was called as a witness to explain Hasidism to the judge and to support the view that the Habad/Lubavitch, unlike certain other Hasidic groups, did not uphold the doctrine that the Rebbe had to live in lavish style in order to bring an abundant flow of divine grace. It was therefore inconceivable that the Hasidim could increase the Rebbe's store of wealth, by giving him a huge and valuable library, for example.

The judge was a son-in-law of the famous Protestant theologian, Reinhold Niebuhr, and appeared to be fascinated by my account of the theological implications of Hasidism. The counsel for the grandson, seeking to discredit me as an expert, asked me 'Is it not true that you had been disbarred by the Chief Rabbi from the Principalship of Jews' College in Oxford?' I found it easiest to take the wind out of his sails by saying, 'That is not true. There is no Jews' College in Oxford.' It was left to the counsel on the other side to point out that my disbarment had nothing to do either with the case or with my expertise on Hasidism.

The case was decided in favour of the Rebbe, and the Lubavitcher Hasidim have declared the date of the victory a minor festival. The nephew appealed on technical grounds but the appeal was dismissed.

The publishing house Keter also commissioned me to write *What Does Judaism Say About . . .?*, a kind of dictionary (running from A to Z) on such topics as 'Alienation', 'Gambling',

'Homosexuality', 'Superstition' and 'Zen', topics not usually found in the standard Encyclopaedias. The idea was to examine the teachings of the Jewish masters that might throw light on contemporary questions. Keter, when commissioning me to write the book, said that they could not afford to let me have royalties but were prepared to offer the sum of £800 for a book of 100,000 words. I suggested that £1,000 would be a more realistic sum but they replied, 'Sorry, we cannot afford to give more than £800 but, if you like, do no more than 80,000 words'! Although my fee remained £800 I was sufficiently attracted to the novel theme to write around 120,000 words. So far as I can tell, of all my books this one has sold the best. I am constantly coming across it in Jewish bookshops. A literary agent would have obtained a better deal for me.

Keter were the publishers of the *Encyclopaedia Judaica*, now the standard Jewish Encyclopaedia, though not superseding entirely the old *Jewish Encyclopaedia*. I wrote many articles for the *Judaica* on Talmudic, theological, mystical and other subjects, including the 10,000-word article 'Judaism'. Professor Zvi Werblowsky, who was associated with the *Judaica*, came to ask me, on behalf of the Editors, to do the article, a well-nigh impossible task, he admitted, since every article in the entire Encyclopaedia is connected in one way or another with Judaism. I sought guidance from the *Catholic Encyclopaedia*, where the author of the lengthy article 'Catholicism' had much the same problem but managed to overcome it with a marked degree of success.

Authors often forget what they have written. More than once I have taken the *Judaica* down to consult an article and have caught myself saying, 'This article is oddly familiar' – only to discover, from the key to authors, that I wrote it myself.

I completed a number of popular books on Judaism for Behrman House. The 'Chain of Tradition' series consisted of five volumes, anthologies of Jewish thought on various themes: *Jewish Law; Jewish Ethics, Philosophy and Mysticism; Jewish Thought Today; Hasidic Thought*; and *Jewish Biblical Exegesis*. Explanatory notes were supplied together with my translation of the texts into English, the notes being printed in the body of the text, wherever appropriate, but in a different type from the text itself. The venture was a success. The publication of the first volume in the series, on Jewish law, coincided with a tour I was taking of the USA and Behrman House took the opportunity of having many copies available for purchase wherever I spoke. My friend Jakob Behrman, of Behrman House, had strong reservations, however, about the saleability of the book on Biblical exegesis and, I surmise, was sorry he had commissioned it. He did not promote its sale – perhaps this turned out to be a self-fulfilling prophecy. In my opinion, the book is one of the best things I have ever written.

The publication of *Jewish Law* in 1968 coincided with the Annual Convention of the Rabbinical Assembly, the organisation of Conservative Rabbis in the US, at Hotel Concord in the Catskills, where I joined them as the 1,000th member of the Assembly and delivered a paper on the use of theological material in preaching. Behrman House seized the opportunity of helping to launch the book by arranging a fish and chips party one evening for the assembled rabbis and their families. The idea was to hail the publication of a book by an English rabbi by providing food peculiar to the English. True to what my American friends imagined to be the correct English way of serving up this gastronomical delight – wrapped in old newspaper – each portion was wrapped in pages from the *Jewish Chronicle*! They knew enough about it not to provide what the Americans call 'chips' (what we call potato crisps), but the 'French fries' they did provide were far too thick to qualify as real chips and, sheer heresy, there was no vinegar. American style was, however, also in evidence in the excellent 'Teachers' Guide' Behrman House provided to help teachers use *Jewish Law* and the subsequent books in the series in schools and colleges.

Two other popular books published by Behrman House are *The Book of Jewish Belief* and its sequel *The Book of Jewish Practice*. These have appeared in a very attractive, glossy format, with photographs, boxed sayings, drawings and all.

The German-type scholarship in which I was trained at University College tended to scorn popular works and, I must confess, this has led me to cringe whenever I see a copy for sale of one of my popular books with its illustrations and attractive cover. However, Anglo-Jewry has a tradition of popular writings on Judaism and I console myself that it is not an entirely unworthwhile aim to help intelligent Jews learn more about Judaism.

Like others who write regularly on Jewish themes, I have contributed to composite works – anthologies, *Festschriften* and memorial volumes. Articles which in themselves might be not too important gain in significance because of the association with the scholar to whom the collection of essays pays tribute or the theme to which the anthology and the like is devoted. A memorial volume for Professor Leon Roth – *Studies in Rationalism, Judaism and Universalism*, edited by Raphael Loewe was published by Routledge & Kegan Paul in 1966, to which I contributed an article entitled 'The Doctrine of the "Divine Spark" in Man in Jewish Sources'. In the table of contents, perhaps with a touch of irony, the editor describes me as 'Rabbi of the New London Synagogue and *sometime* Lecturer, Jews' College, London' (italics mine).

Varieties of Jewish Belief, edited by Ira Eisenstein, was published by the Reconstructionist Press in 1966. This book was a collection of personal statements on Judaism intended to show that a diversity of theologies is both inevitable and desirable. In my contribution to the volume, I described my theological position as that of Liberal Supernaturalism – 'Liberal' in that it refused to ignore the findings of modern critical scholarship and 'Supernatural' in that God is conceived of as Person and as Transcendent Being – not, as some of the other contributors held, only the Force or Power in the universe that makes for righteousness.

In 1972 a series of lectures was delivered at Cambridge University seeking to answer the question of what was the shape of the universe imagined by those ancient peoples to whom all modern knowledge of geography and astronomy was inaccessible. My lecture in the series was on 'Jewish Cosmology'. This was published in 1973 by Allen & Unwin, together with the other lectures in the series, in *Ancient Cosmologies*, edited by Caren Blacker and Michael Loewe. No diagrams being available to illustrate Maimonides' cosmology, based on ancient sources, I had painfully to provide my own; armed with compass, pencil and ruler I constructed a passable picture of the spheres with the earth in the centre. Maimonides, incidentally, knew that the earth was round but shared, of course, the Ptolemean picture of the universe as geocentric.

To mark the 25th anniversary of Rabbi Wolfe Kelman's service as its Executive Vice-President, the Rabbinic Assembly published in 1968 the volume *Perspectives on Jews and Judaism*, edited by Arthur A. Chiel, to which I contributed an article, 'The Responsa of Rabbi Joseph Hayyim of Baghdad'. Rabbi Joseph Hayyim was the foremost Oriental Respondent and Halakhic authority at the turn of this century. He was thoroughly familiar with the famous works on Halakhah by the Ashkenazi authorities but preferred to follow his own original methodology based on earlier Sephardi models. It was fascinating to see how this authority was influenced by his 'Oriental' background, making him, at times, far more lenient than any of the Ashkenazim; at other times, stricter by far than any of them. Working on this essay made me appreciate more than ever the falsity of the picture of the Halakhist as a disembodied spirit uninfluenced by his background, his personal temperament and disposition. I drew on this in my book on the flexibility of the Halakhah, *A Tree of Life*.

Studies in Jewish Religious and Intellectual History, presented to Alexander Altmann and edited by Siegfried Stein and Raphael Loewe, was published by the University of Alabama Press in 1979. Dr Altmann was an old friend and mentor from my Manchester days, Dr Stein my teacher at University College and Professor Loewe a friend and colleague who gave me much support and encouragement during the controversy, so I considered it a privilege to have been invited to contribute to the volume. My article was entitled 'Eating as an Act of Worship in Hasidic Thought'. I tried to show that while Hasidism was not normally ascetic in mood, it certainly did not look upon the gratification of the senses in hedonistic terms but as acts of worship by means of which the 'holy sparks' inherent in all things were rescued from the power of the demonic forces to be restored to their Source on high.

Dr Joseph Heinemann was a man of two worlds. As mentioned in an earlier chapter, he had studied at the Mir Yeshivah and, later, when he came to England as a young refugee from the Nazi terror, at Manchester University. Heinemann was the author of definitive works on the Rabbinic Aggadah and on the Jewish Liturgy. After suffering years of being ignored, he took his rightful place as a Professor of Jewish Studies at the Hebrew University. I knew 'Hans' Heinemann well from my Manchester days and appreciated the invitation to contribute to the volume *Studies in Aggadah, Targum and Jewish Liturgy* dedicated to his memory (edited by Jakob J. Petuchowski and Ezra Fleischer, Magnes Press, Jerusalem, 1981). My article, 'The *Sugya* on Sufferings in B. *Berakhot* 5a, b', sounded a note of caution on the use of the Talmudic Aggadah for the reconstruction of the theological views of the Talmudic Rabbis. My contention was that the Aggadah, like the rest of the Talmud, is expressed in a contrived literary form, so that this famous passage on sufferings is closer to a poem on the theme of suffering than to anything like a precise theological statement.

In 1981 the University of Alabama Press published *Kierkegaard's Fear and Trembling: Critical Appraisals* edited by Robert L. Perkins, to which I contributed an article, 'The Problem of the *Akedah* in Jewish Thought'. In it I considered whether there is anything in Jewish thought corresponding to the Danish thinker's 'teleological suspension of the ethical'.

In my Presidential Address to the British Association of Jewish Studies in 1982, I pursued the idea of literary contrivance in the Babylonian Talmud, particularly in the use of 'sacred' numbers in the arrangement of the material by the final editors. This was put into article form as 'The Numbered Sequence as a Literary Device in the Babylonian Talmud' and published in *Biblical and Other Studies in Honor of Robert Gordis*, edited by Reuben Ahroni, Ohio State University Press (*Hebrew Annual Review*, vol.7, 1983). Professor Gordis has skilfully detected how numbers like five and seven occur frequently in the arrangement of the material in the Bible and the Mishnah. I took up the theme for the arrangement in the Babylonian Talmud.

Before I actually went to Harvard, I was invited, as a Harvard appointee, to contribute to the volume of essays in honour of

Wilfred Cantwell Smith, *The World's Religious Traditions: Current Perspectives in Religious Studies*, edited by Frank Whaling and published by T. & T. Clark, Edinburgh, in 1984. My article, 'The Jewish Tradition', examined Jewish attitudes to the problem of faith and tradition, a problem with which Professor Cantwell Smith had been much engaged.

Speaking of books, it is pleasant to be able to record the six books published by my son David. David is a talented photographer. He was commissioned by Ospreys to photograph American trucks in the USA, a subject that had, and still has, a cult-following also in Britain. David produced a book of splendid colour photographs of trucks and their drivers and contributed the text which described his meetings with these interesting people. The book was an immediate success and further volumes followed. To date six titles have been published in the series with a total sale of over 50,000. The contract for the first book was a magnificent affair, printed on thick, embossed paper in three languages and far superior to any contract I have ever had for my books. But the Talmud penetratingly reminds us that 'a man is envious of everyone except his son and his pupil'.

It has been my lot to write many book reviews, some of them excellent (the books, not the reviews), some of them indifferent, some downright bad. A reviewer owes it to the author to be fair and to give credit where it is due but at the same time he owes it to his readers to warn them against buying or accepting as accurate shoddy or unreliable work. I have always tried to preserve the correct balance but, I fear, have often yielded to the temptation to be too soft-hearted fully to slate a book deserving that treatment.

One advantage of book-reviewing is that the reviewer obtains books he might otherwise not buy to build up his own personal library. Many of the books I own were obtained in this way, including such important and very expensive works as Louis Ginzberg's *Commentary to the Jerusalem Talmud*, the facsimiles of pages from the Babylonian Talmud published in Spain and Portugal before the Expulsion (edited by Professor Dimitrovsky) and the splendid illustrated catalogue of Hebrew manuscripts from the Ambrosiana Library in Milan.

For years I have received a book allowance from the *Jewish Chronicle* and from the Littman Library, which I have spent on building up a collection of original editions and photocopies of Halakhic and Hasidic works. Friends have kindly sent me book tokens as gift which I have used to help build up my library. Shula, indulgent as ever, never complains about my addiction, not even when shelf after shelf in our home is taken over by my books, space she could have used for her own books and ornaments. The result is that my library is now fairly strong in my three special areas of interest: Talmud/Halakhah, Jewish mysticism and theology. There is so little on Jewish theology that it would be difficult for any respectable library not to be strong in the subject.

The few rare books I possess were either bought before such books were sold at auctions at vastly inflated prices or were given to me or left by friends. The most valuable set of old Jewish books I possess is the pocket-size Stephanus Bible published in Paris in the sixteenth century. Every book collector has experienced the thrill of holding in his hands a book that has had a long history of ownership. One of the books left to me by Professor Leon Roth is Gersonides' *Milhamot ha-Shem*, printed in 1560 at Riva di Trento. The printing-press at Riva was established in 1558 by the physician Jacob Marcaria who obtained a licence from Cardinal Madruzzi. The Gersonides book, like the other books printed at Riva, bears the Cardinal's coat of arms with his Cardinal's hat on the title page. My copy of the book had once belonged to the Sadigora Rebbe, Nahum Duber Friedman. It is known that this book collector had three different stamps for his books. Books he had bought himself had the stamped words *Kinyan Kaspi* ('Acquisition by my own money', i.e. bought out of his own pocket). Books he had inherited were stamped *Nahalat Avot* ('Inheritance from Forebears'). The Rebbe was also given presents of books by his Hasidim and on the stamp of these there appears the words *Minhat Shai* ('Gracious Gift'). My copy has these latter words on the stamp. It also has the Rebbe's signature on the fly-leaf and, below it, that of Leon Roth in Hebrew.

It is fascinating to trace the wanderings of a book. Gersonides, an early fourteenth-century Jewish philosopher in Provence, wrote an unconventional book, a copy of which was found in sixteenth-century Italy, where the book was published with a Cardinal's coat of arms on the title page. Passing, evidently, through the hands of a number of owners, it somehow found its way, through the generosity of nineteenth-century Hasidim, into the library of a Hasidic Rebbe in Romania. Eventually, when the Rebbe's library was sold, the book passed into the hands of a bookseller (probably in Israel, where Professor Roth was Chancellor of the Hebrew University) from whom Leon Roth bought it and brought it with him to Brighton when he moved there. In this way, this book by a distinguished Jewish philosopher of the fourteenth century had come to rest in the library of another distinguished philosopher, Leon Roth, in the twentieth century. Whenever I take hold of this book I feel that I am holding history in my hands.

Another book I own which came originally from the library of the Sadegoras Rebbe (this one is stamped *Kinyan Kaspi*) is the Commentary to the Zohar by Mordecai Ashkenazi (thought to be a Sabbatean) entitled *Eshel Avraham*, published in Fürth in the year 1701. On the title page there are illustrations of Moses and Aaron on either side of the title and, beneath it, of Goliath having his head cut off by the youthful David who has killed him with his sling.

A book of special Anglo-Jewish interest is the *Toledot Ya'akov* by Jacob Eisenstadt, the first Hebrew book printed by Jews in London in 1770. Eisenstadt, in this book, fulminates against London Jews who frequent the theatre and coffee houses instead of spending their time studying the Torah.

Another book of Anglo-Jewish interest is a copy of the first edition of the famous Singer's Prayer Book (1891). This copy was given to Simeon Singer by Claude Montefiore and is inscribed 'SS from CGM in memory of many happy and instructive hours spent together over the making of this book, November 1891'. Underneath is written in a different hand (presumably by Singer), 'To Mrs Arnold Gabriel'. When Mrs Gabriel died, her sister, Mrs Winifred Leroy, a member of the New London Synagogue, gave the book to me.

BOOKS

With a library of 7,000 books (at the last count by the removal firm when we were moving house) and a comfortable study, I have had no excuse for neglecting my studies. But I have to confess that I have a partly restless disposition, so that sitting down to study is not always too easy for me. At the Manchester Yeshivah I was regarded as a 'masmid' (a person whose application to study brooks no interruptions) but in those far-off days I had neither duties nor responsibilities to distract me. Yet I have tried to keep my nose to the grindstone, albeit with a struggle. Writing has helped. It is true that the best way to get to know a book is to write a book on it.

18

IN RETROSPECT

According to the rabbis of the Talmud, the wicked are full of regrets. If this is the test of guilt I am not too blameworthy, not at least in my own assessment. Regrets I have. Who does not wish that this or that feature in his career had been different; this or that mistake had not been made; that he had chosen another course from that which he did choose? But *full* of regrets? No. With regard to the Jacobs Affair I am sorry, I hope, for the distress it caused but still believe it was good that it took place.

The major part of this book was written during my convalescence after heart surgery. During this time my thoughts were forcibly turned to the inevitability of death, the dreaded subject normally kept at arm's length. In Judaism repentance is called for every day but especially when danger is close. As Dr Johnson said: 'Depend upon it, Sir, when a man knows he is to be hanged in a fortnight, it concentrates his mind wonderfully.' If I have been wrong all along that was the time for me to acknowledge it. But I recalled with appreciation the story Dov Katz tells in his study of the Musar Movement. One of the Musarists disagreed with the majority of his colleagues, holding that children should be given a good general education in addition to their Jewish education, and he acted accordingly, sending his children to good schools. The man was about to undergo a serious operation. 'Now', one of his colleagues rebuked him, 'is the time to see the error of your ways.' To the man's credit, he refused to be cowed by the threat hanging over him.

Of course, there were mistakes on both sides. Some of these could have been avoided if a greater spirit of tolerance and understanding had prevailed. Speaking for myself, I confess to losing my cool at times, using intemperate language and uttering words best left unsaid and becoming occasionally obsessive on the question of fundamentalism. If, by the Rabbinic definition,

I have not been 'wicked' in this matter, neither have I been saintly, and I have stooped to retaliation. I am not sure whether my grandfather's advice (reported to me by my father) is sound. 'One must not initiate a quarrel but one is allowed to pay back in full' (*man tor nit ton ober man meg oppton*). Yet, sound or unsound, I have acted upon it. For all that, looking back, I find it hard to believe that too much breast-beating is called for. I am certainly not stricken by any remorse for the stand I and my supporters took. Granted the climate that then prevailed in Anglo-Jewry, the row had to come sooner or later. That, through our efforts, it came sooner rather than later is, to my mind, creditable rather than otherwise.

To put it as bluntly as possible, fundamentalism is wrong. It is either ignorant and obscurantist or intellectually dishonest to reject the 'assured results' of historical investigation into the origins of Judaism.

That is the theoretical aspect of the Jacobs Affair. On a more practical level, the Affair exposed the way Anglo-Jewry was going and how right-wing extremists were taking over the community. With the benefit of hindsight, it is clear that here, too, we were right. Increasingly, in the Orthodox community, the theory and practice of the Rabbinic leadership is totally at variance with the theory and practice of those who are being led. At Jews' College the pursuit of critical scholarship, as practised in the days of Büchler, Marmorstein, Wieder and Epstein, has largely been abandoned and the College has virtually given up its chief reason for existence, the training of rabbis for Anglo-Jewish communities. More and more Orthodox pulpits are being occupied by Yeshivah graduates with no training whatsoever in the practicalities of modern synagogal life. Readers of this book will know that I yield to none in my admiration for the total dedication to learning in the Yeshivot, but it does not follow that Yeshivah graduates are automatically equipped to become adequate spiritual leaders in modern congregations: apart from this, it is an open secret that the Yeshivot frown on their better students pursuing the Rabbinate as a career.

I have called attention elsewhere in this book to the increasing rigidity of the London Beth Din in matters of personal status. In other areas, too, the Orthodox community is being fashioned into a replica of Eastern European Judaism, for which only a religious Philistine will fail to have the highest regard, but Shipinshok is not London in the last quarter of the twentieth century. With the removal recently of the mixed choir at the Hampstead Synagogue (they came to us, where they function to the delight of our congregants), the New London Synagogue is the last bastion of the old Anglo-Jewish tolerance and reasonableness. Why should we resist the temptation of saying, 'We told you so'?

I am far from suggesting that all the truth was found on our side, all the error on the other side. What I believe can be claimed is that, through the Jacobs Affair, it has been shown that the idea of a quest is not without religious significance. Judaism can be seen as a great venture into the unknown, with faith in the Unseen, the Lord of all truth.

And it has not been my personal quest. All along those who supported me, for all their personal friendship, cared for the ideas, for the quest itself, and, it is our hope and confidence, the quest will not depend on any particular Anglo-Jewish individual in the future as it has not really so depended in the past. I am not so humble as to deny my part in the Affair, but believe that I have been no more than a catalyst and if it had not been me it would, sooner or later, have been someone else of a similar background, perhaps with greater success. There is at present a degree of peace in the Anglo-Jewish community, at least so far as this particular controversy is concerned. But the Jacobs Affair has not gone away nor will it when I am no longer around.

I would not wish to put it higher than that. Nor do any of us wish to pretend that we have been the only inquirers, even in Anglo-Jewry, to say nothing of the rest of the Jewish world. Indeed, in my travels to America I have often been the recipient of quizzical glances, as if to say, 'So what else is new?'

I have always disclaimed any particular originality in this area. Intelligent Jews all over the world, Orthodox as well as non-Orthodox, appreciate today that the problems raised by the implications of modern scholarship will not simply vanish because they are ignored by officialdom. It has been my fate to have encouraged the quest in a comparatively humble but not entirely insignificant corner of world Jewry. All of us, at the

New London Synagogue, the New North London Synagogue and in the Masorti Movement, must now avoid unbridled personal attacks – even on those who have no such scruples where we are concerned. Above all we must avoid self-righteousness and claims to achievement belied by the sober facts and realities. All we have a right to claim (let us admit it, a pretty big 'all') is that, consciously or unconsciously, we have been helping with inquiries.

GLOSSARY

Aliyah	(*lit.* ascent) the honour of being called to the platform where the Torah is read
Amoraim	teachers (*lit.* speakers) who interpreted the Mishnah and Tosefta, formulated new legal judgments and taught the Torah on the basis of oral transmission (3rd–6th century CE)
Ark	depository for Scrolls of the Law
Av Beth Din	head of rabbinical court
ba'aley teshuvah	born-again Jews; *lit.* penitents
Bar Mitzvah	age of male majority; boys called up to read a portion of Law in the synagogue at age 13
Bava Kama	Talmudic tractate dealing with civil law
Beth Din	rabbinical court, tribunal
bochur	(*lit.* bachelor) student
bubbe (Yiddish)	grandmother
cantillation	chant for biblical readings in synagogue
Cheder	(*lit.*, room) school in which Judaism is taught
chuppah	canopy under which bride and groom stand during marriage ceremony
chutzpah (Yiddish)	cheek, impudence
Dayan	judge in rabbinical court
derashah	sermon
derekh	'way' (of learning)
duchan	priestly blessing of the congregation
epikoros	unbeliever, heretic
frum (Yiddish)	strictly observant
Gedoley Yisrael	great authorities in Jewish law

273

Gemara	lengthy commentary on the Mishnah (digest of oral law), the two together forming the Talmud
get, gittin (pl.)	divorce writ(s)
goy, goyim (pl.)	non-Jew(s)
Habad	Hasidic group
Hafetz Hayyim	prominent rabbinic leader
Haftarah	weekly reading from the prophetic books
Haggadah	the ethical teachings of the Midrash containing philosophical wisdom and folklore written in a popular and impressive style; also the name of the book of the Exodus narrative recited at the Passover Seder service.
Halakhah	that part of traditional Jewish literature concerned with the law
Halakhic	pertaining to Jewish law
Halutzim	Zionist pioneers
Hasid, hasidic	(pious, benevolent person) member of pietist sect
Hevra	a small congregation of traditional Jews
Hochschule (German)	high school
Humash	Pentateuch; see *Torah*
Jüdische Wissenschaft	(*lit.* Jewish Science) movement based on accurate historical research into origins of Judaism
Kabbalah	Jewish mystical tradition
kaddish	prayers recited after the death of a parent
kal va-homer	reasoning *a fortiori*: 'if . . . then how much more so . . .'
Kapparah	atonement ceremony performed before Day of Atonement
kedushah	(*lit.* sanctification) prayer proclaiming the holiness of God (Isaiah 6.3)
kehilla	community
ketubah	marriage contract
Kiddush	Sabbath eve benediction

GLOSSARY

kittel (Yiddish)	plain white overgarment, worn by orthodox Jews on Day of Atonement
Kol Nidre	service on eve of Day of Atonement
Landsleit (Yiddish)	people from the same village
Litvaks	Lithuanian Jews
lomdus (Yiddish)	learning
Lubavitcher	follower of the Lubavitcher Rebbe, also known as Habad
ma'ariv	evening prayers
mahzor	prayer book for holidays
maskil	(enlightened) man versed in Western culture
mechutan	relation by children's marriage
Megillot	five books of Canticles, Ecclesiastes, Esther, Lamentations, Ruth
mensch (Yiddish)	decent, worthy person
minhah	afternoon prayers
minyan	minimum number of people whose presence is required for some religious services to be held, i.e. ten male adults
Mishnah	codification of Jewish laws and precepts, collected by Rabbi Judah ha-Nasi in the late second century C.E. It forms the earlier part of the Talmud.
Mitnagged	opponent of Hasidism
mitzvot	good deeds
Moshe Rabbenu	Moses the Prophet; *lit.* Moses our Master
Musar movement	late 19th-century moral revivalist movement
Ner Tamid	perpetual lamp positioned above Ark in synagogue
Neturei Karta	(*lit.* watchmen of the city) ultra-orthodox anti-Zionist sect
piyutim	liturgical poems
Purim	festival commemorating triumph of good Mordecai over evil Haman
Rabbenu Tam	major 12th-century Tosaphist; grandson of Rashi

275

Radbaz	David Ibn Abi Zimra, Chief Rabbi of Cairo (1479–1573)
Rama	Moshe ben Israel Isserles (c.1520–72), main commentator on *Shulhan Arukh*
Rambam	Maimonides, Spanish rabbi, codifier and philosopher (1135–1204)
Rashi	Rabbi Solomon ben Isaac of Troyes (1040–1105) – renowned Talmudic and Biblical commentator
Rebbe, Reb, Rov	rabbi
Responsa	rabbinic opinions on questions of law
Ribbono shel Olam	prayer, *lit.* 'Lord of the Universe'
Rosh Hashanah	New Year
Sabbatean	follower of the false messiah, Shabbetai Zvi (1626–1716)
Sabra	native-born Israeli
Seder	Passover home service celebrating exodus of Jews from Egypt
Sefer Torah	Pentateuch scroll
Sefirat Ha-Omer	counting of the seven-week period between second day of Passover and Shavu'ot (Pentecost)
Selichot	penitential prayers, said during the period before the Day of Atonement
Semichah	rabbinical ordination
Shabbat Ha-Gadol	Sabbath before Passover
Shabbat Shuvah	Sabbath between New Year and Day of Atonement
shamash	synagogue beadle
shaatnez	mixture of linen and woollen fibres, not worn by orthodox Jews
shehitah	the traditional manner of killing animals for food
Shema	classical Deuteronomic confession of faith – 'Hear, O Israel! The Lord is our God, the Lord is one' (6.4)
sheva berachot	seven blessings recited during wedding celebrations

shidduch	arranged marriage
shiksa (Yiddish)	non-Jewish woman; derogatory term
Shimusha Rabba (tefillin)	a type of tefillin worn only by the most saintly
shohet	a man qualified to perform shehitah
Shul (Yiddish)	synagogue
Shulhan Arukh	Code of Jewish law; *lit.* set table
sidra	weekly Pentateuch reading
stiebel (Yiddish)	small and close-knit Orthodox congregation
stetl (Yiddish)	Jewish community in an Eastern European town or village
tallit	fringed prayer-shawl
talmidey hakhamim	scholars
Talmud	Commentary on the Mishnah together with the Mishnah
Talmud Torah	Jewish day school
tefillin	phylacteries
terefa	non-kosher food
Tisha Be-Av	Ninth of Av–fast day commemorating fall of the Temple in Jerusalem
Torah	(*lit.*, teaching) the Law, of which the Pentateuch is the written record, as revealed to Moses on Mount Sinai
Tosafist	Name given to school of Jewish scholars in Northern France who wrote additions (tosaphot') to Rashi's Talmudic commentaries
Tu Bishvat	New Year for trees
Tzaddik	holy man
tzitzit	fringes worn by men on a four-cornered garment
Vilna Gaon	famous 18th-century Lithuanian rabbi
Yahrzeit	anniversary of a person's death
yarmulka	skull-cap
Yekke	familiar term for a German Jew
Yeshivah	religious seminary
yidel (Yiddish)	little Jew – diminutive term of affection

Yigdal	Sabbath eve hymn
yingel (Yiddish)	little boy
yirath shamayin	the fear of Heaven
Yom Kippur	Day of Atonement
Yom Tov	holy day
Zaide (Yiddish)	grandfather
Zemirot	Sabbath-table hymns
Zohar	principal work of the Kabbalah; *lit.* book of splendour

INDEX

INDEX

INDEX

INDEX